ANDREAS AND THE AMBIGUITY OF COURTLY LOVE

PAOLO CHERCHI

Andreas and the Ambiguity of Courtly Love

UNIVERSITY OF TORONTO PRESS
Toronto Buffalo London

© University of Toronto Press Incorporated 1994
Toronto Buffalo London
Printed in Canada
Toronto Italian Studies

ISBN 0-8020-0577-2

Printed on acid-free paper

Canadian Cataloguing in Publication Data

Cherchi, Paolo
  Andreas and the ambiguity of courtly love

  (Toronto Italian Studies)
  Includes bibliographical references and index.
  ISBN 0-8020-0577-2

  1. Courtly love in literature. 2. André le
  chapelaine. De amore et amoris remedio. 3. Provençal
  poetry. History and criticism. 4. Troubadours.
  I. Title. II. Series.

  PA8250.A236Z64 1994   849'.1209'354   C93-095581-1

University of Toronto Press acknowledges the financial assistance to its
publishing program of the Canada Council and the Ontario Arts Council.

To my wife, Judy

Contents

PREFACE ix

INTRODUCTION xi

The Ambiguity of Courtly Love in
Andreas Capellanus's Model 3

Mezura 42

The *Adynata* 81

Conclusion 124

NOTES 129

BIBLIOGRAPHY 165

INDEX OF NAMES 187

Preface

The idea that informs this book stems from a course I taught several years ago at the University of Valencia, Spain. It was a course on courtly love designed to cover the large area centred on the world of the troubadours, and its repercussions, which were felt as far as Galicia and Sicily. Among the required readings was a selection of troubadour poems and Andreas Capellanus's *De Amore*, which are traditionally considered complementary because they shed light on each other. Andreas's treatise was supposed to help interpret the poems we were reading, but it didn't happen quite that way; in fact, the Latin treatise proved to be a cause of great confusion. Using the poems to interpret the treatise was no less confusing. Both texts present a high degree of ambiguity on their own, and adding one ambiguity to another is not the best way to shed light on a problem. Then another possibility presented itself and appeared to be the most economical solution – namely, denying any relationship between Andreas and the troubadours. However, such a simple and radical solution proved to be not so straightforward after all, because the evidence of many points of contact between *De Amore* and troubadour poetry can be explained only if we assume that some sort of relation between them existed. Something was definitively wrong in the approach, in the way of seeing the rapport between the two objects of study. Things changed when it appeared that studying them together was fruitful only if their relation was understood as a confrontation. In other words, Andreas was not a codifier of courtly love but an adverse interpreter who, in order to carry out his polemic, chose to mimic courtly lovers in the hope of unmasking their supposed deceitfulness. Andreas's unusual kind of parody produced an ambiguous treatise which, even so, helps us to understand some key elements of courtly love. Andreas, however, did not understand the very virtue that made troubadour love poetry ambiguous. This special virtue is *mezura*, a very complex version of *temperantia* that transforms eros into poetry.

Class experience shows that the themes concerning the relationship of Andreas to the troubadours and eros to moral perfection remain crucial for all beginning students of courtly love – hence, the conviction that revisiting them is a useful and still relevant endeavour. The classroom origin of this work surfaces in the presentation of the arguments, in the somewhat scholastic *modus tractandi* of this book; but I would like not to have to apologize for it, especially if in fact this plain treatment encourages students to go deeper into the world of the troubadours.

Introduction

'Mais la poésie médiévale! Reconnaissons-le: dans ces manifestations les plus accomplies, la civilisation des Xe-XIe-XIIe siècles est plus étrangères à la nôtre que celle de la Rome antique.'[1] With these lapidary words, Paul Zumthor synthesized his thinking for decades about medieval poetry. It was an assessment which, in many ways, sounds like a confession of bankruptcy, a realization that his previous work as a historian, cultivated under the aegis of sound philology and history of ideas, had failed to reach the heart of that remote world. In that admission, however, there was no despair: the still young scholar was embarking on a new path which seemed to lead to a novel understanding of early and Romance lyric poetry. The date for this new departure was 1963, a real turning-point in the history of our discipline. How many scholars followed in Zumthor's steps is impossible to say, for one should rather talk of generations of scholars who in the last quarter-century have approached medieval lyric poetry from this new point of view, which, *grosso modo*, can be called formalistic. Its successful results are only too well known, although some may question whether the formalistic approach has ever reached the heart of medieval poetry or has stopped just at its lining. In any case, no one can deny that the formalistic approach has succeeded in enlightening many aspects of that estranged world which is medieval literature.

The lyric poetry of the troubadours has been a privileged testing-ground for the formalistic readers. Paul Zumthor, who would hardly list himself among the Provençalists, in that very same book of 1963, gave a magisterial analysis of a celebrated poem, *Lanquan li jorn son lonc en may*, by Jaufre Rudel.[2] The selection of this text was dictated by a polemical urge rather than by its poetic value, since Jaufre's poem had been previously subjected to sharply diverging interpretations that exemplified quite well the differences in critical approaches. For a long time it was held that the poem had autobiographical content, namely, Jaufre's love for a princess of Tripoli. Such a belief was then jolted by Grace Frank who saw in Jaufre's 'amor de lonh' an allegory of the Holy Land.[3] Frank's interpretation prompted Leo Spitzer to assert that Jaufre's love from afar is nothing but an expression of the troubadours' 'paradox of love.'[4] Zumthor dismissed all previous interpretations. He found that the ambiguity of the poem does not depend either on its allegorical mode or on its paradoxical content, but rather on its approximate construction and on the lack of semantic cogency. Thus the focus was on the form, which was given priority over content, and the poem's ambiguity, which had always been approached from point of view of the theme, was now seen as the result of a formalistic operation. Formal ambiguity was the key phrase, and perhaps Zumthor did not foresee that it would become a key concept in reading troubadour poetry.

Ambiguity, it has often been said, belongs to the very nature of poetical language. One of its most common causes consists in the emphasis on or in the superposition of the poetic function over the referential one, and the result is then a concentration of the poetic message in itself. Troubadour poetry, with its conventionality and its ever-elusive referents, offers an ideal support for this notion. Moreover, some scholars suggest that Provençal is a language which lends itself to ambiguity,[5] and the 'mouvance'[6] in the transmission of troubadour poetry is considered a further cause of it. Hardly any recent reading of troubadour poems misses pointing out their ambiguity.

The problem, however, is not new; the notion of ambiguity has been associated with troubadour poetry since medieval days and it has intermittently surfaced in the ensuing centuries. Andreas Capellanus, a contemporary of the troubadours, found ambiguity in the ethics of *fin'amor*. A sixteenth-century reader like Mario Equicola was unaware of any ambiguity in the Provençal lyrics and he took them as expressions of real love.[7] Later on, such a reader as Stendhal perceived a sense of ambiguity when he saw the troubadour poems as arias of *opera buffa*.[8] In more recent times this sense has surfaced again in interpretations that decode these poems at one time as a religious message, at another as a manifestation of pure eroticism, and at still another as a reflection of feudal tensions, or of medieval narcissism. No other corpus of poetry nor any other cultural movement has lent itself to such disparaging interpretations. The explanation must be *a parte objecti*, in the troubadour poetry itself – above all, in its double message of spirituality and carnality and in the paradox so well defined by Rilke when he spoke of the troubadours as lovers 'who feared nothing more than seeing their wishes fulfilled.'[9]

The scholars of Provençal poetry who approach its ambiguity from a formalistic point of view represent the most recent solution to an ancient problem. The solution is an astute one which presupposes a switch in focus: not any longer the content of troubadour lyric (paradox of love, request of love, hope-despair, narcissism, etc.) but the poem's self-referentiality. This switch, as noticed, has been and still is highly fruitful and stimulating, but it implies that the problem of the ambiguity of troubadour love has been satisfactorily settled and/or that its solution is ultimately useless for the understanding of the formal ambiguity of the Provençal lyric. These assumptions, however, are not completely correct. The present study addresses anew the problem of the paradox of troubadour love with the aim of finding in it the cause of that formal ambiguity which is so specific to Provençal lyrics, not *qua* poetry, and therefore 'ambiguous,' but because they have specific themes that reflect as well as create a particular cultural context.

The best analysis of the ambiguous nature of troubadour love is still Leo Spitzer's; in a few lucid pages, he was able to describe the 'paradoxe amoureux' as being a balance between the opposite elements of eros and moral perfection, an immobile tension between natural desires and social expectations. The brilliance of this essay seems not to have been tarnished by the years. Yet, in reading it almost half a century after its date of publication, it is difficult to overcome a sense of uneasiness for some of its existential overtones; for the idealistic analysis of troubadour poetry, and, above all, for the way in which the paradox of love is understood. Seeing 'désir charnel combattu par la volonté chaste, exaltation semi-religieuse mise à l'épreuve par la passion, désir de contact immédiat et amour lointain'[10] seems a simplification, a mechanical reduction of a paradox to an antithesis which is not unique to the troubadours.

The real paradox – in the etymological sense of a statement 'contrary to a current belief' – is that eros and moral perfection, far from being contradictory, live together in a subtle process of amalgamation in which both become consubstantial – that is, reciprocally necessary rather than reciprocally exclusive. Together, they concur in the mythopoetic creation of a lover who is unique in his dedication, in his suffering, in his moral perfectability and hopes of conquering a lady who is also unique in her beauty and moral value. This process leads us to other questions. Is the troubadour referring to a real or an imaginary lady? And why would this troubadour publicize his own love if one of the self-dictated requisites for conquering her is the utmost secrecy? And just when we are convinced by the 'sincerity' of this one troubadour, if we happened to read other poets of his school we realize how conventional are that sincerity and that dedication to love, for it seems that any troubadour exalts his own image through that of all courtly lovers. Hence comes the conventional and highly formalized poetry of the troubadours; hence, also, that particular form of troubadours' narcissism, which is 'love of the self as reflected in the other.' The key word for this mythopoetic process is *mezura*. This word does not indicate, as it is often said to, the delicate balance between eros and moral expectations, but rather the integration of eros into the ideal of courtliness. *Mezura* transforms nature into culture to such an extent that the origin of love (is it passion or is it literature?) remains ambiguous.

The following pages describe this process of mythopoesis and its ensuing ambiguity. The first step consists in establishing that troubadour love, as a specific manifestation of what is traditionally called 'courtly love,' was a historically new phenomenon. This step would seem unnecessary; but recent discussions have questioned the real novelty of such a phenomenon, and in some cases the existence of a 'courtly love' has even been denied. The second step is an analysis of Andreas Capellanus's *De Amore*. The decision to read anew this treatise rests on two main points: Andreas is the first interpreter of courtly love and he is also the first one to denounce its ambiguity hidden in its combining erotic passion with virtue. Andreas's work has had an enormous impact on modern interpretations, and its importance is unquestionable. *De Amore* – as we will prove – offers a negative interpretation of courtly love, because Andreas could not accept that erotic passion and moral perfection are compatible. The chaplain, however, did not take into account a specific virtue of the troubadours' world, namely, *mezura*, which succeeds in integrating eros and virtue. *Mezura* provides us with the missing link in Andreas's model of courtly love; by using it, we can turn Andreas's negative model into a positive one. The second chapter of this book is therefore devoted to *mezura*. The third chapter departs from the main task of building a model for interpreting troubadour love. It is a sort of historical appendix which surveys troubadour lyrics focusing on the figure of *adynaton*, the emblem, as it were, of the impossibility underlying the troubadours' quest. Such an analysis is meant to provide an insight into the mythopoetic operation undertaken by individual acolytes of *fin'amor*. Also it reminds us that no interpretative model of courtly love, however sound it may be, can suppress the fact that, in a world so prone to conventionality as was the world of the troubadours, poetic voices vary in pitch, and differ in volume and in power to enchant their listeners.

ANDREAS AND THE AMBIGUITY OF COURTLY LOVE

The Ambiguity of Courtly Love in Andreas Capellanus's Model

A tinge of paradox may confuse new students of courtly love who read the critical literature of the last few decades. They will find that the notion of courtly love, especially when applied to troubadour poetry, is threatened with extinction because too much effort is being made to keep it alive. This paradox is proof that neither those who firmly maintain that there is historical justification for that notion nor those who would like to expunge it from the history of literature succeed in making their respective cases persuasive. This debate depends to a great extent on the ways in which courtly love has been understood in the past. Every time a scholar has produced a rigorous definition of courtly love another scholar has had little trouble in proving it approximate and untenable and has countered it with one of his or her own. Every time a historian has enclosed courtly love within sharply defined lines another historian has blurred their neatness, denying the specificity of courtly love to the Middle Ages by pointing out the existence of similar phenomena in other historical periods. Predictably, therefore, one feels quite discouraged by the myriad divergent interpretations,[1] and this constant mirage effect justifies in part the sceptical attitude of some historians who proclaim that courtly love is nothing more than a fabrication by nineteenth-century critics.[2]

Unfortunately problems do not disappear by virtue of simple proclamation. Summary dismissals of this kind are valid only in so far as they question critical approaches and results. As a matter of fact, it is only fair to admit that there is something inherently ambiguous about courtly love, ambiguous at least in terms of our set of values, which explains the unusually large variety of theses. Perhaps we should give up forever the attempts to explain courtly love by tracing its sources (Arab influences, Catharism, medieval Platonism, etc.) because these paths have not led to certain conclusions. Perhaps, also, we should be more careful in using models borrowed from the feudal social system because they are helpful only to a certain point. And once all these roads are closed, we are faced again with a type of love which is different from any other and has its definition in time, and whose most distinguishing trait is a combination of eros and moral perfection, which leads to ambiguity. Of course, all this must be proven, and the following pages aspire to do so.

Before undertaking this task, a clarification is in order. The literature of courtly love is a vast phenomenon which spread from southern and northern France throughout Europe, presenting adaptations and modifications from place to place, from poet to poet. An examination of all these manifestations would result in a study quite different from the present one. I have limited my research to the lyrics of the troubadours. They constitute a relatively manageable *corpus* of poetry and, above all, embody the earliest and the most ambiguous version of courtly love. Throughout this work, I have used the labels 'courtly love' and *'fin'amor'* as equivalent. The latter would seem more specific for troubadour love, but the former, although more generic, has a longer standing; in any case, they both refer to the same phenomenon.

DEFINING THE SUBJECT

Was there ever such a thing as 'courtly love'? The question is hardly an idle one, given the discussions in recent years. It has been said[3] that the label 'courtly love' was first coined by Gaston Paris in a famous article of 1883;[4] therefore, it would be lacking any historical grounds since it was never used by the troubadours. But leaving aside the fact, that in Old Provençal, the expression *cortez'amor* occurs at least once, and that the notions of love and courtliness occur frequently together, and that expressions like *fin'amor* or *amor veraia* – indicating a specific kind of love – are all too common, the argument has no validity. One would not think of dismissing the Middle Ages or Baroque or Metaphysical poetry as historical subjects simply because those labels are not contemporary with the periods or cultural phenomena they describe. This reasoning is what ancient logicians would name 'autoschediasm' and discard as a naïve form of argumentation.

A more difficult and genuine problem is to establish whether the formula 'courtly love,' however approximate, defines a historical phenomenon. Does it qualify a new conception of love; or are the sceptics correct who say that there is nothing unique about courtly love and prove it by recalling many parallel and similar phenomena? Undoubtedly their argument holds some truth in so far as it uses historical evidence to ascertain the presence of love poetry before the blossoming of the Provençal lyric and then proves the similarities between the two. Love is, after all, 'un des aspects éternels de l'homme';[5] thus it is not surprising to see that the ancient Egyptians as well as the Greeks and the Romans had their love poetry. Yet it cannot be called 'courtly love' poetry. Not long ago a well-versed scholar canvassed an immense area from northern Africa to Scandinavia, from the Urals to the Atlantic, and he found the 'courtly experience' everywhere and poetry that resembles in many ways the lyrics of courtly love.[6] Yet what is the true worth of such generalizations? In historical research it is not especially useful to demonstrate that man is a thinking or loving being; what is truly pertinent is to define *how*, in their time and culture, men think and love. Polygenetic observations and studies on origins temper, at best, the dramatic novelty of courtly love, but in no way do they make it less real. Courtly love, like any other historical phenomenon, combines cultural continuity with innovation by adapting a tradition to a new context. Failing to understand this dialectical rapport by emphasizing one component at the expense of the other means seeing in courtly love a phenomenon either much older than the troubadours or mysteriously new.

The closest term of comparison which shows at once the troubadours' respect for tradition and capacity for innovation is medieval Latin poetry, because of its obvious contiguity, and most of all because the troubadours constantly drew from it. The medieval Latin poets were the troubadours' 'classics' – that is, the authors they read in class, the poets upon whose works their literary education was built. Numerous scholars throughout this century, from Wechssler to Roncaglia and Dronke, have shown beyond any doubt the pervasiveness of medieval Latin models in the poetry of the troubadours. There are very few motifs and even fewer rhetorical devices or poetic genres which have not been traced back to a medieval Latin model. This programmatic dependency is explained in part by the aspiration to the status of 'monument' so typical of early vernacular poetry,[7] and in part by the general principle that literature is born from literature.

Yet, if this is true for the thematic and rhetoric aspects, we cannot say the same about the main subject of troubadour poetry – namely, courtly love. Medieval Latin literature, being a luxuriant forest blossoming with all kinds of poetical voices and experiments, incidentally produced a great deal of love poetry that is highly diversified in genre and tone. It is precisely through a comparison with this kind of poetry that one immediately perceives the novelty of courtly love. Discounting a few similarities of minor importance, it soon becomes apparent that the vernacular poets differ on some essential points from their models. For one thing, the troubadours sing prevalently about love. They form, as no group of poets did before, a sort of poetic school enlivened by continuous dialogues or debates on problems of love, or *cortezia*, and although they come from a variety of dialectal extractions, they write in a highly formalized language which is remarkably impervious to dialectal influences. For another thing, the troubadours deviate from tradition by cultivating what may be called a 'conversion to the self': instead of dwelling on the description of the lady so typical of medieval Latin poets, they focus on their own psychology as lovers. The most important innovation, however, is the notion of love about which the troubadours sing.

Venantius Fortunatus, Baudri de Bourgueil, Marbod, Hildebert de Lavardin, and many lesser medieval Latin poets had written about love in a way that bears certain similarities to *cortez'amor*. Yet a closer scrutiny shows that their love is nothing more than 'amicitia spiritualis,' which is essentially an 'amor inter pares,' such as may exist between two men (e.g., love between two warriors), between two women (there are poems of love by a nun to another nun), between a man and a boy, as well as between a man and woman. It is primarily a poetry that celebrates a spiritual friendship free from any sexual or erotic implications. This is not to say that medieval Latin poets never wrote erotic poetry. Indeed there is plenty of erotic verse composed by well-known authors (e.g., Matthew of Vendôme, Serlo of Wilton, Hugh of Orléans, etc.) and plenty of allusions by such authors as Abelard and Pierre de Blois, among others, to their juvenile exercises in writing erotic or even obscene poems.[8] These two types of poetry, however, were neatly separated according to the rhetorical distinction that required different stylistic treatment for each one. In the case of the troubadour lyric, things were less clear. Only occasionally did some troubadours write explicitly erotic or obscene poetry. In general, they tend to combine eroticism with a proclaimed purity of feelings. Troubadour love is not erotic *tout court*, nor is it spiritual friendship. The resulting ambiguity would suffice to measure the innovation of courtly love; but, since this ambiguity remains to be proven in the course of this work, it can hardly be invoked now as a discriminatory element. There are, however, several features that distinguish courtly love from previous types: the insistence on the exclusivity of the relation between lovers, its constancy, its sincerity, the disposition to suffer on the part of the lovers, and other such themes[9] that have as a distinguishing factor their intensity and simultaneous presence more than the originality of each one of them. But, two features of courtly love offer a strong sense of its novelty: one is the notion of *obediensa* and the other is the assumption that love for a lady is the primary source of moral goodness. For the time being we shall confine ourselves to the analysis of *obediensa*.

Obediensa is a key word which describes the relationship between two lovers. It is not a relationship *inter pares* but between the poet (the lover who speaks in the first person) and a lady who is socially and/or morally superior to him. The poet devotes his own self to such a high person; he repeatedly declares his obedience and total submission to her, who, he claims, is an incomparable model of goodness and social grace. The concept, if not the word, is already present in a poem attributed to Guilhem IX of Aquitaine, the first troubadour:

> E ja, per plag que m'en mueva
> no·m solvera de son liam.
> Qu'ans mi rent a lieis e·m liure,
> qu'en sa carta·m pot escriure   (ed. Pasero, ll. 6–9)[10]

> [And yet, however much she may harass me, she will never untie me from her. On the contrary, I give and entrust myself to her in such a way that she can write me up among her possessions (she can consider me as her servant)].

It is interesting to observe that Guilhem, who was the most powerful lord of France in his day, pledges obedience in quite explicit legal terms to the person he chooses to be his lady. The same situation and imagery are used by another lord, Raimbaut, Count of Orange:

> Dona, vostre domini ser
> Crezet me ...   (ed. Pattison XXII, ll. 57–8)

> [Lady, believe me your feudal serf (Pattison's translation)];

or in this example:

8 Andreas and the Ambiguity of Courtly Love

> De midonz fatz dompn'e seignor   (XXVII, l. 25)

[I make a lord and master of my lady].

Perhaps the most dramatic case is that of King Alfonso of Aragon:

> Tant mi destreing sa bontatz,
> sa proez'e sa beutatz,
> qu'eu n'am mais sofrir en patz
> penas e dans e dolors,
> que d'autra jauzens amatz
> grans bes faitz e grans socors:
> sos homs plevitz e juratz
> serai ades, s'a leis platz,
> davan totz autres segnors   (ed. Riquer, 1975, p. 569, ll. 28–36)

[So much do her goodness, moral and physical beauty distress me, that I prefer to suffer in silence pains, damage, and hurt rather than enjoying the love of another woman with great rewards and relief. I will always be her committed and sworn vassal, in front of all the other lords, if she so desires].

A king who professes obedience to a subject!

Less incongruously, but no less firmly, Folquet de Marselha recalls 'sella cui obedis' (ed. Stroński, III, l. 18: 'That one whom I obey'); Giraut de Bornelh calls himself obedient servant, 'sers obediens' (ed. Kolsen, VII, l. 78); Arnaut de Maruelh says 'sui vos obediens' (ed. Johnston, VI, l. 33: 'I am obedient to you'); and Cadenet proclaims himself 'humils et hobedienz / Per far vostres mandamenz' (ed. Zemp V, ll. 22–3: 'humble and obedient to comply with your orders'). The list of examples could go on, especially if the inquest were extended to the whole semantic field of *obediensa* and considered adjectives like *aclin* and *humil* or verbs like *servir*,[11] which occur frequently. Also included in this semantic field is a neologism coined by Guilhelm: it is the word *midons*, that is, *meus dominus*:

> Totz jois li deu humeliar
> e tot'autr'amors obezir,
> midons, per son bel acuillir
> e per son bel douset esgar   (ed. Pasero, IX, ll. 18–21)

[Every joy must bow before her and every other love must obey my lady, because of her gentility and sweet looks]

or

Si·m vol midons s'amor donar,
pres soi del penr'e del grazir (IX, ll. 36–7)

[If my lady wants to give me her love, I am ready to accept it and thank her].

The term *midons* becomes a fixture of troubadour language.[12]

Obediensa is a notion that possibly has a religious[13] or a legal feudal origin, but the troubadours give it a different connotation. In any previous usage, the word suggested a static situation, a relationship never to be changed.[14] The troubadours, instead, consider their permanent submission as a means of obtaining equality (*paritas*) with their lady. This paradox is easily explained: the *paritas* (*paria*, in the troubadours' language) is the gift of love, the goal always pursued and practically never attained. *Obediensa* is, then, the first step on a sloped road which should take the troubadour to the highest level of perfection he can achieve. To reach this point, he channels all of his energies in an upward direction, incessantly aiming at the top. This is one of the major innovations brought about by courtly love. To be sure, the concomitance of love and equality is not unknown to medieval Latin poetry, but usually the loved person is asked to descend to the lover's level so that the *paritas* is reached in the lowest point of a descending vector: it is very much a relationship of love based on the model of Christ's love for mankind.[15]

This new way of understanding *obediensa* is evident in a series of verbs like *s'enantir* (to rise), *se melhorar* (to improve oneself), *s'esmerar* (to refine oneself), *s'enriquecir* (to become morally rich) and several others which occur frequently in the language of the troubadours of all generations. These verbs underline the perfecting tension inherent in courtly love, representing very well that upward dynamic which engages all the virtues, all the moral energies of the lover, and showing how love is the cause and the end of moral perfection. Also these verbs have a social connotation; as will be shown later, courtly love is, to a large extent, a social phenomenon. The social dimension is at the root of endless ambiguities, and it distinguishes courtly love from previous and parallel phenomena. It distinguishes it, for instance, from the sort of courtly love sung about by the medieval Arabs, which presents strong similarities to that of the troubadours, even in the concept of *obediensa*. However, as specialists tell us, the love of the Arabic poets, besides often being of a pederastic nature, never had a social implication[16] as does troubadour love. The Arabic love did not mould a society; courtly love, by contrast, did so, because it was the lever of *cortezia*.

The notion of *obediensa* leads us, through its moral and social implications, to the most distinguishing element of courtly love – namely, the notion of *proeza*, the moral beauty inextricably tied to erotic love. However, since it is a central element in our argument, we must postpone its treatment until Andreas Capellanus brings us back to it. For the moment, it will suffice to have highlighted one feature which is unique to courtly love. While having identified that feature is sufficient to give us the confidence to talk about courtly love as a unique phenomenon, to understand it we need a model.

THE NEED FOR A MODEL

The preceding pages, as those that follow, may convey the idea that the troubadours were engaged in elaborating a rigorous ethical system. Nothing could be farther from historical reality. This impression is, no doubt, created by our search for and use of a 'model' of courtly love, a model that – to borrow a scientific notion – reproduces, through schematization of its essential features, a phenomenon in order to understand it. But it would be wrong to deduce from this operation that courtly love was born as a complete doctrine, defined once and for all by the troubadour.[17] Actually, there was never such a complete or perfect *doctrine*, and, in any case, the first known troubadour – given his Janus-like attitude towards love – would be the last person to be considered as a coherent codifier of courtly love. The Duke of Aquitaine, however, provided the basis for a new way of understanding love and the relationship between lovers simply by declaring *obediensa* to his lady, by recognizing his being *aclin* ('obedient') to her. Many other elements that were to concur in the notion of courtly love came much later, with the poets of the so-called generation of 1170. It was a splendid generation, rich in strong artistic personalities such as Peire d'Alvernhe, Raimbaut d'Aurenga, Bernart de Ventadorn, and Giraut de Bornelh, who refined *cortez'amor* under the pressure of the moralistic teachings of Marcabru's poetry. They accepted the notion of *obediensa*, but they also sang of *fin'amor* as the source of moral goodness. The poets of the generation of 1200 formalized and conventionalized the notions they had inherited, showing a slight tendency to temper the erotic element and emphasize the spiritual overtones. This long and uneven history was enlivened by numerous controversies and debates among poets and different stylistic schools, and was marked by poetical conversions, and even by occasional objurations. Fortunately, under that very agitated surface, there exist strong elements of continuity and stability that legitimize and facilitate the creation of a critical model.

In a sense all interpretations of courtly love have relied on models in order to bring out what their authors perceive to be the persistent features of troubadour love poetry. For sure, the need for building a model of courtly love is as old as the troubadours themselves. They never felt it necessary to analyse in logical terms the principles of their moral world: they just sang them. Only occasionally they discuss themes of love, nobility, and virtue. But either the novelty or the ambiguity of their singing compelled at least one of their contemporaries to build a model of courtly love, essentially to exorcize it. This man is Andreas Capellanus, the first militant interpreter of courtly love. Our model of *fin'amor* makes great use of Andreas's interpretation, since it is indeed invaluable. Andreas's familiarity with the world of courtliness, his critical approach, and his concern for moral problems allowed him to focus on what we consider to be the core of all ambiguity and originality of courtly love – namely, the relationship between love and virtue, between sex and *proeza*. Yet the ultimate goal of this study is to get rid of Andreas. Paradoxically, Andreas's *De Amore* has constituted the greatest impediment to the understanding of courtly love.[18] The major responsibility for this fact rests on Andreas's readers, who take his treatise to be a manual, a codification of courtly love rather than an interpretation of it. The minor responsibility rests on the work itself, on the way in which Andreas develops his argument.

De Amore cannot be considered, as it has been,[19] just one of the many *artes amandi* written during the twelfth and thirteenth centuries. These *artes* deal in general with courtliness, not specifically with love. If, for instance, we examine the *Facetus* – the treatise that bears the closest resemblances to *De Amore* – we can see that its author is hardly concerned with the subject of love. In the section devoted to it, he presents a set of dialogues between men and women, as does Andreas; but, while all the dialogues in the *Facetus* have a happy ending, those in *De Amore* do not. In the *Facetus* the dialogues are followed by a bitter misogynistic tirade comparable with *De Amore*'s third book. However, the differences are decisive: Andreas condemns women on moral grounds, whereas the author of the *Facetus* condemns them on purely aesthetic and physical principles. Thus, if the *Facetus* is the closest any *ars amandi* can get to *De Amore*, there is no question that Andreas stands alone as the author of a singular book concerned exclusively with the problem of love, completely indifferent to matters of courtly etiquette or to any other mundane subjects which make up the main bulk of the various contemporary *documenta* or *ensenhamens*. It is a distinction that has led to repeated misunderstandings of Andreas's work, misunderstandings which, in turn, have greatly confused the interpretation of courtly love.

Andreas's treatise is usually considered a *vademecum* of courtly love,[20] and it is quite common practice to quote from it whenever a troubadour poem presents themes, ideas, or motifs found also in *De Amore*. No thought is given to questions of chronology, or to the fact that no troubadour ever mentions Andreas, and that Andreas never quotes a troubadour. These difficulties are not insurmountable,[21] but they very much discredit the idea that *De Amore* was ever a *vademecum*, a manual from which the troubadours could draw materials for their poems. What is even more discrediting is that, in *De Amore* there are many elements (e.g., the definition of love that opens the treatise; the notion of youth; the anti-feminism of the third book) that are totally inexplicable in a supposed manual of courtly love. The relation between Andreas and the troubadours becomes much clearer and more meaningful if we understand his treatise to be an interpretation of courtly love rather than a simple codification of it. Only with this understanding it is possible to make full use of Andreas's treatise. As a preliminary inquiry as we read *De Amore*, we must see what materials Andreas drew from the troubadours' world so as to be sure that he was talking about courtly love and not other forms of love. Then we will reconstruct his method of argumentation to see how he denounces the critical fault in the 'system' of courtly love – how he denies the philosophical possibility of building an ethical system on eros, demonstrating that this assumption central to courtly love is nothing but hypocrisy. If we follow Andreas that far, his analysis will have shown clearly how the relation between passion and reason is at the core of courtly love. This is the point, however, where our interpretation must part company with that of the chaplain. His notion of hypocrisy (reason disguises passion) will be replaced by that of 'ambiguity' (reason and passion are consubstantial).

The Ambiguity of Courtly Love 13

In order to stay as close as possible to Andreas's model it is essential to use only the materials to which he presumably had access. We must therefore accept the most conservative dating of the work – namely, the last decade of the twelfth century (very likely between 1186 and 1196).[22] Such dating makes sense from the historical point of view because it places the composition of *De Amore* in the context of the animated poetic climate of the troubadours of the 1170 generation. Of lesser importance is the question of the place where the treatise was composed. Some archival documents, as well as some internal evidence, indicate that it was written in northern France;[23] some other elements point instead to southern France.[24] Whichever may be the case, its location is not particularly decisive: notwithstanding some differences,[25] the courtly love phenomenon was common to both parts of France, and the exchanges between both traditions were much more intense than is normally suspected.[26] Moreover, one must always bear in mind that Andreas's model, by its very nature, was sparse in specific historical references, and it can therefore be used to fit many versions of courtly love. Traditionally, however, Andreas's work is related to the world of the troubadours for thematic similarities and because its characters seem to portray the southern 'gentlemen' rather than the northern knights.[27] Indeed, we shall see that many motifs and themes of troubadour poetry are present in Andreas's treatise, making his knowledge of it a virtual certainty.

ANDREAS'S MODEL: ITS COURTLY MATERIALS AND
THEIR FUNCTIONS

Andreas explicitly puts forward the principle of *obediensa* as a commandment of love: 'Dominarum praeceptis in omnibus obediens semper studeas amoris agregari militiae' [Being always obedient in all things to ladies' commands be eager to join the army of Love].[28] This is one of the rules of love contained in the fifth dialogue of the first book; but the duty of *obediensa* is implied in all the other dialogues as an indispensable principle of love.[29] This principle, as stated above, was already expressed, as we saw, by Guilhem IX, who died in 1126.

In the ninth chapter of the first book, Andreas talks about love acquired with money, 'de amore per pecuniam acquisito.' Perhaps this problem is discussed because the troubadours mention it several times. We find it in Marcabru (ed. Dejeanne, XXI, ll. 32 ff. and *passim*); it is the subject of a debate between Giraut de Bornelh and King Alfonso which took place around 1172 (ed. Kolsen, LIX); it is touched upon by the *trobairitz* Azalais de Porcairagues,[30] and by Bernart de Ventadorn (ed. Lazar, VII, l. 18; XLI, l. 35) and it is found in the work of Guilhelm de Saint Didier (ed. Sakari, III, l. 43) among others. It is superfluous to say that, for the troubadours as for Andreas, love that can be bought or sold does not deserve any praise. But if the question arises among the troubadours it does so because they reject the identification of wealth with nobility in favour of that of nobility with virtue.

In the dialogue between a man of higher nobility and a commoner (*nobilior plebeiae*), the lady expresses her concern about the *detractores*, the malevolent gossipers who could stain her honour. The nobleman acknowledges the possibility of provoking 'vaniloquia vulgi et insidiantium suspectos rumores' [the empty gossip of the mob and the dubious rumours of spies, p. 115]; but he minimizes the effect they might have upon a happy love, which always causes envy in the crowds. These *pravi homines* are a counterpart of the omnipresent *lauzengiers*, the vile gossipers who oblige the troubadour lovers to be extremely discreet.

Chastity is a theme upon which *De Amore* touches several times. Once, for instance, it appears in a rule of love: 'Castitatem servare debes amanti' [You must maintain chastity for your beloved, p. 106]; later, a reference to this rule is made in the closing sentence of the last dialogue: 'Non enim iuxta praeceptum amoris castitatem videtur amanti servasse, cuius impudicus conatus mentem detegit impudicam' [A lover whose lewd attempt reveals a shameless mind does not seem to have maintained chastity for her lover according to the precept of love, p. 219], where the 'impudicus conatus' refers to philandering with other women in order to forget the one the man loves. The context makes it clear that *castitas* is not abstinence but faithfulness, and it is thus an expression of *obediensa*. Indeed, 'amor reddit hominem castitatis quasi virtute decoratum, quia vix posset de alterius etiam formosae cogitare amplexu, qui unius radio fulget amoris' [Love makes a man as though he is adorned with the virtue of chastity, for he who shines with the light of just one love can hardly think of embracing another woman however beautiful, p. 10].

An identical notion of chastity is found among the troubadours. It is figuratively expessed by Folquet de Marselha:

> Trop vos am mais, dona, qu'ieu non sai dire,
> e quar anc jorn aic d'autr'amor desire

no m'en penet, ans vos am per un cen,
car ai proat l'autrui captenemen (ed. Stroński, II, ll. 41–4)

[I love you, lady, much more than I can tell you, and since I never had a desire of another love, I do not regret it; on the contrary I love you a hundred times more, having experienced (i.e., observed) the behaviour of others].

It is a motif used by Raimbaut d'Aurenga:

Autra non poria amar ges
Per nulla beltat qez agues (ed. Pattison, XXIII, ll. 105–6)

[I could not love any other woman, however beautiful she may be]

and again:

[...] midons, c'aixi·m lia
Que vas autra no·m apel (XXIX, ll. 46–7)

[... my lady who binds me so that I do not address myself to any other woman]

or in Guilhem de Cabestanh:

En sovinensa
Tenc la car'e·l dous ris,
Vostra valensa
E·l belh cors blanc e lis;
S' ieu per crezensa
Estes vas Dieu tan fis,
Vius ses falhensa
Intrer'em paradis;
Qu'ayssi·m suy, ses totz cutz,
De cor a vos rendutz
Qu'autra joy no m'adutz:
Q'una non porta benda
Qu'ieu·n prezes per esmenda
Jazer ni fos sos drutz,
Per las vostras salutz (ed. Långfors, V, ll. 31–45)

> [I keep in my memory your face and your sweet smile, your elegance and the beautiful body so white and smooth; if I were so faithful to God I would be worthy of entering Paradise while still alive. Because, without any thought, I have given myself to you so heartily that no other (woman) can bring me joy. There is nobody among those who wear a wimple (i.e., all women) with whom I would like to sleep or whose lover I would like to be, rather than to have your greetings]

or Arnaut de Maruelh:

> car lei qu'eu plus am e desir
> non aus mon talan descubrir
> ni altr'amor non posc voler   (ed. Johnston, XIV, ll. 5–7)
>
> [since I do not dare to manifest my wish to the one I love and desire, and I cannot wish another love]

or in the intensely lyrical lines of Arnaut Daniel:

> D'autras vezer soi secs e d'auzir sors
> qu'en sola lei veg e aug e esgar   (ed. Perugi, XV, ll. 8–9)
>
> [I am blind to seeing other women and deaf to hearing them, because I see and hear and contemplate only her].

For the troubadours as well as for Andreas, chastity means loyalty to a lady. It is for this reason that the semantic field of *castitatz* contains words such as *fizel, firm, cert, leial* (faithful, firm, certain, loyal), which also fall under the general heading of *obediensa*, and more specifically within the realm of devotion. In view of this fact it appears wrong to interpret, as do some scholars, a line by Guilhem de Montanhagol: 'e d'amour mou Castitatz' (ed. Ricketts, XII, 18; and chastity springs from love) as if it were an indication of a new spiritual orientation of courtly love.[31]

The definition of *amor purus* found in *De Amore* is very famous:

> Et purus quidem amor est, qui omnimoda dilectionis affectione duorum amantium corda coniungit. Hic autem in mentis contemplatione

cordisque consistit affectu; procedit autem usque ad oris osculum
lacertique amplexum et verecundum amantis nudae contactum, extremo praetermisso solatio; nam illud pure amare volentibus ex-
ercere non licet. (p. 182)

[Pure love is the one which binds together the hearts of two lovers
with a total affection. It consists in a mental contemplation and in
the affection of the heart; it goes as far as kissing on the mouth and
embracing with the arms and a pure contact of the naked loved
lady, without the ultimate solace because this is not allowed to
those who want to practise pure loving].

The expression *amor purus* is – as far as I know – quite uncommon (was
it coined by Andreas?), and it has often been considered as corresponding to *fin'amor*. In its definition there are three important points that
represent three stages of love: the first two are the union of hearts and
the kiss, both studied by R. Nelli;[32] the third is the *concubitus sine actu*,
also studied, but less successfully, by R. Nelli. These three stages of
amor purus have ample correspondences in troubadour poetry. For our
purpose, the last stage is the most interesting one because lying with
the lady without possessing her seems quite a strange practice, and the
fact that we find it in both *De Amore* and troubadour poetry cannot
easily be the fruit of mere coincidence.

This amorous test – some instances of which are also recorded in
northern France – is known by a technical term among the troubadours:
it is called *assag* or *assai*, meaning 'assay,' 'test.' There is some question
whether the poets of the early generation ever used this motif, which
occurs fairly frequently in the poetry of the later generations.[33] For example, it appears highly dramatized in an episode of *Flamenca*. R. Nelli,
who first studied this motif, does not sufficiently document it. He supports his thesis with passages from the poem of Beatritz de Dia and
Azalais de Porcairagues, and with the episode of *Flamenca*. The texts of
the two women poets, however, could be interpreted differently,[34] and
Nelli's thesis would seem rather weak. There are, instead, other texts
that explicitly refer to the *assag*. One is by Raimbaut d'Aurenga:

Mas mandatz mi per plans essais,
Per tal cobrir sol sapcha·l cais!
Qu'eu irai lai de grant eslais.
Qu'ie·n pert la color e·l sanc

> Tal talent ai que·m desvesta
> C'ab vos fos ses vestimenta
> Aissi com etz la plus genta   (ed. Pattison, XV, ll. 47–53)

[But ask me for a plain *assai*: do it so secretively that only the mouth knows. I will go to it with great haste. I am losing my colour and my blood, because I have such a desire of undressing myself so as to be with you without clothes, as you are the most gentle one].

It is not uncommon to find in the poetry of the earliest troubadours expressions of their desire to lie next to their lovers in the nude (see, for example, Cercamon, ed. Jeanroy, II, ll. 45–9; VIII, ll. 41–2; Comtessa de Dia, ed. Kussler-Ratyé, III, ll. 9–12) as a possible allusion to an *assag*. In passages such as these,[35] one is allowed to see a situation where the *amor purus*, that is, 'extremo praetermisso solatio' is practised with enjoyment. Raimbaut d'Aurenga bluntly says that it is possible to enjoy love without consummating it: 'E feira·m ses faitz esgauzir' (ed. Pattison, VI, l. 46: And she would make me enjoy without the *faitz*).[36]

But there are more explicit occurrences of *assag*. One is in the *partimen* between Gaucelm Faidit and Peirol. Here the latter asks the question:

> Gaucelm, diguatz m'al vostre sen
> qals drutz ha mais de son plazer?
> cel c'ab sa bona dona jai
> tot'una nueit, e non lo fai;
> ho cel qui ve a parlamen
> e no a lezer gaire
> mas quant d'una vetz faire,
> e aqui meteis torna s'en?   (ed. Mouzat, LX, ll. 1–8)

[Gaucelm, tell me, in your opinion, which one of the two lovers has the greater pleasure, the one who lies the whole night long with his good lady and does not 'do it,' or the one who goes to visit her and has hardly the time to 'do it' only once and goes away immediately?].

The discussion goes on for a while – the poem is incomplete – and Gaucelm firmly maintains that the first lover is the happier one. But Peirol argues that refraining from the *faitz* is a cruel test:

> Gaucelm, ben ha gran espaven
> aquel qu'es en autrui poder,
> que trastot'una nueit i jai
> de lonc cella que plus li plai,
> e non pot aver son talen
> ni sa voluntat faire,
> don trai negus pecaire,
> ins en enfern, aital turmen. (ll. 17–24)

[Gaucelm, he really has a great fright who is in another person's power, and who lies the whole night alongside his dearest one and cannot have his pleasure nor have his own wish. No sinner in hell receives such torment].

The same subject is picked up by Aimeric de Peguilhan, who asks Elias d'Ussel for advice:

> N'Elyas, conseill vos deman
> De lieis c'am mais c'autrui ni me,
> Qe·m ditz qe·m colgara ab se
> Una nuoich, ab qe·il jur e·il man
> Que non la fortz part son talan,
> Mas q'eu estei baisan tenen.
> Del far digatz m'al vostre sen:
> S'es mieils c'aissi sofra et endur,
> O part son voler me perjur.

And Elias answers:

> N'Aimeric, e·us vauc conseillan
> Que, s'ab si·us colga, faitz l'o be,
> Car, qui sa dompna en son bratz te,
> Fols es s'aillor la vai cercan;
> [...]
> Car, s'ieu era ab midonz jazen
> E n'avia faich sagramen,
> Faria l'o, so·us assegur,
> Qui que m'en tengues per perjur (ed. Shepard and Chambers, XXXVII, ll. 1–18)

['Sir Elias, I ask your advice about the lady whom I love more than anyone else or myself. She told me that I might lie with her for one night, provided that I swear to her and promise not to force her against her wish, and to be content with kissing and hugging. Tell me your opinion about the fact, whether it is better to suffer and endure, or to perjure myself against her will.' – 'Sir Aimeric, if she lets you lie with her, my advice to you is to do the *faich* for her; because he who holds his lady in his arms is crazy if he seeks for her elsewhere [...] If I were in bed with my lady and had sworn to her, I would do the *faich*, I can assure you, whoever may consider me a perjurer on that account'].

This text, dated around 1208 by the editors, is perhaps too late to be known by Andreas; even so, it is of great interest because it confirms the vitality of the *assag* motif. In general, *partimen* discuss fashionable themes, and it is therefore not surprising if the dilemma just seen is chosen at least once more as the subject of another *partimen* where Donna H. poses to Rofin the problem: 'My lady agrees to let me lie with her provided that I limit myself to discreet embraces; shall I keep my promise or violate it?'[37]

Such predicaments are all too common in the poetry of the troubadours. It is naïve, however, to believe that they refer to real situations. Nelli's analysis of the *assag* theme has found little credit precisely because it assumes that this test was actually practised by courtly society. If this were the case, evidence would very likely be found elsewhere than in the poems of the troubadours. The *assag* theme undoubtedly contains the most explicit allusions to the sexual component of courtly love but is in no sense closer to a historical reality than is any other courtly love theme. Andreas, as a matter of fact, does not emphasize this theme any more than the others used in building his model of courtly love. From his polemical point of view, the *amor purus* mentioned by one of the characters proves the hypocrisy of courtly lovers, and the *assag* is nothing but a device of seduction, as are many other arguments used by courtly seducers. Thus, equating *amor purus* with *fin'amor* is wrong and impedes the understanding of courtly love. The *assag* is just a way of dramatizing *fin'amor*, which is *mezura*. The second chapter of this book will deal in some detail with other themes that have the same function. Discussing the *assag* now was necessary to support the idea that Andreas relies on troubadour themes in building his model, and this one in particular highlights the erotic component of courtly love.

There are many more thematic similarities between *De Amore* and the poetry of the troubadours than seen so far,[38] and all of them could support the idea that Andreas had in mind the troubadours as his ideal interlocutors; but since these themes add very little to the interpretation of *fin'amor*, we do not lose very much by neglecting them in order to focus on a study of the theme that Andreas considers most important. It is the theme of *probitas morum*, of spiritual beauty, which, significantly, is treated in *De Amore* and in no other *ars amandi* of Ovidian lineage. This theme occupies the most extended part of Andreas's treatise and involves the problem of the relationship between virtue and love, between love and *proeza*, which in the world of the troubadours are interrelated.

Whenever Andreas uses the word *probitas*, the fourteenth-century Italian translator[39] renders it with *prodezza* and the French translator, Druart La Vache, with *prouesse* (cf. English 'prowess'). These vernacular renderings carry a vaguely military or, at least, chivalric connotation, due in part to the epic tradition.[40] Such is not the case in Provençal, where the adjective *proz* seldom has the meaning of 'valiant,'[41] and *proeza* (a back formation on the adjective) always means spiritual beauty. There is, thus, a perfect correspondence between Andreas's *probitas* and the troubadour's *proeza*. We have an indirect proof of this equivalence in a Provençal text which translates the Latin word *probitas* with *proeza*:

> Per aysso dit Boeci, un gran doctor, que s'apela en sancta gleyça mosenher Sant Sever: 'magna nobis, ubi dissimulare non velimus, indicta probitatis necessitas, cum agamus coram occulis iudicis cuncta cernentis': gran proeça nos fay mestiers, si doncs no volem dissimular, com nos sapiam e siam sert que totas nostras obras sian preçens davant los uelhs de nostre iutge, que tot o ve.[42]

Proeza is a word that appears in the vocabulary of the earliest troubadours, including William IX (ed. Pasero, II, l. 15; XI, l. 25). It indicates the sum of all courtly virtues. As such, it found a passionate singer in Marcabru, the poet of rectitude, the nostalgic moralist whose criticism of his contemporary world was, to a great extent, a bitter lament about the disappearance of *proeza*:

> Tant cant bos Jovens fon paire
> Del segle e fin'Amors maire,

> Fon Proeza mantenguda
> A celat et a saubuda,
> Mas er l'ant avilanada
> Duc e rei et emperaire (ed. Dejeanne, V, ll. 37–42)

[As long as good *joven* was the father of the world and *fin'amor* was its mother, *proeza* was kept up, both privately and in public. But now dukes, kings, and emperors have degraded it].

So *proeza*, the personification of moral rectitude, often appears as the victim of moral upheaval, and it remains the implacable antagonist of *avoleza* and *malvestat*:

> Avoleza porta la clau
> E geta Proez'en issil (XXXIII, ll. 19–20)

[Wickedness holds the key and throws *proeza* into exile]

or:

> Qui ves Proeza balansa
> semblansa fai de malvatz (XVIII, ll. 5–6)

[He who hesitates (to embrace) *proeza* shows himself to be a base person].

Proeza alone, for Marcabru, has the monopoly on courtliness; actually it is courtliness itself, so that it is better defined as the antonym not only of *avoleza* and *malvestat* but also of their social or worldly expression as *escarsetat* and *vilania* (cf. e.g., XXIV, ll. 16 ff.; XXXVI, ll. 13 ff.).

So powerful was Marcabru's personification of *proeza* that it outlasted him. At one time as the antagonist of baseness, at another time as the inspirer of liberality and of good manners, *proeza* lives in the poems of troubadours such as Peire d'Alvernha (ed. Del Monte, VI, ll. 13 f.; XV, ll. 9 ff.), Cercamon (ed. Jeanroy, V, l. 25; VI, l. 14), and Alegret (ed. Dejeanne, I, l. 19). *Proeza*, as the highest moral value, is embodied in the lady whom the troubadour loves: for example, she may be the lady of a Folquet de Marselha (ed. Stroński, XXI, l. 29) or of a Giraut de Bornelh (ed. Kolsen, VIII, l. 1). *Proeza* is the source of *joy*, as explicitly stated by Rigaut de Berbezilh (ed. Varvaro, XI, l. 41) or by the Monge de Montaudon (ed. Klein, VIII). *Proeza* – moral beauty – combined with *pretz* – the social prestige that comes from it – holds an irresistible fascination, as Beatritz de Dia (or la Comtessa de Dia) well knew:

> Proesa grans q'el vostre cors s'aizina
> e lo rics pretz q'avetz m'en atayna,
> c'una non sai loindana ni vezina,
> si vol amar, vas vos non si' aclina   (ed. Kussler-Ratyé, IV, ll. 22–5)

> [(I am so awed by) the great *proeza* which rests in you and by the great *pretz* that you have, that I know no lady, be she far away or close by, who, if she is ready to love, does not give herself to you].

Every troubadour, every acolyte of courtly love must be *pros*, must live in conformity with *proeza*. So important was this concept that it was subjected to a detailed analysis – a unique case in the troubadour *corpus* – by a poet of the 1170 generation, Arnaut de Maruelh, who devoted an *ensenhamen*, a short didactic poem, to this subject.[43] Written before 1196 but no earlier than 1162 – unfortunately there is no internal or external evidence to date it more precisely – this composition by Arnaut, rather than being a typical *ensenhamen*, is a sort of manifesto meant to vindicate *proeza* from any falsification and especially from a simplistic identification with the aristocratic status.

Whoever wants to be courteous, Arnaut says after a few opening lines, must love and fear God and must be conversant with the history of all peoples, inquire about their habits, and know how good and bad persons act; he must know and retain everything on that account. After this description of the first cardinal virtue, *sapientia*, Arnaut introduces us to *proeza*:

> Ja non aura proeza
> Qui no fug avoleza
> E non la pot fugir
> Qui non la sap chauzir   (ed. Eusebi, ll. 77–80)

> [He will never have *proeza* who does not avoid wickedness; and one cannot avoid it unless he is able to sort it out].

Proeza stands here in sharp contrast to *avoleza*. The choice between the two is easy, provided that one is able to discern the dangers of *avoleza*,

24 Andreas and the Ambiguity of Courtly Love

and wise enough to embrace *proeza*, distinguishing it from any counterfeit. This discernment helps us to recognize wise people and to love their company, tells us when it is time for mirth and for earnestness, and teaches us to be humble with good people and proudly diffident towards wicked ones: 'C'onz sia humils als bos / Et als mals ergulhos' (ll. 107–8); for this is a sign of true nobility.⁴⁴ Any man who acts according to these principles of wisdom is *pros*, regardless of his social status. *Proeza* is indeed a moral quality which

> Ges no nais ni comensa
> Segon autra naissensa,
> Qu'ins el cor, so sapchatz,
> La noiris voluntatz;
> E nous sia veiaire
> Si filhs fo de bo paire,
> C'onz pros es meravilh
> Si non pareys al filh.
> Terras Pot honz laissar
> E son filh eretar
> Mas pretz non aura ja
> Si de som cor nol tra   (ll. 147–58)

[(*Proeza*) is not born and does not begin anywhere else but in the heart. Know that the will nourishes it. It should not seem strange to you if a *proshomme* who was born to a good father does not, in turn, have a son similar to him. One can leave lands and his son can inherit them; but he will never have *pretz* if he does not draw it from his own heart].

Pretz, the prestige or respect accorded to people who have discernment, is derived only from *proeza*, not from nobility of lineage or from riches:

> Paratje d'auta gen,
> Poders d'aur ni d'argen
> Nous daran ja bon pretz
> Si ric cor non avetz
> Ric cor sens desmezura   (ll. 163–7)

[High and noble extraction, power of gold and silver, will not give you esteem unless you have a noble heart, a noble heart without any arrogance].

Such a noble heart is basically *proeza* itself:

> Proeza eis de coratje,
> Veus lo melhor linhatje (ll. 169–70)

[*Proeza* springs from the heart. There you have the best lineage].

And it brings *pretz* because *proeza* is:

> Conoissensa e sabers,
> Sens, largues'e poders
> Dono pretz per tos temps
> Quils sap aver essem (ll. 173–6)

[Discernment, knowledge, good sense, liberality, and power always give *pretz* to those who know how to have all these virtues at the same time].

Proeza, then, is the sum of the cardinal virtues: *conoissensa* and *sabers* correspond to *sapientia*; *sens* is essentially *temperantia*; *largueza* falls under the realm of *iustitia*; and *poders* is *fortitudo*. *Proeza*, we might say, is similar to the Latin *honestum*, moral beauty, a concept to which we shall return later.

Conoissensa and *largueza*, Arnaut continues, are the key to *proeza*; *poder* is its lock: who does not know how to open it gently cannot sustain his *pretz* for long. It is, therefore, appropriate for *sen* to hold the key while *saber* becomes the gentle messenger able to talk and to do lovely and endearing things. The combined and simultaneous presence of these qualities constitutes perfect *proeza*. But such perfection is very rare. Often we hear that some knights or clergymen or ladies have *pretz*; they, however, do not necessarily have *proeza*, but only a greater or lesser share of some specific virtues. *Proeza* cannot be divided, nor can it exist in lesser or minimal degrees.

In closing his poem, Arnaut reiterates his attacks against the common notion that aristocracy is the depository of *proeza*. It is possible he says – repeating an idea which is also expressed by Andreas Capellanus – that the creation of a superior social class responded to an original need of mankind to select as leaders those people in whom the feeling for mercy, temperance, liberality, and justice ('E merces e mezura/e larguez' e dreitura,' ll. 313–14) was stronger than in anyone else. Today, however, the noblemen are not worthy of their origins.

This conclusion shows the polemic nature of Arnaut's teaching. His *ensenhamen* is in many ways an attack on the hereditary aristocracy; its lines and tone unmistakably recall the moralistic verses of Marcabru. Arnaut, like many troubadours, recognizes *pretz* only in those who live with *proeza*, forming a new aristocracy of noble hearts.

Arnaut makes no mention of love: his exclusive interest is in describing *proeza* and in seeing its relationship to nobility. The problem had remote origins;[45] but it acquired deep social and moral implications only in the twelfth century. It is, therefore, not surprising that it became a fairly common topic of discussion.[46] The most appropriate genre for this discussion was the *partimen*. Besides the already mentioned *partimen* between King Alfonso and Giraut de Bornelh, several others are devoted to the same question. Some of them were composed in Andreas's day – for example, the debate between Perdigon and the Dalfin d'Alvernhe. Others, such as the *Ensenhamens d'onor* by Sordel, were composed later. The theme of nobility acquired through virtue, however, is not confined to these debates alone. It pervades the poetry of the troubadours and involves the notions of *obediensa, paria*, and so on delineated at the beginning of this chapter. Andreas was thus very perceptive in making the *probitas morum* one of the pivotal elements in his model of courtly love.

For Andreas, however, the problem was not so much one of accepting the notion that virtue and nobility coincide as the role that physical love played in that equation, and whether love really generated virtue and, consequently, nobility. It is too bad that Arnaut de Maruelh did not touch upon the problem of the connection between love and proeza: given the didactic and theoretical nature of his work, his treatment of such a problem would have been enlightening. The troubadours never engaged in a discussion of this problem either. Their general assumption, however, is that love causes *proeza*, and this assumption is repeatedly stated in their lyrical language. Arnaut de Maruelh himself opens a poem with this strophe:

> A gran honor viu cui jois es cobitz,
> que d'aqui mou cortesi'e solatz,
> enseignamenz e franques'e mesura,
> e cors d'amar et esfortz de servir,
> e chausimenz, sabers e conoisensa,
> e gens parlars et avinens respos,
> e tuich bon aip, per qu'om es gais e pros   (ed. Johnston, XXI, ll. 1–7)

[Who has been granted joy (of love) lives in great honour, because from it are derived courtliness and pleasure, education, frankness and temperance, loving heart and desire of serving (love), discernment, wisdom and knowledge, beautiful conversation and appropriate answers, all the qualities through which a man is joyful and virtuous].

Here it appears that the virtues which, when combined, constitute *proeza* are caused, or at least brought to life by the joy of love. Marcabru had already said: 'Ai! fin'Amors fons de bontat' (ed. Dejeanne, XL, l. 36: Ah! *fin'Amors*, source of goodness), and even if there is a sarcasm in this line, it could not be understood unless it was directed against a common assumption.

There are also more persuasive passages containing explicit reference to the filiation *fin'amor–proeza*. Here is one by Arnaut Daniel:

Amors es de Prez la claus
e de Proes'us estancs
don naisso tut li bon frug
s'es qui lialmen los cueilla (ed. Perugi, XI, ll. 9–12)

[Love is the key to *prez* and it is the pool of *proeza*: thence come all the good fruits if there is someone who knows how to pick them]

and another one by Bernart de Ventadorn:

Per re non es om tan prezans
com per amor e per domnei,
que d'aqui mou deportz e chans
e tot can a proez'abau (ed. Lazar, XI, ll. 25–8)

[Nothing makes man so worthy as love and courting ladies: because from this comes all joy and singing and anything that pertains to *proeza*].

Love, source of virtue! This is the fundamental principle upon which the universe of troubadour poetry is based. Yet it remains a simple assumption, never philosophically demonstrated. This is the weakest point of the 'system' of courtly love, and Andreas exposes it as its major critical fault. In his demonstration it will be clear that the filiation physical love–virtue is simply an insidious *petitio principii*.

Now that we have isolated the main components in Andreas's model, it is time to consider how he organizes them in order to build his argument against courtly love.

ANDREAS'S POLEMIC AGAINST COURTLY LOVE

Andreas's treatise opens with a definition of love:

> Amor est passio quaedam innata procedens ex visione et immoderata cogitatione formae alterius sexus, ob quam aliquis super omnia cupit alterius potiri amplexibus et omnia de utriusque voluntate in ipsius amplexu amoris praecepta compleri (p. 3)

> [Love is an inborn suffering resulting from the sight of and immoderate thinking about an image of the other sex; so that a man desires above anything else to enjoy the embraces of the other sex, and by common wish, to carry out all the precepts of love in the other's embrace].

Andreas then analyses all the elements of his definition. Love is suffering (*passio*) because, until it reaches fulfilment, it is constantly plagued by fears of all kinds (e.g., fear of being rejected because one is poor or ugly), it knows the torment of jealousy, and it must always defend itself against gossip. This suffering is inborn, produced by an uncontrolled meditation on an image. When a man sees a woman who attracts him, he begins thinking incessantly about her so that her image obsesses him. He constantly wonders about her limbs and he lusts for her. Love, in sum, comes from seeing and meditating; yet not all meditation on an image can be called love, but only that which is exaggerated and obsessive.

Andreas's definition of love is so strictly physiological that it closely resembles a definition given by medical authorities. Constantinus Africanus, writing about the disease of love in his *Pantegni*,[47] says: 'mor autem est animae sollicitudo in id quod amatur et cogitationis in ipsum perseverantia' [Moreover love is an anxiety of the soul for what is loved and a persistent meditating upon the same].

Another example, even closer to Andreas's definition, can be found in Avicenna's *Canon*:[48]

> Haec aegritudo est sollicitudo melancholica, similis melancholiae, in qua homo sibi iam induxit incitationem cogitationis suae super pulchritudinem quarundam formarum et figurarum quae insunt ei
>
> [This disease (i.e., *kukjbut*, the Arabic word for the disease of love) is a melancholic distress in origin, similar to melancholy; it is produced when a man excites himself with an intense meditation upon the beauty of certain forms and figures which are in him].

Andreas, it appears, took the key elements for his definition of love from medical authorities rather than from Ovid[49] or the church *doctores*, as it has often been stated.[50] One of these elements is *cogitatio*, a term present in all three definitions given here. *Cogitatio* is an operation not of the intellect, but rather of the *vis cogitativa*, one of the internal senses, which has a clearly sexual origin in Andreas's view as well as in the medical treatises, since they specify that love can exist only between two people of opposite sex. Moreover, for Andreas as well as for his sources, the *cogitatio amorosa* is different from all types of *cogitatio*, in so far as it is immoderate.[51] Andreas's emphasis on the medical aspects of love are proven not only by an explicit quotation from the writings of the Arabic physician Johannicius – a quotation which appears when Andreas is describing, *iuxta phisicalem auctoritatem*,[52] the pathological effects of love – but also by other elements such as his setting physiological limits to love:

> Et scire debes, quod omnis compos mentis, qui aptus est ad Veneris opera peragenda, potest amoris pertingi aculeis, nisi aetas impediat vel caecitas vel nimia voluptatis abundantia. Aetas impedit, quia post sexagesimum annum in masculo et post quinquaegesimum in femina, licet coire homo possit, eius tamen voluptas ad amorem deduci non potest, quia calor naturalis ab ea aetate suas incipit amittere vires, et humiditas sua validissime inchoat incrementa fovere atque hominem in varias deducit angustias et aegritudinum diversarum molestat insidiis, nullaque sunt sibi in hoc saeculo praeter cibi et potus solatia. Similiter ante duodecim annos femina, et ante decimum quartum annum masculus non solet in amoris exercitu militare (pp. 11–12)
>
> [And you should know that everyone of sound mind capable of carrying out Venus' works can be reached by the arrows of love

unless age, blindness or an excess of passion prevents it. Age is an impediment because after the sixtieth year for a man and the fiftieth for a woman, although one can have intercourse, his pleasure cannot grow into love, because by that age his natural heat begins to lose its strengths while his humours begin to grow very much and it leads him into various troubles, tormenting him with the dangers of several ailments; so that he cannot have other pleasure in this world except eating and drinking. Likewise a female before her twelfth year and a male before his fourteenth year do not serve in Love's army].

This extensive quotation is taken from the fifth chapter, entitled 'quae personae sint aptae ad amorem.' In this chapter Andreas also explains why blind people cannot love because seeing is a necessary prerequisite for loving, and why people who are victims of immoderate concupiscence cannot sustain just one *cogitatio*, as they get excited by any image.

Unquestionably, thus, Andreas understands the origins of love in purely physiological terms and devotes many pages to the notions of *humores*, age, and other related physiological aspects. In this respect, *De Amore* should be classified among works such as Aldobrandino da Siena's *Le Régime du corps*.[53] No one would establish a similarity between Andreas's notion of age and the key concept of *joven*, which the troubadours use without attaching to it any physiological connotation.[54] Andreas clearly presents love not as *phylia*, to use Aristotle's terminology, but as *phylesis* – a passion that hampers the intellect's operations and, in contrast to *phylia*, exists only between individuals of the opposite sex.

Andreas's chapter on the physiology of love is preceded by several observations on the effects of love,[55] which lovers take to be virtue. The *dispositio* of these arguments is not very logical, so one cannot help drawing the disconcerting conclusion that virtue is no longer attainable for a man after his sixties or for a woman after her fifties! Love does indeed cause dramatic changes:

> Effectus autem amoris hic est, quia verus amator nulla posset avaritia offuscari, amor horridum et incultum omni facit formositate pollere, infimos natu etiam morum novit nobilitate ditare, superbos quoque solet humilitate beare, obsequia cunctis amorosus multa consuevit decenter parare (pp. 9–10)

[And such is the effect of love that a true lover cannot be stained by avarice; love causes anyone who is uncouth and uncultivated to be distinguished for his elegance; and it can bestow nobility of mores on anyone who is of very humble extraction; it blesses the proud person with humility; and the man who is in love becomes accustomed to rendering appropriately many services for everyone].

Faced with such miraculous effects, Andreas cannot refrain from uttering his bewilderment:

O, quam mira res est amor, qui tantis facit hominem fulgere virtutibus tantisque docet quemlibet bonis moribus abundare! (p. 10)

[Oh, what a wonderful thing love is, since it makes a man shine with so many virtues, and teaches him, whoever he might be, to abound in many and good habits!].

This exclamation is obviously ironic because Andreas was aware that virtue – infused or acquired – never represents a temporary possession strictly related to the duration of love. Indeed, he hastens to add that, if love could really originate virtue, he would not hesitate to embrace its laws. These laws are actually quite unjust because, as we shall see, love carries two weights in its hands.

Having established the origin and nature of love, Andreas begins the sixth chapter. Judging by its length (it covers almost two-thirds of the entire work), this chapter is the most important of the whole treatise. Judging by its content, it constitutes a small treatise all by itself, presenting an idea of love quite different and opposed to that maintained thus far by the author. This section is a sort of *dragmaticon* made up by eight dialogues between men and women of different social extraction. Each dialogue presents an example of how to conquer love: the chapter, as a matter of fact, is entitled 'Qualiter amor acquiratur et quot modis,' that is, 'In what manner and in how many ways love can be won.' The argument used by the male character echoes in many instances that of the troubadours, to the point that it is justified to see *De Amore*'s lovers as counterparts of the Provençal poets. It is not surprising, therefore, that Andreas's readers have widely utilized this chapter to reconstruct what they assume to be his courtly code. Unfortunately, this way of reading *De Amore* has caused endless misunderstandings of the work, as well as of courtly love, by attributing to the author the thoughts that belong, in fact, to his characters. Andreas's lovers are *dramatis personae*, not spokesmen for an author who is so unsympathetic towards his characters that he never helps them to succeed in their aim. It is indeed a strange fact that these *personae*, who are supposed to exemplify how to win love, are instead systematically rejected by the ladies they love. If we understand why this happens, we will have the key to Andreas's model of courtly love.

Andreas, who is committed to teach his pupil Walter how to win another's love, says that there are five means for doing so: physical beauty (*formae venustas*), moral beauty (*morum probitas*), eloquence (*copiosa sermonis facundia*), great wealth (*divitiarum abundantia*), and readiness in granting what has been asked (*facilis rei petitae concessio*). It is obvious that only two out of these five means – elegance of speech and moral beauty – can be the subject of discussion because they are the only ones that, to a certain degree, can be taught. Compared with them the other means of winning love are shallow, short-lived assets.

Probitas alone wins love ('sola ergo probitas amoris est digna corona,' p. 18). No beauty, no wealth deserves to be loved unless it is accompanied by moral excellence. *Probitas morum* is indeed such an important force that it is at the root of social-class differences. Andreas, the author, says:

> Nam quum omnes homines uno sumus ab initio stipite derivati unamque secundum naturam originem traximus omnes, non forma, non corporis cultus, non etiam opulentia rerum, sed sola fuit morum probitas, quae primitus nobilitate distinxit homines ac generis induxit differentiam (pp. 17–18)
>
> [For since all of us men are descended originally from one stock and we all had a birth according to nature, it was not beauty or physical care, or even wealth but moral beauty alone which brought distinction of nobility among men and introduced difference of class].

The idea that men come from a common root is a very old one, and it is found also among the troubadours. Equally old and known to the troubadours is the idea that probity is the origin of nobility.[56] The troubadours, however, do not share Andreas's view that social differences were established forever by our ancestors, even if the chaplain recognizes that many noblemen of his day are not worthy of their lineage.

Eloquence, fluency of speech, wins love, although this is not always the case:

> Sermonis facundia multotiens ad amandum non amantium corda compellit. Ornatum etenim amantis eloquium amoris consuevit concitare aculeos et de loquentis facit probitate praesumi (p. 18)
>
> [Oftentimes, fluency of speech will move to love even the hearts of those who are not in love. Indeed an elegant talk by a lover usually arouses the arrows of love and creates a presumption of moral beauty for the speaker].

How can this be so? Andreas has an explanation which, again, is based upon the differences of social class. A woman may belong to one of three classes: the middle class, the low nobility, or the higher nobility. The same is true for men (not counting the noblest of them all, the priests). But, while for men there is no social mobility, for women it is possible to move on the social ladder just by marrying someone of different rank. At first, this seems a strange explanation, but it is actually quite astute because it sets the frame, as it were, for the dialogues to come. The nature of the rank of both speakers – be it equal or not – should determine the *topoi* of the dialogues, in accordance with the first requirement of elegant eloquence – namely, the appropriateness of words to things. Elegance of speech creates the 'presumption' of moral beauty. The diversity of social ranks leads the discussion to focus on the *probitas morum* as a quality that reinstates equality. For women, social differences can be enticing or not, given their 'mobility' on the social scale.

Now the frame for the dialogues is set and their subjects are more or less defined. Andreas's characters can begin to act in order to ensure for themselves a presumption of probity. They feel entitled to do so by the fact that they love, and love – they will say, contrary to their creator's opinion – is the source of moral beauty. We are then ready to observe the dialectics between *probitas morum, nobilitas*, and *amor*, or, in the parallel terminology of another language, between *proeza, pretz*, and *amors*.

The distribution of the dialogues is as follows: both the commoner and the high aristocrat speak to three different women, each representing one of the three social classes; the low aristocrat talks only to a lady from the low class and to one of his peers. In all, there are eight dialogues. They seem a few too many, considering that the book was meant to be a guide for Walter, Andreas's pupil, who, we can assume, belonged just to one social class, so that four dialogues at the most would have prepared him for any possible encounter. But the spectrum of Andreas's characters is broad to the point that the discussion on nobility is seen in all possible combinations of viewpoints. What his characters maintain is opposite to the view of their creator, who had in his own voice defended the difference of classes. His male characters, instead, consider moral beauty as the only sign of nobility; and in doing so they sound very much like the troubadours.

The commoner opens this attack on social institution by boasting to have in himself that *probitas morum* which allows him to claim to be a real aristocrat:

> 'nobilitatem tibi non generis vel sanguinis propinavit origo, sed sola probitas et compositio morum digniori te nobilitatis specie ditaverunt. Nam homines universos ab initio prodiit una natura, unaque omnes usque ad hoc tempus tenuisset aequalitas, nisi magnanimitas et morum probitas coepisset homines nobilitatis inaequalitate distinguere.' (p. 23)

> ['You did not derive your nobility from your descent or your ancestors but only from goodness of character and manners which made you more worthy of nobility. As a matter of fact, just one nature created all men at the beginning and it would have kept us all equal until the present had it not been that magnanimity and probity began to differentiate men through the inequality of (levels of social) nobility'].

If the *plebeius* hopes to win love by arguing, as in this case, against the social notion of nobility ('quum ab eodem Adam stipite derivemur,'[57] he says at a certain point), the *nobilior* hopes for the same thing by renouncing his social rank when dealing with love:

> 'Ibi quisque debet sibi postulare amorem, ubi amoris suasione constringitur. Ille enim est amor electus, qui in quocunque ordine ex placibilitate et delectatione formae cuiusque solummodo sumpsit originem, non qui ob generis tantum quaeritur praerogativam. Amoris itaque non subverto praecepta, si ex minori ordine mihi

curem amorem eligere, sed eius in hoc videor mandatis obsecundare. Est namque tale praeceptum amoris: Qui vero cupit amore potiri, propriae fines non audeat voluntatis excedere nec ordines discernat amori, qui ex quolibet genere suum vult exornare palatium, et omnes in sua curia aequaliter militare nulla ordinum praerogativa servata. Plebeia ergo in amoris curia aequali cum comite vel comitissa meruit ordine permanere. Quum in vos tota mei animi dirigatur voluntas, sine omni vos possum reprehensione eligere, nec ex hoc parva sed valde magna petere iudicabor. Nam quum honorabili amoris curia digna permaneatis [honore] et ad vestrum voluntas me cogit amorem, inter magnanimes vestra me debet prudentia reputare. A meo igitur non est abstinendum vobis amore, nisi bonis me videritis moribus destitutum et a bonis actibus alienum' (pp. 112-13)

['Every man should ask for love where force of Love compels him. Indeed that Love is excellent which arises solely from pleasure and delight in the beauty of someone of whatever class, and which is not sought because of the privileges of rank alone. Therefore I do not violate Love's rules if I choose my love from a lower class: actually I seem to be obeying them in this. For there is this precept of Love: he who desires to have a control over true love must not dare to go beyond the limits of his own desire or to make distinctions of classes in matters of Love which desires to adorn its palace from every class and to have everyone in its court serve on equal terms with no special privileges of rank. Thus a middle class woman deserves to remain in the court of Love on an equal level with a count or a countess. Since my whole heart's desire is directed towards you I can choose you without any blame whatsoever and I will be regarded to be aiming not at low things but rather at very great ones. Therefore since you remain worthy of the honorable court of Love and Love compels me to love you, your wisdom ought to count me among the magnanimous persons. You should not then refrain from loving me unless you see that I lack moral beauty and that I am stranger to good deeds'].

There are many passages of this tenor in the dialogues, and their message is quite constant. The lovers aspire to reach a *paritas* with their desired counterparts, an equality which is beyond class differences. Between two lovers, class rank is not a real obstacle because 'aequalibus eos oportet in amoris aula gradibus ambulare' ['in the court of love they must walk with equal steps,' p. 116]. Andreas's character is expressing an idea which is common among the troubadours. Arnaut de Maruelh puts it better than anyone else: 'paratges es vas Amor aclis' (ed. Johnston, XV, l. 28: 'nobility by birth bows to Love'), or:

> Mais Ovidis retrais
> qu'entre·ls corals amadors
> non paratgeia ricors (XXV, ll. 8–30)

[But Ovid says that between sincere lovers wealth does not create ranks].

How is one to achieve that moral beauty which levels all social differences? There is only one answer, and all the characters of these dialogues have it ready: moral beauty comes from love. The sagacious *plebeius* is the first one to enunciate the principle:

'Profiteor etenim, quod magnis sunt digna praeterita facta muneribus, verumtamen universis constat hominibus, quod nullum in mundo bonum vel curialitas exercetur, nisi ex amoris fonte derivetur. Omnis ergo boni erit amor origo et causa. Cessante igitur causa eius de necessitate cessat effectus. Nullus ergo poterit homo facere bona, nisi amoris suasione cogatur. Petitum itaque largiri debes amorem, ut benefaciendi causa mihi a te videatur indulta et per te valeam bonis moribus informari et stabili semper in firmitate durare' (pp. 28–9)

['I admit that past deeds are worthy of many rewards; yet everybody is aware that no good is done nor courtliness is practiced in the world unless it derives from the fountain of Love. Love is therefore the origin and the cause of all good. Once the cause ceases its effects necessarily cease. Thus no man may do good unless compelled by the persuasion of Love. You should then grant my request of your love so that people will think you did it to cause me to do well and that through you my manners may be improved and may firmly last forever'].

The *nobilior* is no less convinced about it:

'Nam amare aut est bonum aut est malum. Quod sit malum, non est asserere tutum, quia satis omnibus constat et est manifestum, et amoris hoc nobis doctrina demonstrat, quod neque mulier neque masculus potest in saeculo beatus haberi nec curialitatem nec aliqua bona perficere, nisi sibi haec fomes praestet amoris. Unde necessario vobis concluditur ergo, bonum esse amare et appetibile' (p. 118)

['Love is either a good thing or a bad thing. It is not safe to say that it is a bad thing because it is fairly clear to everyone and the teachings of Love show us that neither a woman nor a man in this world can be considered happy or well-bred, nor can he do any good unless the source of Love inspires him. Wherefore you must necessarily conclude that loving is a good thing and a desirable one'].

Many passages similar to this one assert over and over again that Love is the *summum bonum* and the source of moral beauty. 'Amor enim iste [i.e., purus] tantae dignoscitur esse virtutis, quod ex eo totius probitatis origo descendit':[58] it could be the epiphenomenon that sums up this principle.

The 'system' of courtly love now begins to be clear, and so do its contradictions. A major flaw, a sort of vicious circle, is readily identifiable in this system. Love, the characters say, is the origin and cause of all good. Yet this good is nothing other than the effects of love itself. Love, then, is *causa efficiens* and *causa finalis* at the same time. This simultaneity imposes serious limitations on the moral autonomy and value of *morum probitas*.[59] If one remembers that love, as defined by Andreas at the outset of his treatise, is *passio*, a purely irrational force, then it is wrong to consider it as *causa finalis* because, in so doing, we would be denying the very nature of morality. No moral system can ignore the notion of finality, but no finality is morally meaningful when there is no freedom of choice or possibility of decision, as is the case when a *passio* determines behaviour with the blindness of fatality. Therefore, a causal relationship between love and *probitas*, the world of virtue, is proclaimed by untenable statements which, at best, offer a pretext for an exercise in philosophical discourse. A futile exercise indeed: the lovers try to extenuate their *passio* with eloquent appeals to their *probitas*, but they never succeed in persuading their ladies to love them in return. The ladies point out, often hilariously,[60] that behind all the apparatus of courtliness and the presumption of moral beauty on the part of their interlocutors, there is only a desire to *coire*. The ladies defend their moral freedom with arguments that are more persuasive than those of their male counterparts. These men construct a metaphysical entity, a God of Love who, according to their reasoning, has created a universal order to which no creature can claim indifference. Yet this god, the ladies reply, is not a fair one because he rules by an uneven scale (*inaequale pensum*) and because his arrows hit blindly: plainly said, the ladies will reciprocate only if wounded by the arrows of love.[61] Thus, all these elucubrations on love fall short of their aim. Contrary to what the title of the chapter promised, none of these lovers wins love. If these dialogues achieve anything it is the disclosure of the passional nature of love, and ultimately the impossibility of building upon it a coherent notion of moral beauty.

The concluding chapters of the first book are, in a way, corollaries that further prove the main points made in the dialogues. Andreas does not spend much time speaking about the love of the clergy, because the *clerici* have a God-given nobility and thus do not need to dwell on the argument that nobility comes only from *probitas*, which, in turn, comes from love. Andreas then reviews the implications of love for nuns. Its treatment is even more summary, because this kind of love reveals only too clearly its sexual motivations since it is impossible to conceal them under promises of marriage or under the exaltation of an adulterous relationship. Finally, Andreas touches upon the love of peasants and love of prostitutes. The first is so similar to the love of animals that peasants cannot even begin to ennoble their passion with ambiguous and deceitful moral arguments. As for love acquired with money, it is obviously a passion other than sexual, and it can more properly be called *avaritia*.

If it is not yet clear that Andreas sees in courtly love a deceiving rationalization of erotic passion, let us follow him into the second book of *De Amore*. Here the mischievous chaplain teaches Walter how love can be maintained and, if it happens not to be perfect, augmented. But with the same scientific detachment Andreas also shows how love can diminish and die, especially if other related passions (jealousy, for instance) intervene to upset love's apparent beatitude. Moreover, Andreas again stresses in this book the physiological nature of the love discussed in his treatise. The implicit lesson emerges clearly: a love which can increase and decrease cannot in any way be considered a *summum bonum* because it lacks the attribute of permanency, which is inherent in all perfect things. Andreas knew – as did his contemporaries – that the true *summum bonum* is God and that only from knowing God comes *probitas*, the virtue which is a habitus, a constant norm of behaviour. How ridiculous and vain those oaths of eternal love, so predominant among the *topoi* of the troubadour lyric, appear now, when seen in the light of the ephemeral nature of erotic love!

The lesson is not yet over, for Andreas closes his second book with what may be taken as a triumph of the God of Love, who dictates his rules and is celebrated in the court of Love. But this triumph shows once again how courtly love confuses reason and passion. The *iudicia amoris*, the judgments pronounced in the courts of love,[62] offer emotional solutions to legal problems, and the *regulae amoris* given in the most 'fantastic' section of this 'philosophic' treatise represent a sort of legal codification of emotional matters.

While the condemnation of courtly love in the first two books takes the form of a sustained *insinuatio*, its denunciation becomes explicit only in the third book. Any reader of *De Amore* is aware that this *reprobatio amoris* constitutes a most vexing problem. Some interpreters have seen it as recantation inspired by the church's censorship; others maintain that Andreas wanted to dramatize the two souls of the Middle Ages[63] or the Averroistic double truth by contrasting two views of love;[64] some explain this contradiction by making up biographical assumptions;[65] some have introduced sophisticated notions like 'gradualism' to soften the contradiction;[66] some have proposed still more daring explanations. But those who have followed our interpretation so far will not be surprised by this supposed about-face of Andreas. Indeed, Andreas had no trouble in denying what the reasoning of his courtly characters had not been able to demonstrate – namely, that love is the highest good. The third book, therefore, constitutes quite predictably an exhortation to mistrust courtly love, or as he often calls it, carnal love. Even in this book the physiological aspects of love are present, and this time Andreas stresses the pathological consequences of carnal love. A misogynous tirade, quite conventional in its motifs, associates such a love with all kinds of pain. Andreas praises instead friendship and charity, the only forms of love which never fade because they are born from the notion of the true highest good.

This is not to say that Andreas condemns erotic love: it is, after all, a natural function which fulfils a providential law in so far as it promotes the perpetuation of the species. This function is, therefore, blessed by the sacrament of marriage.[67] What Andreas opposes – if it must be repeated – is the exaltation of erotic love made by courtly lovers, an exaltation which, in his view, perverts all values by considering sexual desire as the source of moral beauty and by ignoring its main function, which is procreation.

De Amore, in spite of its unusual way of building an argument, is quite lucid in its message. Andreas did not write a vademecum of courtly love – as is often repeated – but a *vade retro*. Even so, for the reasons already stated, *De Amore* is very valuable as the first attempt at creating a model of courtly love.

Andreas's model of courtly love is in many ways more sophisticated than the twentieth-century model. Andreas sees and combines the two essential elements of courtliness whereas modern scholars tend to emphasize just one of them under the pressure of dissolving the ambiguity ensuing from that combination. Only too well known are the attempts by a Wechssler or by a Casella to reduce *fin'amors* within the frame of mystic literature; equally well known are the attempts by a Briffault or by a Lazar to reduce it to pure erotic literature.[68] Andreas would have found both interpretations partial because they dissolve the dialectics of courtly love. One should agree with the chaplain. Both eroticism and spirituality are overwhelming in troubadour love poetry, so that is impossible to think of this love as pure *amicitia spiritualis* or as pure *libido*. It is fruitless, therefore, to create a model of courtly love without considering these two components, and seeing how they relate to each other and assessing the nature of the paradox they create. Andreas's perception of both elements was rather insightful, and his lesson should not be forgotten.

There are, however, many reasons for disagreeing with Andreas. He worked at his model not as a detached observer, but rather as a passionate moralist. Passion sharpened his sight, and he was able to identify the major components of courtly love. But passion distorted his findings. For him the *probitas morum* of his courtly characters was just a means to disguise their sexual aims, so courtly love is a deceitful practice since it exalts eros while preaching virtue. Yet, a more serene analysis could show that, in *fin'amors*, eros and moral perfection are consubstantial, forming an ambiguous synthesis. How this happens remains to be proven; and it can be done by questioning some of Andreas's findings as well as enriching his model. Had Andreas questioned the nature of *fin'amor*'s eroticism (had he, for instance, asked himself how erotic the desire of a never-seen person can be) he might have come to the same conclusions at which we will arrive. Had Andreas ever suspected that all troubadours' lyrics he might have heard were not promoting a new kind of love as much as creating an ideal type of gentleman, his stance against courtly love would have been quite different; actually he would have understood that the troubadours were celebrating Natura, the goddess who had so many unquestionable admirers in the twelfth century. Andreas, in sum, missed altogether the notion of *mezura*, which regulates the rapport between eros and virtue and is therefore fundamental for the interpretation of *fin'amor* because it is the fundamental virtue on which the whole ethics of courtly love is based. Had Andreas had the historical perspective we enjoy he would have come to realize that the association of love and virtue made by the troubadours, however philosophically weak, was the basis on which lyrical love poetry thrived in the Western civilization for many centuries to come.

When the historical chapter of *fin'amor* was closed, and after Jean de Meung reduced it to pure eros and Dante to pure spirituality, Andreas's *De Amore* enjoyed an unpredictable popularity.[69] It was translated into French and Italian. It seemed that only this treatise could restore the secret of courtly love, presenting anew the dyad eros/virtue; and in the late fifteenth century someone called it *De arte honeste amandi*, thus underlining the chaste love it preached as well as the 'eloquente' nature of its characters. This was the highest tribute an era full of nostalgia for courtly love could pay to Andreas; but his guidance into that world where love has contradictory manifestations was bound to create some confusion which lasts to our day.

Mezura

Dante, with his customary acumen, gives an engaging definition of courtliness which offers an excellent basis for the construction of an interpretative model:

> Cortesia e onestade è tutt'uno: e però ne le corti anticamente le virtudi e li belli costumi s'usavano, sì come oggi s'usa lo contrario, si tolse quello vocabulo da le corti, e fu tanto a dire cortesia quanto uso di corte [1]

> [Courtliness and *onestade* are one and the same: and since in the courts of yesteryear virtue and beautiful habits were cultivated – just as today the opposite is done – that word (i.e., courtliness) was derived from the 'courts,' and 'courtliness' came to mean the same as 'custom of the Courts'].

This definition is based on the principle of identity,[2] which succeeds in clarifying a concept only if one of the two terms is clear. Considering how difficult it is to give a global definition of *cortesia*, we may perhaps fare better by defining *onestade*. Again, Dante himself, in another passage of the *Convivio*, opens the way. There he touches upon the Stoics and the moral end:

> Furono adunque filosofi molto antichi deli quali primo e principe fu Zenone, che videro e credettero questo fine de la vita umana essere solamente la rigida onestade; cioè rigidamente, senza respetto alcuno, la verità e la giustizia seguire, di nulla mostrare dolore, di nulla mostrare allegrezza, di nulla passione avere sentore.

E deffiniro così questo onesto: 'quello che senza utilitade e senza frutto, per sé di ragione è da lodare'[3]

[There were, thus, very ancient philosophers, the first and the prince of whom was Zeno. They understood and believed the end of life to be only the rigid onestade; that is rigorously, without any concern, to follow truth and justice, not to show pain about anything, not to show joy about anything, not to show a shadow of passion about anything. And they defined this onesto in the following way: 'That which without expediency and without any fruit, is to be praised for its own reason'].

This is a technical definition of *onestade*, a term that cannot be rendered in English as 'honesty.' Its closest equivalents is 'unselfishness' or 'disinterestedness,' but these terms actually reflect a predicate of *onestade* and are not true synonyms. Indeed, the meaning of *onestade* today is completely lost to English as well as to other languages that derive from Latin. Only history and philology can give us back the full meaning of *onestade*, and we must solicit their help, because a correct understanding of *onestade* sheds light on the cultural context of the troubadours as well as on some pivotal principles of *fin'amors*.

HONESTUM

Dante found his definition of *onestade* in Cicero's *De finibus bonorum et malorum*: 'Honestum igitur intellegimus quod tale est, ut detracta omni utilitate, sine ullis praemiis fructibusve per se ipsum possit iure laudari' (II, 45: By *honestum* we understand that which is of such a nature that, though devoid of all utility, it can justly be commended for itself apart from any profit or reward). It is a Stoic definition given by Cato, one of the characters of the dialogue. *Honestum* for him is moral beauty or perfection, a value measured only by itself, so that nothing else can enhance or diminish it. It is Virtue, which is sought for its own sake, not as a means to anything else – otherwise it would be expediency. It is, in other words, the ultimate goal pursued by the true sage because only in *honestum*, the perfect realization of virtue, does he achieve beatitude. In this sense *honestum* corresponds to the Greek *to kalon*, the Beautiful. A fuller treatment of this subject is also given by Cicero in his *De officiis*, where he follows the thought of the Middle Stoa, aiming at defining the mean morality of the *vir bonus* who, not being the perfect Stoic sage, cannot live up to the *honestum* but only to the *similitudo honesti*. Essentially this is a practical reduction of the *honestum*, which must take into account man's limitations and asks him only to know himself, to live according to reason and to the circumstances. A *vir bonus* must operate in accordance with the fundamental virtues – wisdom, justice, fortitude, and temperance – whose value is always established by their rapport with *honestum*. *Honestum*, in sum, is not a virtue, but is paramount among all virtues. It is the criterion that allows us to see whether a virtue – and its respective duties – is practised for its own sake without selfishness. Indeed, the opposite of *honestum* is *utile*, unless this overcomes the limits of a particularized interest to become useful for everybody. If this happens – if, in other words, *utile* has as its goal the whole society – then *honestum* and *utile* coincide. A typical example can be a heroic deed: if it is done for vanity or glory or reward it is not *honestum*, but if it is done for the good of the society it is at once *honestum* and *utile*.

De officiis became an immensely influential work, one of the main sources of Western humanism, a work that as late as the eighteenth century was still considered by Frederick the Great to be 'le meilleur ouvrage de morale qu'on ait écrit et qu'on écrira.'[4] It is mainly from this work that Western civilization has received the notion of *honestum*, having its possible antonym in *utile*. *De officiis* was adapted to Christian thinking by St Ambrose in his *De officiis ministrorum*, which follows Cicero's ideas very closely. The notion of *honestum/utile* was rejected by St Augustine, who – especially after a polemic against Pelagius and Julian of Escalona – replaces it with the dyad *frui/uti* and denies any finality to *honestum*. Yet, notwithstanding Augustine's authority, the Ciceronian teaching survived in works such as Martin of Bracara's *Formula honestae vita*, also known by the title *De quattuor virtutibus* (later translated into Provençal), in many *florilegia* (the best known are the *Excerpta Ciceronis* by Hadoard of the ninth century), and even in the teaching of grammar.[5]

The *De officiis* received special attention in conjunction with that cultural ferment known as the twelfth-century Renaissance. It is difficult to say whether Cicero's work contributed to such a renaissance or whether the attention paid to *De officiis* was caused by the nature of the discussion on ethics that took place in that century. At the present stage of historical knowledge the second explanation seems more likely. *De officiis* was adapted in a work attributed to Guillaume de Conches, entitled *Moralium dogma philosophorum*, and known also as *De honesto et utili*.⁶ This work, which had an exceptionally wide circulation, was composed around the years 1146–50. By that time a long discussion had been under way, prompted in part by the naturalism of the school of Chartres but mostly by the repeated intervention of Abelard in the field of ethics. By stressing the autonomy of the will and by defining the nature of the moral act through the *intention* of the doer, Abelard opened the way to an ethical rationalism which again made possible the discussion of *honestum*. It is too technical a discussion to survey here. Its aspiration, however, is quite clear: it strives to establish a constructive relationship between the *summum bonum hominis* (this is the expression used by the philosopher, a character in the *Dialogus inter philosophum, judaeum et christianum*)⁷ and the highest Christian good, and it also involves the relationship between the cardinal and theological virtues. As everyone knows, this is an immense problem which has engaged the greatest minds for over two centuries,⁸ since it concerns the connection between Nature and Revelation, which is likewise the link between the classical and Christian world. This is the problem dramatized in Dante's *Comedy* with the invention of Limbo. Through the hundreds of treatises which touch upon these subjects, the notion that *honestum* represents a degree of spiritual and social beauty worthy of being pursued for its own sake strongly emerges. Behind this theorization one senses the rise of a new social ethics which is both aristocratic and lay, an ethics which places great value upon honour and earthly fame, and it seems therefore to meet the horizon of values promoted by a class educated in the schools of the cathedrals rather than in the monasteries, because it is oriented towards noble worldly values.⁹ In short, it is the courtly ethics which celebrates the values that Cicero would place under the heading *honestum*. It is not by chance, then, that Cicero's works (*De finibus, De officiis, De inventione, Academica*, etc.) form the basis of the definitions of the virtues privileged by that class.

In the context of the discussions on ethics, the *Moralium dogma philosophorum* represents just one episode, but a very special one. This book, which was meant to be a manual for the schools, presents an organic and exclusive treatment of the *honestum/utile*, showing no concern for theological virtues: actually it is so faithful to its classical authors (Cicero and Seneca who appear to William in a dream) that it never mentions God but rather emphasizes the gods! William strictly follows Cicero's *De officiis* in the division of the arguments' parts, but in the division and classification of the virtues he may follow Cicero's *De inventione* or Macrobius's *In Somnium Scipionis*. The subject of the first book is *honestum* 'quod sua vi nos trahit et sua dignitate nos allicit' (which attracts us by its force and entices us by its dignity); the subject of the second book is *utile*, and the third is devoted to the problem of whether any conflict exists between *honestum* and *utile*.

An indirect proof that the *Moralium dogma* is not just any one treatise among the many written in those days on the cardinal virtues (also called 'political' virtues) is the attention it has enjoyed among modern scholars, and not only with respect to problems of authorship, date, sources, and diffusion. In fact, since 1919, when Gustav Ehrismann published a now famous article on the 'Chivalric system of the virtues,'[10] *Moralium dogma philosophorum* has been considered by the Germanists as a key work in the formation of courtly ethics. In 1943 and again in 1948 E.R. Curtius[11] attacked Ehrismann's thesis and denied any connection between the Latin treatise and the chivalric moral system Ehrismann had reconstructed through the works of Hartmann von Aue and Wolfram von Eschenbach. But Curtius was wrong, both in his details and in his main contention.[12] Ehrismann's fault, if any, lies perhaps in overly rigorous systemization and in the aggrandizement of the role of Guillaume's work. Indeed, as previously mentioned, the discussion of *honestum/utile* was widespread in the twelfth century, and *Moralium dogma philosophorum* shared its popularity with works such as *Formula honestae vitae* by Martin of Bracara, and *De quattuor virtutibus vitae honestae* by Hildebert of Lavardin (d. 1136), which is concerned with human perfection.[13] Yet William's limpidity of definitions, the agility of his argumentation, the Ciceronian division of his materials give, better than any other work, the sense of what the civilization of the twelfth century understood *honestum* and *utile* to be. It is no wonder, then, that Ehrismann took the *Moralium dogma philosophorum* to be an organic codification of moral perfection on which the chivalric world could base its system of virtues. Codes, like words, not only reflect realities and aspirations; they help to create them as well.[14] The twelfth century, in its search for *honestum*, in the celebration of the Beautiful unstained by base expediency, helped to create or identified the aspirations of its civilization, indeed of the 'courtly civilization.'

Courtliness is, in its essence, living according to the cardinal virtues in a celebration of the man's nature at his best. Ultimately it is a manifestation of magnanimity, that desire and capacity of conceiving and pursuing great deeds and honour through virtue. The courtly society is meant to be an aristocracy of great souls, and only by being part of it can an acolyte of courtly values attain his highest moral goodness,[15] the *honestum*.

In theory, *honestum* is indivisible, because he who possesses one virtue possesses them all. Yet, in the practical world, individuals as well as cultures may emphasize one virtue over the others. This is true for the courtly civilization which evolves along two directions clearly defined by geographical and linguistic boundaries: one in northern France in *langue d'oïl*, and the other in southern France in *langue d'oc*. Generalizing a bit, it is possible to say that the world of northern *courtoisie* places the virtue of justice above the other three. The knight of the North – the hero of so many romances – cultivates friendship (*amicitia*), purity (*innocentia*), religion (*pietas*), compassion (*humanitas*), liberality (*liberalitas*), beneficence (*beneficentia*), and other minor virtues traditionally classified as expression of justice. The gentleman of the South – the troubadour – privileges *temperantia* over justice; he emphasizes elegance, as it were, over right and duty, esthetics over every other value. In northern France, we can say, courtliness lives through *aventure*; in the South, it lives through *mezura*.

MEZURA

With the notion of temperance, we finally return at to our main subject. At first we must see how the Ciceronian *temperantia* was interpreted in the twelfth century and how, in its new version, it coincides with *mezura*. Once again, the best analysis of this virtue is to be found in William of Conches's treatise. He says that temperance is 'dominium rationis in libidinem et alios motus importunos'[16] (the absolute rule of reason over passions and any other unfit impulses). Temperance can show itself as *modestia*, which shuns any excess in matters concerning attire; it demands elegance in walking and any other movement, and prescribes the acts that are appropriate for each age, as well as the kinds of speech and tone one must use for particular circumstances. Temperance also appears as *vercundia*, the bashfulness by which we avoid scurrilous language or an inappropriate tone (e.g., saying something sad while laughing). Temperance restrains us from prying into people's lives and betraying confidences. Other virtues subsumed by temperance are *abstinentia, parcitas, honestas,* and *sobrietas* (which is the opposite of lust and homosexuality). This classification goes back to Macrobius, but in the background Cicero is clearly present. It is from him that William takes the idea that it is almost impossible to distinguish *temperantia* from *honestum* itself, just as it is difficult to think of a fresh complexion as distinct from good health. From Cicero he also takes the idea that no other virtue embellishes man like temperance. There is, however, a remarkable difference between Cicero's and William's treatments of *temperantia*, a difference perspicaciously underlined by Delhaye: temperance for Cicero has a subjective component because it is nothing more than living according to *one's own* nature; for William, instead, temperance has an objective quality, and it 'connaît un devoir qui s'impose à tous.'[17] William was addressing himself, not to the *vir bonus* as did Cicero, but to the *clericus* and to the courtier who live in a strongly conformist society where the duties of each virtue are uniformly codified for everyone. William's audience could have been made up of gentlemen of southern France because they also lived in a conformist society and understood *temperantia* exactly as the northern philosopher did, even though they called it *mezura* in their own language.

The correspondence between the two terms is unobjectionable. The clearest proof can be found in the *romanz* of Daude de Pradas on the four cardinal virtues, a work which represents the Provençal version of *Formulae honestae vitae* by Martin of Bracara. When Daude comes to analyse the virtue which, in his model, is called *temperantia*, we read:

> La terza vertutz es tan bona
> Que de totz bes porta corona.
> Honesta es, neta e pura
> E per aquo a nom mesura,
> Contenenza o atempranza   (ed. Stickney, ll. 738–42)

[The third virtue is so good that it bears the crown of all goodness. It is beautiful, neat and pure; and for this reason is called *mezura*, continence, or temperance].

This correspondence is known even to Cicero, who sometimes uses *mensura* as synonym of *temperantia*, *modestia*, *continentia*, and other virtues.

The correspondence, however, goes far beyond a linguistic level. Everything William says about *temperantia* can be found in the many didactic poems, the Provençal *ensenhamens* that run parallel to the lyrical experience of the troubadours.[18] Beginning with the earliest authors of the genre – from Garin lo Brun (who died in 1156 and who was a contemporary of William of Conches) or from Arnaut Guillem de Marsan (who flourished around 1170, and who was, therefore, part of the great troubadour generation of 1170) to the last poets of the late thirteenth century (Sordel or N'At de Mons) – one repeatedly finds precepts about the way of dressing, walking, talking, eating, drinking, receiving guests, decorating the house, choosing servants, and, most of all, acting according to the circumstances. *Mezura*, however, is not just 'good manners' or simple practical wisdom. Those external acts manifest a spiritual composure nourished by wisdom. When Marcabru, for instance, says that 'mezura es de gen parlar'[19] (consists of gentle speech), he is expressing an idea which is found in many *ensenhamens*. The 'gen parlar' is different from mere *urbanitas*. It closely resembles that 'civil conversazione' in which the Italians of the High Renaissance expressed their ideal of elegance and spiritual communion in celebration of Beauty.

This moral dimension which is behind courtly 'good manners' explains why the word *mezura* is often combined in a syntagm with *sen* and *razo*, two words meaning wisdom: not the wisdom gained from the knowledge of earthly and divine things, but a special one which enhances and integrates *mezura*. N'At de Mons calls it a combination of *discressio* and *membransa*. Describing *sens*, N'At says that it consists of three virtues. The first is *apercepemen* (perceptiveness); then

> L'autr' es discressios
> Et entendemens bos,
> Que tri'e devezis.
> Si's bo co abelis.
> D'aquesta veramens
> Nais genhs e pessamens
> E razos e mezura,
> Per que homz fa drechura
> Et enten falhimen;
> Est'es razitz del sen,
> Que·l mal e·l be balansa.
> E la ters'es membransa,
> Escrins et archadura
> On estuja mezura
> So que·l platz ni·l sap bo;
> Car anc thezaurs no fo
> Ses servar amassatz[20]   (ed. Bernhardt, ll. 300–17)

[The second is *discressio* and good judgment which chooses and decides how it pleases if it is good. From *discressio* indeed behaviour, thought, reason, and *mezura* through which man operates justly and understands faults. This is the root of wisdom which balances the bad and the good. The third is memory: case and coffer, where *mezura* stashes away what pleases it, and finds to be good. No treasure was ever built up without putting aside].

Here *discressio* translates the Latin *discretio*; but *discretio*, an act of reason, remains a difficult and somewhat elusive concept, although widely used. Francesco Di Capua,[21] who has studied it, explains it with an example which we can borrow. Let us imagine, he says, a general who, on the battlefield, must make a tactical move. Obviously he has not time to consult any of the manuals of tactics from which he has learned the art of war, nor does he have time to recall them; however, the success of his move proves that he has been using them almost spontaneously, for they have come to be his second nature, a habit no longer aware of itself. The same can be said of a poet who composes a poem without always being aware of the rhetorical precepts he is using because he has integrally assimilated them and made of them his second nature. In both cases, that learned spontaneity with which difficult things are carried out can be called *discretio*.[22] That spontaneity is, in fact, attained through assiduous application and, once achieved, can never fade away; hence the notion of *membransa* found in the writing of N'At de Mons. This spontaneity is a superior form of elegance, free from any sign of strain or trace of affectation and ostentation. It is the elegance which produces admiration and good reputation. The courtiers of Castiglione would call it 'sprezzatura'; the troubadours called it *mezura*.

Mezura is the expression of an internal composure which comes only with the possession of all the courtly virtues. There is no authentic temperance without a consistent moral excellence, and the courtly world knows the difference between a gentleman *ab mezura* and a hypocrite who reduces temperance to the purely external manners. Guilhem de Montanhagol, in a *canso* which is a sort of *ensenhamen*, voices this general notion:

> Qui vol esser agradans e plazens
> a totz vuelha dir e far sa honors
> a cadaun si co·l devers es lors,
> e no sia autius ni reprendens,
> ans ay'ab si mezur'et abstinensa,

e si' aitals en cor cum en parvensa,
quar atressi deu esser vergonhos
del mal pessar cum del dir totz hom pros.

Quar anc non dec caber fals pessamens
en lial cor, ans tanh que·s vir alhors
e·l cambi tant que non hiesca clamors;
ni no·l vengua en cor nulhs fols talens,
qu'om non es pros qu'us fols volers lo vensa,
ni es razos de far desconoyssensa,
quar en totz faitz deu gardar totz hom bos,
ans que·l fassa, si·faitz li er dans o pros.

Res no es tan grazit entre las gens
cum mezura, quar als non es valors
mas qu'om valha segon qu'es sa ricors:
quar mezura non es mas solamens
so que de pauc o de trop tol falhensa;
entr'aquestz dos la forma conoyssensa
e fai vertut d'aquestz vicis amdos
tolhen los mals d'ambas las falhizos   (ed. Ricketts, XIII, ll. 1–24)

[He who wants to be pleasant and gracious must honour everybody with words and deeds, according to what is due to each one. He should not be haughty and not too prone to blame; he should, on the contrary, have *mezura* and discretion. And he must be in his heart just as he is in appearance, because otherwise a gentleman should be ashamed of his bad thought as well as of his bad words.

Indeed, no bad thought should live in a loyal heart; quite on the contrary, this gentleman should dodge and change it in such a way that no sign of it shows up, and no foolish desire comes to his heart. And a man is without *proeza* if a senseless desire can overcome him, and there is no reason in being ungrateful. In every action a good man must consider, before doing it, whether it is going to be to his detriment or to his advantage.

Nothing is honoured more among people than *mezura*, because value consists in acting according to one's own nobility: because *mezura* essentially is what compensates for 'too little' and for 'too much': wisdom creates it (i.e., *mezura*) between these two, and makes a virtue out of both vices, eliminating from both defects their respective negatives].

The poet is talking about moral rectitude, which is rewarded by good reputation, and calls it *mezura*. It is this virtue which integrates the sphere of private morality into public life, because the moral beauty of the individual coincides with the aspirations of society. In other words, *mezura* is the conquest and the celebration of the self through the code of social values. Men of great soul pursue distinction and good reputation because by doing so they celebrate courtliness, the highest ideal of their world. *Mezura* means belonging to the courtly world and living up to its aspirations. Where *mezura* is attained, the identity between *honestum* and *utile* has been reached. Such an ideal balance or integration of private and public values is courtliness itself, as Folquet de Marselha put it, 'Courtliness is nothing but *mezura*':

Cortesia non es als mas mesura.[23]

Understood in this way, *mezura* promotes the two main attitudes of the courtly world which seem to contradict each other. On the one, hand there is the impulse given by *mezura* to excel in moral beauty; this is the clue to the subtle vein of narcissism present in many aspects of courtly literature, beginning from the predominance of the lyric genre, the tendency of the *gap* or boast, to the assumption of the lyrical *I* as a model of perfection, and culminating with that sense of complacency with which a troubadour treats his lot and his artistic achievements. On the other hand, there is the imperative to conform to society implied in the notion of *mezura*; this explains another overwhelming feature of courtliness, that is, its strong propensity for conventionality, a propensity quite antithetical to the striving for distinction. The 'father of Romance philology,' F. Diez, described the lack of originality in the troubadours' lyric in a memorable way: 'One could think of this whole literature as the work of just a single poet, yet expressed in a thousand voices.'[24] Diez's notion of originality was a Romantic one, and today's formalist criticism has shown that the originality of the troubadours is to be found in their formal features rather than in their sentimental expression. It is impossible, however, to deny the conventionality of troubadour lyrical poetry when one constantly finds the same themes, the same motifs, the same clichés, the same language in thousands of poems, especially in those written by the poets who flourished in the thirteenth century.

This seemingly paradoxical combination of claims to uniqueness and conscious obedience to conformism is, in fact, not surprising if we understand that courtliness is a sort of *paideia*, civilization having an intrinsic (that is, necessary) didactic vocation, which demands that its literature, culture, and education be an ideal reflection of its own social structure.[25] The numerous *ensenhamens* express that vocation very clearly, even in the denomination of the genre. The same is true for the moral and satirical overtones present in much of the lyrical production – from Marcabru to Peire Cardenal, and even to poets writing far away from southern France[26] – who find their natural matrix in the courtly *paideia*. Otherwise how can we understand the endless debates on courtly values? They are instruments and expressions of that *paideia* which demands constant awareness of the aims pursued. In this sense *mezura* emblematizes the didactic vocation of the courtly world, where uniqueness, too, has an exemplary and didactic function.

The temperance idealized by the Provençal culture is akin to that illustrated in William of Conches' treatise: it is an individual virtue but also one shared with everyone else. *Mezura* presupposes a well-established set of values and conventions to which a gentleman, who is truthful to his social status as if it were his own nature, must conform. *Mezura* does not encourage 'originality' in the Romantic sense; actually being an 'original' in the world of the troubadours would have meant committing a sin of *desmezura* against courtliness. The only originality courtliness allows – indeed demands – must be worked out within its own code. *Mezura* is – and this sounds like a paradox – a form of prescribed originality. A courtly gentleman (the troubadour) will emphasize his being unique in his love as well as in his virtues; but his audience would not find these statements unpredictable because he is acting according to its expectations. This is *mezura*, the courtly *prepon*, the ennobling gentleness of any virtuous person who exalts himself in celebrating the ideals of Beauty shared by all courtly people. The ultimate result seems to be a disinterested celebration of Beauty.

MEZURA AND SOME THEMES OF FIN'AMOR

How does *mezura* affect *fin'amor*; what does it mean for a phenomenon which is one of the major expressions of courtliness? At a superficial glance, *mezura* and troubadour love would seem incompatible, for the latter appears to privilege the world of desires, which are both subjective and intemperate. A closer look, however, shows that *fin'amor* is the most efficacious dramatization of *mezura*. Actually it is through love that temperance is attained, as Peire Vidal says: 'Que mesura d'amor fruitz es' (ed. Avalle, XXXIV, l. 46: *Mezura* is the fruit of love).

This point is of the utmost importance and, properly understood, justifies the troubadours' claim that it is possible to derive virtue from eros, that same claim which prompted Andreas Capellanus's philosophical attack. The major themes of troubadours' lyrics often go in opposite directions: one is positive and the other is negative; the first tells of the irresistible strength of passion; the other presents what checks it. On the whole they balance each other in a sort of tense immobility which is one of the most frequent phenomena of *mezura*. We should analyse some of these themes.

It would be appropriate to start with the theme of *obediensa*, which, as we saw, is fundamental to courtly love. However, since we have dealt with it before, a brief allusion to the paradox it contains may be sufficient. Indeed, the service of love puts the troubadour in a contradictory situation. On the one hand, by serving he hopes to gain his lady's love; on the other, serving means to comply with the lady's wish of not granting her love. From obedience, therefore, simultaneously stem hope and despair, desire and suppression of it. The dialectic between these two contradictory elements has no solution; its only synthesis is *mezura* by which feelings such as hope and despair, which under normal circumstances are always temporary, acquire the connotation of perpetuity in an insoluble and immobile drama.

The most important and common theme of troubadour poetry is the conflict between intense love and what impedes its fulfilment. Tragic as it may sound, this essential conflict is quite artificial because the impediments are all self-imposed. They are personifications (the main ingredients in medieval *fictio*) meant to dramatize that 'dominium rationis in libidinem et alios motos importunos' which William of Conches saw as the capital function of temperance. A clear instance comes through the most obvious of troubadour paradoxes. The troubadour makes public his love through his poems;[27] yet his poems are filled with complaints against the curiosity of gossipers (the *lauzengiers* or *malparliers*). He may be calling for the solidarity of his audience against them, but he also feeds their malice. He sings his hate for those whose suspicions he should not arouse – namely, his lady's husband (the *gilos*) and her guardian (the *guardador*). The troubadour artfully wards off any possible trouble by concealing his beloved's identity under a *senhal*, a nickname. His listeners, however, know he is resorting to a convention.

The *senhal* underlines the poet's discretion but it also opens the way to another contradiction. Indeed, the supposedly loved lady is given a name to singularize her; but when the troubadour describes her she is indistinguishable from any other lady. What distinguishes her from any other is a mere *flatus vocis*, because the ladies for whom troubadours die are all alike. Their physical portraits are highly conventional, despite the fact that each lady is supposed to be a miracle of unique beauty and elegance, superior to any other lady on earth. For example, there is little difference between Bernart de Ventadorn's lady:

> Bela donna, ·l vostre cors gens
> e·lh vostre belh olh m'an conquis,
> e·l doutz esgartz e lo clars vis,
> e·l vostre bels essenhamens,
> que, can be m'en pren esmansa
> de beutat no·us trob egansa:
> la genser etz c'om posch' el mon chauzir,
> o no i vei clar dels olhs ab que·us remir (ed. Lazar, III, ll. 49–56)

[Beautiful lady, your gentle body and your beautiful eyes have conquered me, together with your sweet glances and clear face and beautiful manners that when I think of it I don't find anyone who rivals you in beauty: you are the most beautiful one that a man can find, or I am not seeing clearly through the eyes with which I contemplate you]

and the lady sung of by Gaucelm Faidit:

> Tan aut me creis Amors en ferm talan
> per una bela flor e·l sieu clar vis!
> Blanca, vermeill' e mesclad'ab robis,
> plus d'autra ren es de gaia semblansa;
> c'ab sos bels hueils amoros e plazens
> m'a si ferit e nafrat doussamens,
> que tornat soi en la bon' esperansa (ed. Mouzat, VI, ll. 1–7)

[Love makes grow in me a firm desire for a beautiful flower and for her clear face! White, pink, and mixed with rubies, she is more attractive than any other thing; she has so sweetly struck and wounded me with her beautiful eyes that I have gained again new hopes].

Gaucelm continues expressing his admiration for the 'cors blanc e lis' (white and smooth body) of his lady, for her 'gens cors' and her moral qualities as well. The more poems we read, the more we realize that all these unique beauties are blonde (no troubadour ever loved a brunette!); have fair complexions, high foreheads, white teeth; are plump and yet slender, proud, and elegant: on the whole, a conventionalized portrait, a stereotype which matches the ideal of feminine beauty in the courtly world. It often happens that a detailed portrait is found which follows the classical pattern (from the hair to the feet), forming a sort of catalogue of conventionalized beauty.[28] One may quote a single example taken from Arnaut de Maruelh's *salut*, 'Dona, genser qe no sai dir':

> Vostre gen cors cuende e gay,
> Las vostras belas sauras cris,
> E·l vostre fron pus blanc qe lis,
> Los vostres huelhs vairs e rizens,
> E·l nas q'es dreitz e be sezens,
> La fassa fresca de colors,
> Blanca, vermelha pus qe flors,
> Petita boca, blancas dens,
> Pus blancas q'esmeratz argens,
> Mento e gola e peitrina'
> Blanca co neus ni flors d'espina,
> Las vostras belas blancas mas,
> E·ls vostres detz grailes e plas,
> E la vostra bela faisso ...   (ed. Bec, I, ll. 84–97)

[Your gracious and pleasant body, your beautiful blonde hair, and your forehead whiter than a lily, your dark and smiling eyes, your straight and well built nose, the fresh complexion of your face, red and white more than a flower, your little mouth, your white teeth, whiter than fine silver, your chin, your neck and your bosom, white as snow or hawthorne, your beautiful and white hands with your thin and neat fingers, your beautiful demeanour ...].[29]

Given the identical features of the ladies beloved, it is not difficult to infer that their lovers are also identical, as well as the obstacles seen above – the jealous husband, the guardian, the gossipers, all people who are reduced to a simple fictional function in a highly predictable lyrical situation.

Responding to the audience's expectations, the troubadour imagination multiplies the impediments. They provide an occasion to show fortitude and perseverance while at the same time they stress the intensity of the lover's passion. They dramatize the old Ovidian principle: 'Nitimur in vetitum semper cupimusque negata; / Sic interdictis inminet aeger aquis' (*Amores*, III, 4, ll. 17–18: We strive for what is forbidden and always want what is denied to us; just as a sick person ardently craves for the water which is denied to him), a principle which Andreas Capellanus incorporated in his treatise [30] and which was certainly known to the first troubadour:

> Per tal n'ai meins de bon saber
> quar vueill so que non puesc aver   (ed. Pasero, VII, ll. 19–20)

[Because of this, I have less pleasure: because I want what I cannot have].

By imagining his beloved as a married lady, the troubadour creates a difficult obstacle. This theme caused critics of several generations to state that courtly love is essentially adulterous in nature; but recent studies[31] have discredited this thesis. Marriage is but another 'impediment' theme which promotes a constellation of other themes and motifs – the *gilos*, the gossipers, the rules of secrecy which in turn produce yet more obstacles. Besides being married, the lady often belongs to a higher social rank. This fact, again, may not have any historical foundation, but what matters here is the degree of difficulty it creates for the fulfilment of love. We have already seen how this impediment becomes a source of moral energy, as the troubadour strives to ennoble himself in order to rise up to the lady he loves.

Another impediment to the fulfilment of love comes from the lady's good reputation, which, paradoxically, is what initially awakens the poet's love. The clearest explanation of this standard impediment is provided by a passage in Sordel's *Ensenhamens d'onor*. A lady, he says, should never love anyone who is not a complete gentleman because he will tarnish her fame with his vile requests of love. Yet she does not lose her good reputation in loving a fine knight, provided that they both know how to restrain themselves as it is proper to do ('ab que sapchan l'amor guardar / aissi com si cove a far' (ll. 1091–2):

> Qar la plus neta res del mon
> es amors, qui be ve preon,

> adreicha; mas non vai adreig
> pos que mesura i pert son dreig,
> e son dreig i per pos neteza
> n'es menz ni·n cor deslialeza
> qu'om no ama be lialmen,
> si tot autretan coralmen
> non ama, ses cor camjador,
> de sa dopna·l prez e l'onor
> quom son cors ni s'amor a prendre.
>
> Per so·s deu dopna car tener,
> qu'il non pot amor ni plazer
> far ni dir, si tot s'a beleza,
> mas aitan quan a de careza (ed. Boni, ll. 1093–1103, 1117–20)

[Because, if one thinks deeply, the purest thing in the world is the right love; but it does not proceed on the right path after *mezura* loses power over it; love does not have any force when purity fades away and disloyalty arises, for a man does not love loyally if he does not desire with his whole and unchanging heart the valour and the honour of his lady as much as he desires her body and her love.... A lady must be very reserved because – although she has beauty – she cannot show love or say pleasant things unless they are in proportion to her own reserve].

Here we see why the troubadour must refrain from passionate love. If he does not, he ruins his lady's reputation and thus destroys the very beauty that aroused his love in the first place. He must love her because she does not concede love, because she never grants a 'facilis rei petitae concessio,' as Andreas Capellanus says. Yet the troubadour dreams of a situation where his and his lady's will come to agree one day, as Berenguer de Palol puts it:

> Doncs s'ieu ja·m vey dins vostres bratz enclaus,
> si qu'ambeduy nos semblem d'un voler
> meravil me on poiria·l joy caber (ed. Beretta-Spampinato VIII, ll. 36–8)

[Thus, if ever I see myself in your embrace, so that both of us seem to have just one desire, I wonder where such a joy could be contained] where one perceives a similarity with Andreas Capellanus's sentence 'omnia de utriusque voluntate in ipsius amplexu amoris praecepta compleri,' which appears in his definition of love at the opening of *De Amore*.

Highly imaginative and poetically successful are the themes and motifs indicating the control of erotic passion produced along temporal and spatial lines. Temporal distance projects the revelation of love into the past and creates the desire and the hope for repeating the encounter in the future. Memory and hope define the realm in which love is consummated only in meditation. The tone of nostalgia, the frenzy of desire, the praying and the cursing, occupy an empty present and provide the bulk of materials for the troubadours' songs.[32] This empty present is filled by the psychology of the troubadour. He studies his *cossir*, he analyses his reveries. Prompted by a sudden memory, he records his fantasies, and erotic love lives only in those distant times.

The distance is also physical. Who does not remember: 'Luenh es lo castelhs e la tors / On elha jay e sos maritz' (ed. Jeanroy, III, ll. 17–18: Far away are the castle and the tower where she and her husband lie), an image by Jaufre Rudel which still dazzles our imagination by its simplicity and its vagueness, an image which has shaped our vision of the courtly world. The lady in a castle: this symbol of elegance and inaccessibility is the most frequent and concrete representation of the impossibility of ever being close to the beloved. Sometimes the lady is imagined as residing in a different region, and the troubadour, longing for her, turns his eyes in that direction, hoping somehow for a vision to overcome that distance. A most beautiful occurrence of this situation is this by Arnaut de Maruelh:

> Ves lo païs, pros dompna issernida,
> Repaus mos huoills on vostre cors estai,
> E car plus pres de vos no·m puosc aizir,
> Tenc vos el cor ades e cossir sai
> Vostre gen cors cortes, qui'm fai languir   (ed. Johnston, VIII, ll. 25–9)

[Towards the country where you reside, noble and distinguished lady, I turn my eyes; and since I cannot be closer to you, I keep you in my heart and imagine your gentle and gracious body which makes me languish].

Sometimes the distance is bridged by the wind, the sweet medium which caresses the lady's body and brings her perfume to the poet. This poet may be Bernart de Ventadorn:

> Can la freid'aura venta
> deves vostre païs
> veyaire m'es qu' eu senta
> un ven de paradis   (ed. Lazar, XXVI, ll. 1–4)

[When the cold wind blows from your country, it seems to me I feel a wind from paradise]

or Peire Vidal:

> Ab l'alen tir vas me l'aire
> Qu'ieu sen venir de Proensa   (ed. Avalle, XX, ll. 1–2)

[With my breathing I inhale the air which I feel coming from Provence]

or any other poet who repeats this classical theme.[33]

The most beautiful theme based upon physical distance, one which is immediately associated with the courtly world, is the *amor de lonh* made unforgettable by the melancholic accents of Jaufre Rudel and by his imitator, who, incidentally, never sensed any allegorical dimension in their model, as have modern readers. This theme of classical origin celebrates a love's *ses vezer* (without seeing), love *ex auditu* – as Saint Augustine calls it[34] – a love which is purely noetic and which alters the notion of distance.[35] In this love from afar, the poet does not find in his memory the image of his lady, but creates it with his *curiositas*; there is not a particular time or an encounter to remember, but rather an anticipation for an encounter to be. The *amor de lonh* coordinates distance and time to dramatize a vague hope and sublimate desire.

All these themes, and many others that one could choose convey a message of impossibility; but, since the obstacles to the fulfilment of love are self-imposed, one wonders whether that impossibility is really sought after and whether the real message is 'fear of seeing love fulfilled,' as Rilke said. Whatever the answer may be – and it seems that no univocal answer is possible – these impediments work against the consummation of love and intensify the desire for it. But they also change the nature of love by transferring it from the realm of the 'blind passion,' analysed by Andreas, to the realm of fiction. It becomes a love of loving in a refined way, which says more about the elegance of the lover than about his erotic passion; or, if one prefers, it says a lot about erotic passion but only in so far as it offers a pretext to aggrandize the uniqueness of the lover. It all sounds like a melodrama, and when Stendhal thought of the troubadours' poems as being arias of 'opera buffa,' he was in part correct.[36]

Tormented by memories, elated by hopes, the troubadour lives on a constant sentimental see-saw, in a state a psychologist would define as cyclothymia.[37] Joy and pain alternate in the same song, and no firm position as regards either is ever attained. Yet, the troubadour's love, despite his constant moving from one mood to its opposite, remains in a state of restless immobility. Its moving is not for real; it reminds us of a car in neutral gear with the driver pressing the gas pedal: the noise is great, but the car goes nowhere. By checking his passion, by denying it any real outlet or solution, the troubadour can afford to push it to a paroxysm: the result will not be the conquest of physical joy, but it will make beautiful literature. The asseveration of desire and the firm impediments to fulfilling it do not create a gratuitous play. Their combined function is to show how magnanimous the lover is in accepting that his love will not succeed and yet how perseverant, loyal, devoted, and judicious he can be in pursuing his desired lady.

The troubadours were able to sustain such a fragile and paradoxical enterprise on a fact which is too often forgotten. Their lyric poetry has no story or narrative requiring development, nor situations to be resolved. Therefore, the conflict between desire and impediment can be kept alive forever. This is not the case in a narrative work, not even in the world of the troubadours. Indeed, when stories are told in the Provençal world, when we have the 'eccezione narrativa,' as Alberto Limentani[38] defines it, the opposition love/obstacle finds a solution that the lyric situation could postpone indefinitely. In a long poem like *Flamenca*, for instance, a protracted but impeded desire takes the main protagonists ... to bed! But, for the troubadours, the situation cannot conclude in the same way because theirs is a drama without a plot.

This is always the case in troubadours' lyrics. Even the Provençal genres, which are different from the lyrics and seem more suited to a narrative mode, show the depth of the incompatibility of *fin'amor* with any sequence of events that may constitute a story. *Pastorelas* and *albas* are a case in point. Twenty-five *pastorelas* (a relatively small number) have reached us, and several of them — certainly the first, *L'altrier jost'a una sebissa*, written by Marcabru — are in fact anti-*pastorelas*. They satirize the mixing of *cortezia* and *vilania* found in other *pastorelas* because that mixture leads to 'uncourtly' consequences. The same can be said for *albas* which always present a situation in which two lovers separate after having spent one night together. An *alba*, always begins when the action is over, so that the lyrical tone prevails over the narrative one.

It may be worthwhile looking closely at this courtly idiosyncrasy to any narrative experimentation because it ultimately is a manifestation of *mezura*. A good example is a poem by Guiraut Riquier, a poet who belongs to the last generation of the troubadours. Guiraut Riquier wrote six *pastorelas* — they are unique in that they all present the same shepherdess over a period of twenty-two years, from youth to marriage and motherhood — and a piece, unique in its genre, called *serena*, which is a variation of the *alba*. Whereas in the *alba* the lover curses the dawn which puts an end to a night of pleasure, in the *serena* the lover anxiously waits for the evening (*ser*) to come. The following is the text:

>   Ad un fin aman fon datz
>   per sidons respiegz d'amor,
>   e·l sazos e·l luecx mandatz;
>   e·l jorn que·l ser dec l'onor
>   penre, anava pessius
>   e dizia sospiran:
>   – Jorns, ben creyssetz a mon dan,
>   e·l sers
>   auci·m e sos loncx espers.
>
>   Tant era l'amans cochatz
>   de la deziran ardor
>   del joy que l'er'autreyatz,
>   qu'elh se dava gran temor
>   que·l ser non atendes vius.
>   E dizia sospiran:
>   – Jorns, ben creyssetz a mon dan,
>   e·l sers
>   auci·m e sos loncx espers.

Nulhs hom non era de latz
a l'aman de sa dolor
no conogues, tant torbatz
era ab semblan de plor;
tant li era'l jorns esquius.
E dizia sospiran:
– Jorns, ben creyssetz a mon dan,
  e·l sers
auci·m e sos loncx espers.

Mout es greus turmens astratz
a selh qu'ab nulh valedor
no·s pot valer; donc gardatz
d'est aman en qual langor
era·l jorn d'afan aizius.
E dizia sospiran:
– Jorns, ben creyssetz a mon dans,
  e·l sers
auci·m e sos loncx espers   (ed. Riquer, *Los Trobadores*, pp. 1613 f.)

[A loyal lover was given a tryst by his lady – she set the time and the place. And during the day before the evening on which he was supposed to receive the honour, he was pensive and would say, sighing: 'Oh! day, to my sorrow you last too long; and the evening kills me and (so does my) long wait for it.'

So tormented was the lover by the burning desire for the joy which had been granted to him that he was very much afraid that he would not live till evening. And he would say sighing: 'Oh! day, to my sorrow you last too long; and the evening kills me and (so does my) long waiting for it.'

No one who was close to him could help but notice his pain, so agitated he was in his tearful appearance: so burdensome was the day to him. And he would say, sighing: 'Oh! day, to my sorrow you last too long; and the evening kills me and (so does my) long waiting for it.'

A great torment is the lot of him who cannot be helped by any aid. Consider, thus, in what anxiety the lover found himself on the day which was so full of torment. And he would say, sighing: 'Oh! day, to my sorrow you last too long; and the evening kills me and (so does my) long waiting for it'].

The use of the refrain, as well as the *unissonas* rhymes, gives an initial impression of unity to the poem, and defines the vast semantic field of *amor-onor-ardor-temor-dolor-plor-valedor-langor*, which encompasses all the painful effects of love in the tormenting *espers*.[39] This unity, however, is deceiving. The poem is divided into two parts, made up, respectively, of the first three *coblas* and the last one. The first part is cast in a narrative mode; the second in a didactic one. Moreover, each strophe is divided into two parts; in the first, we hear the narrator's voice; in the second, that of the protagonist-lover. The distribution of the verbal tenses underlines such a division. The narrator's voice in the first three strophes uses the past tenses – perfect, and most often imperfect. In the *refranh*, there are three verbs. One still belongs to the narrator's voice and is in the imperfect; the other two, used by the pained lover, are in the present tense.

The division could not be sharper, and its meaning is also clear. Using Harald Weinrich's interpretation of *tempora*[40] we can say that the past tenses in the poem present the 'narrative' parts, and the present the 'commentative' ones. Indeed, the poem opens in the best of narrative modes, presenting a character bound by what we may call a 'contract,' which, according to A. J. Greimas,[41] is one of the syntactic structures in the grammar of narration. This *fin aman* is introduced by the indefinite article *un* which conveys little information, but, as we will see, prepares us for some 'post-information.' The character lives in a different time from that of his creator. This difference is not necessarily a chronological one, but it is of such a nature as to confer autonomy on the world which is the object of the narrative. The past tense may not refer to a chronological past; it can actually be very close in time to the narrator's present; but, in any case, it creates that distance which is indispensable to the narrative mode.

But do we really have a narrative? Frankly, I do not know of any narratological model in which Guiraut's 'suspended narrative' could fit. The contract is accepted by the *fin aman*; but this hardly matters to the narration. The *fin aman* is not taking any decision, is not rejecting or pursuing any possibility, is not facing any test or impediment – he is only waiting, just fighting against time. The contract does not set in motion a sequence of events, as we would expect. It is precisely this situation of immobility that prompts the 'comments' of the lover. The second and third strophes elaborate on this situation without adding any narrative information. The fourth *cobla* departs from any suggestion of narration. The narrator speaks in his own present, 'commenting' on the history that he actually never finished for us. He switches to the didactic mode, which explains to us that *un fin aman* was meant to be *any* noble lover. Thus the indefinite article, which means 'all possible lovers,' is elevated to an exemplary level. The refrain in the last strophe, which seems so loosely tied to the preceding lines (one would expect a personal pronoun *el*, anticipated by the demonstrative *est*, rather than a conjunction) turns out to be a 'contiguous commentary' which is valid for all courtly lovers.

Indeed, the lot of courtly lovers is that they must 'wait' for ever. *Mezura* requires them to live in a perpetual state of restless immobility. They can only comment on the joy and pain experienced while imagining an event which never precipitates a chain of events. The love of the troubadours, rather than risking the 'closure' of a story, prefers to comment upon the endless alternation of joy and pain, desire and frustration. What is remarkable is that plotless dramas such as those of the courtly lover may require a vast stage.

The stage[42] belongs completely to the troubadour. There he is able to show how tormented he is by passion, and how he can win love. Torn between desires and constraints, the troubadour presents to his audience his cyclothymic self. Joy and pain compete to reach the higher note. Wisdom and madness alternate in a delirium that can cause the lover to express himself in different languages (as it happens in the *descort* by Cerveri de Girona or Bonifacio Calvo) or to do other foolish things.[43] It is a superb performance of a titanic fight which draws the applause and approval of the audience. The troubadour sings to it about his reasons for singing; he protests his status of victim while hoping to become conqueror; he proclaims that he will win by surrendering. This solo performance provides an opportunity to display both moral power and a singular artistic virtuosity. The poet insists, to the point of boasting, on the uniqueness of his situation and on his particular way of controlling it. Thus, he assures his listener of the sincerity of his love. We know very well, however, as does he, that the audience is calling the tune and judging how the troubadour's performance conforms to its ideals. His successful integration into society's horizon of expectation is an indication that the lover has attained *mezura*.

In performing his drama of *fin'amor* the troubadour renounces the most immediate and selfish *utile* – his sexual satisfaction – and pursues an *utile* of a higher order – the fame of his lady and the perpetuation of the courtly values. His lonely fight, conducted as it is under the severe eyes of courtly society, is truly a parable in *mezura*. In conforming to social ideals, the poet transforms the *femna* (female) into a *donna* (a lady), and sublimates his passions by directing their primordial energy into an ethically and socially superior sphere. *Fin'amor* exists only with *mezura*, and the troubadours can say with some justification that love is the source of all courtly virtues. *Mezura* exorcises the demon of eros by exposing it, by prescribing its ways of expression. Virtue does not come from passion (this was Andreas's understanding of the troubadours' statements), but it is present and active only when passionate love (the *fol'amor* or the 'exagitata cogitatio') is tamed, and temperate love (the *fin'amor*) is attained. Both passion and contenance (personified by the obstacles to love) are present in the fictional agon of troubadour lyrics, but the first is there only as a testimony of the ultimate victory of the second. In this victory eros has not been suppressed but given a new direction: *mezura* does not consist, as it is generally believed, in the elimination of physical desire but in reorienting it. Modern scholars who debate whether courtly love is primarily erotic or platonic rely upon specific statements by the troubadours, overlooking the fact that their message is not univocal but is given by the simultaneous presence of the two referents. Out of their contradiction and ambiguous interaction springs forth the conquest of *mezura*, which is bound thereby to contain a strong degree of ambiguity.

NARCISSISM

This degree of ambiguity is increased by the sense of complacency which runs through troubadours' verses of love. We have seen that *mezura* demands its acolytes to be magnanimous; accordingly, the troubadour extols a monument to his own uniqueness as lover in order to call himself *amaire ab mezura*. The danger of narcissism implied in this operation is quite strong; indeed, that sense of complacency we just mentioned betrays its presence. But *mezura* casts doubt on the real nature of a troubadour's passion because it prescribes that he 'be in love.' Is this love just a pretext on which to build his own image of courtly lover? And is it not this image the very object of a troubadour's love, so that his poems, rather than aiming at conquering a lady, constitute a monument to the troubadour's self, who only through his calculated self-love can be dubbed an acolyte of *fin'amor*?

These questions bring us to the problem of troubadour narcissism. A proper understanding of its nature should further our comprehension of *mezura*, its ambiguity and its role in creating some peculiarities in the *corpus* of troubadour lyrics.

First, we should be aware that the word *narcissism* has a special meaning for modern post-Freudian interpreters, a meaning unknown to the medieval mind.[44] To a twentieth-century reader, the myth of Narcissus immediately suggests the notion of *libido* having its object in the Ego; for a medieval reader, the abnormal feature of Narcissus's love is not his loving himself but his loving a shadow. Indeed, there is no trace of neurosis beneath the troubadours' restless immobility; there is, instead, a type of 'narcissism' which preserves some features of that 'love for a shadow' of the original myth.

We have reached a point which is of the utmost importance because it teaches to understand at last the nature and the origin of troubadours' *libido*. We may start by calling once again on Andreas Capellanus who gives a definition of erotic passion which reflects the thinking of his day about such a matter. Let us examine anew the definition of love he gives at the outset of his treatise:

> Amor est passio quaedam innata procedens ex visione et immoderata cogitatione formae alterius sexus, ob quam aliquis super omnia cupit alterius potiri amplexibus et omnia de utriusque voluntate in ipsius amplexu amoris praecepta compleri.

In the translation given in the first chapter of this book, the word *passio* is rendered as 'suffering.' What is the nature and the cause of this suffering? An answer is provided by rendering *passio* in another way which is equally acceptable and authorized by that medical tradition from which Andreas drew his definition of love. According to this tradition, *passio* is a violent 'movement of the concupiscible soul' towards a desired object. 'Passio est motus sensibilis appetitivae virtutis in apparitione boni vel mali' (Passion is a sensible movement of the appetitive power in the presence of the good or the bad); or 'Passio est irrationalis motus animae per susceptionem boni vel mali' (Passion is a non-rational movement of the soul toward the possession of the good or the bad); or, in a more general way, 'Passio est motus ex altero in alterum' (Passion is a movement from one person towards another). These definitions,[45] given by Nemesius of Emesa by way of the translation of the Bishop Alfanus of Salerno, are not incompatible with that of *passio* as suffering. Actually both notions are complementary because the 'movement' towards an appearance of goodness or badness causes a pain that is relieved only when the movement reaches its goal, and the desire rests in the attainment of its object.

This explanation takes us into the realm of the internal senses, which play an essential role in the process of becoming enamoured. In the Middle Ages, medical doctors as well as the philosophers dealt at great length with the process of knowledge, which originates in the external senses and culminates in the intellect after traversing the internal senses.[46] The process of love follows the same route. Simplifying it as much as possible, one can say, with Andreas, that love begins with a *visio*, a sight, which is transmitted through the eyes to the *sensus communis*, the internal sense which receives all external sensations. When the object causing the sensation is no longer present, the sensation is preserved by the *phantasia* or imagination. Both powers have their organ in the front ventricle of the brain. The imagination has an active power and transmits the retained image to the central ventricle of the brain, where the imaginative power exists. This sense differs from the imagination (*phantasia* or *imaginatio*) in so far as it has the faculty of combining images whereas the imagination can only record them. If the combining of images is done according to the senses it is called *vis imaginativa*; if it does so according to reason it is called *cogitatio*.[47] In the back part of the central ventricle is the organ of the *vis aestimativa*, which perceives the *intentiones* of things seen. In order to understand the notion of *intentiones*, one may recall Avicenna's example: a sheep fears a wolf because it perceives its hostile nature, and such a perception can be made only by the *vis aestimativa*.[48] The *vis aestimativa* corresponds to what is known to us as the instinct: it judges – not rationally – whether one thing is good or bad, useful or dangerous, pleasant or unpleasant to the subject. The whole chain of perceptions is then stored in the memory, or *vis memorativa*, which has its organ in the third or back ventricle of the brain. At this point the perceptive process is over and can be transformed into a concept if reason intervenes. The process of love, however, might not engage the reason. Once the original vision reaches the *virtus aestimativa*, it is perceived as the cause of great delight, so that the will moves the appetitive soul towards that cause. This movement is the *passio*. As Andreas knew, such a movement cannot generate virtue because it has its origins in the *vis aestimativa* rather than in the reason (the only power capable of judging the good and the bad), whereas virtue is rooted only in rational judgment. A lover considers the source of his delight to be the *summum bonum*; but this is a confusion which hampers the intellect and may even degenerate into a disease.[49]

Does any or all of this apply to courtly lovers? Yes, of course, in so far as they pretend to be persons subject to passions like anyone else. A troubadour insistently recalls the vision of a woman; tells how he was struck by her poise and by her complexion; occasionally he even hints at an intimate moment when his lady allowed him to lie next to her. The memory of the vision or of that moment is as implacable as an obsession: it is the 'exagitata cogitatio' which torments any normal lover. It could not be otherwise, mainly for mimetic reasons: no lover would be believable without experiencing sorrows and joys. But the voice which utters those words of love (and here it is not important whether it is the voice of the poet or of his persona – namely, the troubadour) also expresses words which refer to virtue and moral perfection. This combination – which scandalized Andreas – is unusual in other love poetry; and this anomaly, even from the philosophical point of view, compels us to consider whether the sexual desire of courtly lovers stems from the same reality of all other lovers – if, in other words, it comes from a real vision of a beauty. If this is not the case, then we must assume that the process of falling in love for courtly lovers is of a kind of its own, which is actually the case.

Several facts that have already been analysed lead us to suspect that there is something anomalous in the passion sung about by troubadours. One is that the person they love is a stereotype with insignificant variations. Another is that often they have never seen their beloved persons. A troubadour may have heard her beauties celebrated, in which case the origin of his love seems to be of literary origin, a love born from a literature-like situation. Regardless, the process of falling in love does not correspond exactly to the one described by Andreas, who, incidentally, thought it impossible for blind people to fall in love. But a third element accentuates the anomaly of troubadours' love: for them both loves – the one born from sight and the other from hearing – are equal in intensity. This situation is untenable, be it from a psychological or from a medical point of view. The first Italian poet, Giacomo da Lentini, imbued with medical science, tells us that these two loves are not comparable in intensity:

> Bene è alcuna fiata om amatore
> senza vedere so 'namoramento;

> ma quell'amor che stringe con furore
> da la vista de li occhi ha nascimento.[50]

What is one to infer from this unusual situation of *fin'amor* where the beloved ladies do not exist or, if they do, they have never been seen? The simplest conclusion is that the toubadours were not 'sincere.' But the 'sincerity' in troubadours' plotless stories of love, a problem which still concerns scholars of our generation,[51] should not be questioned unless we understand 'sincerity' in the autobiographical sense. The 'sincerity' of the troubadours must be understood in the artistic sense. In reading troubadour poetry one is often reminded of what Diderot dubbed the 'actor's paradox':[52] the more sincere and spontaneous an actor appears to be, the better he is playing his role which he has learned by heart; and in this paradox he reaches the perfection of the artistic illusion. The troubadour is indeed an actor. He is an hypostasis of the poet who has created him. Provençal poets are like all poets described by Fernando Pessoa in a poem entitled 'Autopsychography': 'The poet is good at pretending; he pretends so well that he even arrives at fictionalizing a pain that he really feels.'[53] A Provençal poet fictionalizes his own feelings in the troubadour. This character might have his creator's name, but he is not the same person any longer. He is an idealized lover who is supposed to love intensely and, at the same time, draw virtue from this irrational feeling. Thus what was deemed philosophically impossible by Andreas turns out to be possible at the level of a fiction which combines eros and virtue because they are both of a literary nature. Thus the more deeply one looks for signs of real life in troubadour poetry the more elusive they become, because they evanesce in the literary sublimation. But that hypostatization is not an empty literary exercise; in fact, it celebrates the ideals of *cortezia* in the figure of a gentleman whose main ambition is not to sing about passionate love and virtue, not even to conquer love, but to demonstrate that he is a lover *ab mezura*.

This lover *ab mezura* must claim to be unique in every respect, be it the beauty of his beloved or the intensity of his feelings; but his uniqueness is again one of a literary kind for it must match the sublimity of his literary heroes. If the author idealizes himself in the troubadour, his own image becomes moulded by other exemplary lovers – namely, the other troubadours or mythic lovers of the classical or Romance world. The troubadour, in other words, projects his own image on a mirror made of ink and paper, a mirror having a mythopoetic power. The troubadour is pleased to see his own image aggrandized by this mythic dimension, and, of course, he loves it, as his sense of complacency makes it clear. It is a love for a shadow, it is true; but it is a shadow that has the reality of the ideals and the fascination of the myths; and through this self-love the troubadour attains his *Dasein*, his belonging to courtliness.

Strange mirror, that of a troubadour! When one is convinced that its surface is all covered by one image, at closer inspection one sees that surface becoming opaque – made of ink and paper as it were – reflecting the image of myriad lovers singing altogether about joy and pain in the same chords and tunes, although each of them claims to be singing a *solo*. It is a choir where the supposed individual voices seem to express a collective aspiration for which we have a name: *mezura*. So troubadours' narcissism has its ambiguities, too, although not those one usually associates with neurosis. It is the love of the self in the other; and in that dialectic between these two entities it is impossible to decide how much of its own the first sacrifices to the second, and how much the second is enriched by the first: they live in each other, giving each other light; and in the process each risks being the shadow of the other.

The songs of the troubadours come out of the playing of mirrors and images where the reality of the outside world becomes a pale shadow. In that game of mirrors and images, the superior reality of *mezura* is ciphered and celebrated. Any celebration should have its music and its literature; *mezura* had plenty of both – actually, so much so that *mezura* could seem a pretext, and the real aim of that choir was singing for the sake or for the beauty of singing. Such is the perception of the formalist readers of troubadour poetry, and it is hard to refute in a categoric way: above all because it seems to meet that nuance of disinterestedness of the *honestum*. But we have seen that *honestum* and *utile* coincide when the latter is not just selfishness. Even when a troubadour stresses his egoistic and possessive desires, he is paying tribute to *cortezia*; his formalistic exercise is ultimately a tribute to Beauty, the collective ideal of *cortezia*. It is not an exaggeration to say that Provençal literature was the first extensive phenomenon of art for art's sake; but the paradox and the ambiguity are that the principle for justifying 'l'art pour l'art' were taken not from art itself but from the ethical and social aspirations of *cortezia*.

At the point of concluding this chapter, it may be appropriate to read *in extenso* a poem and find support for some of the basic ideas presented above. The text chosen is a poem by Folquet de Marselha which is typical in so far as the themes and the topoi are concerned, but it is quite remarkable as an artistic achievement to the point that a connoisseur of Dante's stature used it as a supreme example of *tragica coniugatio* (*De vulgari eloquentia*, II, 6):

I

Tant m'abellis l'amoros pessamens
que s'es vengutz a mon fin cor assire,
per que no·i pot nuills autre pes caber
ni mais negus no m'es dous ni plazens,
qu'adonc viu sas quan m'aucizo·l cossire
e fin'amors aleuja·m mo martire
que·m promet joi, mas trop lo·m dona len,
qu'ap bel semblan m'a trainat longamen.

II

Be sai que tot quan faz es dreiz niens!
Eu qu'en puesc mais s'Amors mi vol aucire?
Qu'az escien m'a donat tal voler
que ja non er vencutz ni el no vens;
vencutz si er, qu'aucir m'an li sospire
tot soavet, quar de liey cui dezire
non ai socors, ni d'allors no l'aten,
ni d'autr'amor no puesc aver talen.

III

Bona dona, si·us platz, siatz sufrens
del ben qu'ie·us vuel qu'ieu sui del mal sufrire,
e pueis lo mals no·m poira dan tener
ans m'er semblan que·l partam egalmens;
pero, si·us platz qu'az autra part me vire,
ostatz de vos la beutat e·l dous rire
e·l bel semblan que m'afollis mon sen:
pueis partir m'ai de vos, mon escien.

IV

A totz jorns m'etz plus bel'e plus plazens;
per qu'ie·n vuel mal als huels ab que·us remire,
quar a mon pro no·us poirian vezer
et a mon dan vezon trop sotilmens;
mos dans non es, sivals pos no·m n'azire,
ans es mos pros, dona, per qu'ieu m'albire,

si m'aucisetz, que no·us estara gen,
quar lo mieus dans vostres er eissamen.
    V
Per so, dona, no·us am saviamens
qu'a vos sui fis et a mos ops trayre;
e vos cug perdr'e mi no puesc aver,
e·us cug nozer et a mi sui nozens;
pero, no·us aus mon mal mostrar ni dire,
mas a l'esgart podetz mon cor devire,
qu'ar lo·us cuich dir et aras m'en repen
et port n'als huels vergonh'e ardimen.
    VI
Trop vos am mais, dona, qu'ieu no sai dire,
e quar anc jorn aic d'autr'amor desire
no m'en penet, ans vos am per un cen,
car ai proat l'autrui captenemen.
    VII
Vas Nems t'en vai, chanssos, qui qe·s n'azire,
que gauch n'auran, per lo meu escien,
las tres donnas a cui ieu te presen   (ed. Stroński, II)

[So pleasing is to me the amorous preoccupation which came to dwell in my noble heart (so that no other thought can find a place in it and no other thought is sweet and pleasant to me) that I live in health when these thoughts kill me, and *fin'amors* alleviates my pain, because it promises me joy but delivers it too slowly, since for a long time it has led me on with nice appearances.

I know too well that anything I do (is worthy) a pure nothing! What can I do if love wants to kill me? Knowingly it gave me such a wish that I will never be won and it will never win either. Oh yes, I will be won because my sighs will very sweetly kill me, since I do not get any help from her whom I desire, and I do not hope for it either, nor can I feel a desire for another love.

Excellent lady, if it pleases you, be tolerant of the love I feel for you, because I am the one who suffers the pain: this pain won't hurt me if it will seem that we share it evenly. But if you want me to turn in another direction, remove from yourself your beauty and your sweet smile and your beautiful appearance which makes my mind go crazy; then I will depart from you with full awareness.

Every day you are for me more beautiful and more pleasant; and for this reason I hate my eyes with which I contemplate you, because they could not see you to my advantage, they see too subtly to my damage. In fact it is not my damage, lady, so that I do not get sad, but in my interest so that I imagine that if you kill me it will not be to your own advantage, considering that my damage will be yours as well.

Therefore, lady, I do not love you wisely, because I am loyal to you and a traitor to my own interests; and I think that I am losing you and (in fact) I cannot have you; and I think that I am causing you damage and actually I am hurting myself. Yet I do not dare to show or tell you about my pain; but you can understand my intention from my glances, because the sooner I repent, and I have in my eyes bashfulness and daring.

I love you more, my lady, than I can say; and since I never had a desire of another love, I do not regret it; on the contrary, I love you one hundred times more, because I have experienced someone else's behaviour.

Song, go to Nemes – who ever may object – because, as far as I know, the three ladies to whom I am presenting you, will derive pleasure from you].

The deixis of the first stanza focuses on the lyric *I*. It appears in the first line, which also introduces an exceptional situation (*tant*) created by the paradox (*m'abellis / l'amoros pessamens*). The subject, however, is not the lover but his *amoros pessamens*. The lover is indicated by a pronominal object (*me abellis*), which, given the strong middle voice nuance of *abellis*, could be an ethical dative or an accusative direct object. This situation remains unchanged throughout the stanza: *m'es dous, m'auciso, aleuja·m, que·m prome, lo·m dona, m'a trainat*. This deictic sign of the pronominal object appears seven times (but one should add to the same account the possessive adjective *mon fin cor* and *mo martire*) in eight lines. There is only one verb in the first person (*viu*), which occurs in the middle of the stanza and introduces the second paradox of living through death. The message is clear: Love is the active force that rules over the lover's life, confining him in a closed place where pain and joy will keep him company.

The situation varies but essentially remains the same in the second stanza. The lover confesses to his impotence, his useless doing. *Amors* retains its power over him (notice, again, *mi vol aucire* and *m'a donat*). Two passive verbs (*er vencutz*) and an active one (*qu'aucir m'an*; its subject is *suspire*, a metonimic agent for *Amors*) present the lover as self-absorbed in considering – through rhetorical questions and contrary to fact hypotheses – his privileged situation of being a powerless victim of love. In this self-absorption appears a *liey*, the lover's lady. Her presence lacks denotative signs: she is 'the lady' by antonomasia, born, as it were, from the association of thoughts rather than from an outside reality. Her presence prompts a series of negative considerations: *non ai, no l'aten, no puesc aver*, which are made in the first person and further seclude the lover from his lady's world, which only desire can reach.

The lady who first appears in a mute way now dominates the third stanza as a silent addressee, as an idealized interlocutor whom the lover implores and mentally tries to win by a contract. He offers her two possibilities: either (*si us platz*) to share his passivity (*siatz sufrens*) so that a sort of *paritas* (*que'l partam egalmens*) can be achieved in joy and pain; or to be altogether another person, without any of her physical beauty so that he can easily depart from her. Both alternatives are unrealistic. As a result the lady appears even more remote, and her beauty is diminished by distance. Her lover's folly has the intensity of all passions which are disproportionate to the object of their desire, and are consummated in solitude.

This timid and completely fantasized attempt at a dialogue is carried on in the following stanza, where the discourse becomes highly emotive. The *hic* deixis is again emphasized by the frequency of personal pronouns in the subject case and in oblique cases, as well as by the recurrent use of the possessive adjective *mon*. This self-centred world has its outermost boundaries in the eyes of the lover. They convey an image which produces the paradox of joy/pain, or a constant immobile tension resulting in a state of 'non-sadness' (*no·m n'azire*) on the part of the lover.

The final stanza shows more clearly that the dialogue between the lover and his lady is actually a monologue. We have here a series of considerations on the paradox of love, more specifically on the alternation of *pros* and *dans* treated in the previous stanza. *Pros* and *dans* are the positive and negative poles of that paradox seen from the point of view of the self. In this final stanza, the situation seems to go towards a solution, for the lover appears to take an active role – as shown by the first-person pronouns. But the majority of the verbs are denoted either by a negative particle (*no·us am, no puesc, no·us aus*) or by a negative meaning (*perdre, nozer*). When they are not negative they are copulative (*sui fis, sui nozens*) or auxiliary (*cug*) or reflexive (*m'en repen*). In their totality, these verbs indicate an inability to free the paradoxical situation and open this self-perpetuating circle to the outside world. The only manifest sign of that inner turmoil can be read in the lover's eyes; but the message is ambiguous, for it conveys daring and bashfulness at the same time.

These cursory observations prove that the world of this fictionalized lover is self-focused and closed, almost like a perfect monad. Other considerations could bring further evidence of this fact. The majority of the verbs in this poem are *verba sentiendi*, verbs which express feeling, opinion, fear, calculation, regret, desire, and hope; verbs which define an emotional state of self-analysis, of frustrated dreams of success. Active verbs like *viu* and *aucire* are semantically ambiguous because life is felt through death, and death is accepted with joy. An active verb like *remire* has a nuance of passivity for we can render it with 'I contemplate.' The prevalence of *verba sentiendi* and the choice of verbs with a dim active meaning depend on the fact that the situation which they predicate teems with paradoxes. The paradox, being by its nature a closed ring, does not allow any 'way out,' and imposes instead a perpetual and unvariable reflection over the tension created between its positive and negative poles. The *verba sentiendi*, focusing on that unresolvable situation, convey an impression of psychological stasis in spite of the underlying restlessness.

The poem does not build a linear discourse, but it proceeds in a circular way in which the same situation of paradox is repeated over and over again. The *rimas unissonans* support this impression of continuity in immobility or, if one prefers, of continuity in contradiction, since most rhymes recall by association a series of antonyms: *pessamens-plazens-niens-sufrens*, etc. Also the syntax supports this impression. Folquet, who is known as the most 'logical' of the troubadours, is actually not better than others when he attempts to solder two stanzas into a linear, constructive argument. Folquet's logical ability is limited to the setting of each stanza. In the first two stanzas we see that the consecutive construction prevails. The third – the central one – is woven along a hypothetical construction. In the fourth and fifth stanzas, the declarative and causal sentences dictate the syntactic construction. This division alone – corresponding to (a) declaration of love and its consequences; (b) an unrealistic desire of winning it; (c) resignation to Love's power) – attests to Folquet's artistic craft as well as to a vague design of a constructed discourse. But this construction is really too vague. The only syntactic tie between two stanzas in the whole poem is the conjunction *Per so*, at the beginning of the fifth stanza. The liaison, however, is very weak because it does not introduce a 'consequence,' but just a variation of what is stated in the previous stanza without adding any new information.

From this circular discourse we learn several things. The main point is that the world of a courtly lover finds the key to its existence in repetition. The lyric *I* is self-centred, engaged in what amounts to a monologue whose subject-matters are pain and hope. The vague references to the outside world hardly interfere and provide any weight to upset the balance between the two. The lover is thus caught in his contradictory situation, incapable of resolving it – actually, not eager to resolve it, since it is that very contradiction which nurtures his plotless story of love. The lover is therefore bound to express pain and joy endlessly without ever hoping or wanting to bring his story to closure. The first *tornada* of Folquet's poem hints at this fact. Here the lover says: '*Trop* [in symmetry with the opening *tant vos am mais, dona, qu'ieu no sai dire*.' One recognizes the *topos* of 'ineffability'; but underneath the clichés one reads the reason for that repetitiveness: words are approximate so the speech can present only an illusion of progression by accumulation.

Yet, that 'not saying enough' has created a poem. Also it has created a persona, a lover who is self-absorbed and whose monologue conveys the pathos of his being unrequited and yet hopeful, loyal and unique in facing the alternatives of love's forces. Torments and joys are accepted with a sense of complacency because their uniqueness makes exceptional the person who endures it all. This persona loves his own being in love, because love distinguishes him and causes him to sing with a distinct voice. The whole is a crafty mythopoetic operation whose aim is not a confession but a composition centred around the ideal of a *fin aman*. But since this courtly lover is a poetic fiction, his love, too, is of literary origin, even if it borrows as much as possible the language of real passion. The second *tornada* supports our conclusion. When the poet's *discressio* imposes the closure of the poem, he distances himself from his fictionalized persona who has allowed him to write a poem which is then offered as a gift to three ladies. It is possible to establish the historical identity of these ladies; however of the lady sung to by the troubadour we have no trace because very likely she never existed.

Would these three ladies enjoy the poem? The sender has no doubt about it (*'gauch n'auran per lo meu escien'*) because they know all the secrets of his supposed love: they know it is a ritual. As connoisseurs they appreciate what a deftness the making of a poem takes; they recognize all the *topoi* and catch even some close echoes of other poems, as in the *'dreiz niens'* of line 9 which reminds us of William IX, or line 26 which is so close to Bernart de Ventadorn *'O no·i vei clar dels olhs ab que·us remir'* (ed. Lazar, III, l. 56). These ladies will not be scandalized by the hints to the obscure world of passion because its intensity is purified into literature, into elegant rhythms which seduce just as all art seduces. Above all they would enjoy the subtle projection of the poet into his persona, which is so like the personae of other poets. It is not a frivolous play, they understand: because that projection is seen as a striving towards the ennobling force of *mezura*. In sum, these ladies will look into the troubadour's mirror and see themselves in the poet (his art) and in his image (his and their ideals). They, like us, will find it impossible to isolate just one image in that mirror. It contains a trinity where poets, their idealizations as lovers *ab mezura*, and audience expectations come together in a harmonic consubstantiation. If we undo that trinity we may be accused of heresy; but, what is ever worse, we would miss the enchantment we derive from troubadour poetry.

It is interesting and yet by now predictable to observe how such 'great loves' as were those of the troubadours remain recorded only in their songs. Not a single one of these 'unique loves' – with the exception, perhaps, of Guilhem de Cabestanh's – has left a trace in history like, say, Abelard's love for Heloïse. What happened of so much desiring, of so much passion? The great paradox is that *mezura* encouraged it and *mezura* curbed it because it made it acceptable only in combination with virtue. In this respect *mezura* is kindred to *Natura*, the twelfth-century goddess who, in the daring affabulations of the Chartrian school,[54] brings together natural desires and virtue. Provençal poets, too, were in their way singers of Natura;[55] but they placed their *summum bonum* not in God, but in the God of Love whose sphere of power was limited to the world of the *honestum*. The celebration of this God of Love did not require complex treatises of theology, but only lyric poems. Through the invention of this earthly divinity loving and singing became inseparable for many centuries to come.

Mezura shaped the world of *fin'amor* and (it is another paradox), was the major cause of its extinction. The strong call for conformism implied in *mezura* impeded any rejuvenation. Not the crusades against the Albigensians – as scholars maintain – but the normative force of *mezura* caused the poetic vein of the troubadours to dry up. The voices of the troubadours of later generations have a uniform and rather monotonous pitch, hardly sufficient to give new life to old themes and motifs which, by the middle of the thirteenth century, had the sterile beauty of things past. Even if there are plenty of remarkable poets (Guilhem de Montanhagol, Cerveri de Girona, Sordel, Bertran d'Alamon, and many others), they invented very little that was new. Their position of 'post-classics,' as it were, explains the propensity in some of them (Guilhem de Montanhagol and Sordel are the best examples) for codifying the principles of *fin'amor*; and their codification means both that *fin'amor* has exhausted its creative energy and that *mezura* has succeeded in shaping a civilization, indeed in creating a language.

What was left of the troubadours' myths? When the last troubadour remained silent, a splendid chapter in literary history was closed. Many poets perused it, but none of them was able to reproduce that subtle interplay of eros and virtue without ultimately settling for one or the other; no one was able to understand that *mezura* was one and the same substance with love. What was left besides the identity of love and poetry was a series of themes and motifs which, in new contexts, lost their original meaning. Hence came the temptation – still alive today – to take literally what the troubadours said. In that temptation is the great danger of confusing literature with life. This danger has its unforgettable victims: one may be Francesca, who justifies her life through literature; and the other may be Don Quixote, who justifies literature through his life. Don Quixote is the last of courtly lovers, but his uncourtly contemporaries called him a fool. He was, like many troubadours, 'enamorado de oídas,'[56] a lover by hearsay. When a duchess challenged him to describe the beauty of his Dulcinea 'because there is not such a lady in the world: in fact she's a fantastic being, a creature of your imagination, painted with all the charms and perfection you desired,' Don Quixote replied: 'On this question much might be said. God knows whether or not there's a Dulcinea in the world, real or imaginary: these are not things the truth of which can be proven. I neither engendered my lady nor brought her forth, but simply think of her as she needs must be, as one whose parts can make her famous in all those of the world: beautiful without blemish, distinguished without pride, tender and yet modest, gracious from courtesy and courteous from good breeding; last of all, noble of lineage, since, with family as a background, beauty shines forth and excels with more degrees of excellence than with the fair of lowly birth.'[57] A troubadour, if pressed to answer the same question, would have given the same answer; but he would not have been alone in doing so, and none of his listeners would consider him a fool. Many other troubadours like him were fighting for the same lady, whom they wound up sharing because her name was *mezura*.

The *Adynata*

The concluding paragraphs of the previous chapter have perhaps left the impression that the poems of the troubadours, given their repetitious and conventional qualities, could be interchanged among themselves. This impression may result from our attempt to construct a 'model' of courtly love to which even the most distinct poetical personalities are sacrificed. It is clear, though, that no reader, however insensitive, would ever mistake a poem by Raimbaut d'Aurenga for one by Guiraut Riquier, or a poem by Arnaut Daniel for one by Bertolme Zorzi. The differences in poetic diction and lyrical intensity are usually so sharp that there is no room for confusion. In fact, some of these differences are programmatic, because they depend as much upon a poetic school as upon the personality of the poet. Yet the problems of attribution in the tradition of Provençal poetry are more frequent than in any other tradition, problems which do not depend only on normal accidents in textual transmission and cannot always be resolved on thematic and stylistic grounds. Indeed, even the most original voices pay tribute to conventionality, not because of poetic inertia but because adherence to a convention is an intrinsic feature of courtly poetry. This inherent quality becomes increasingly more prominent with the succession of generations of poets. Concomitantly, the poetics of the *troubar clus*, the hermetic style (with its variants of *trobar ric*, *trobar prim*, *trobar brau*, etc.) which allowed a higher degree of distinct expressivity, tends to fade away, leaving room for the plain style, the *trobar leu*.[1] It is, therefore, an unfair and fruitless endeavour to look for that kind of originality which the Romantic Diez sought in troubadours' lyrics. The originality of any troubadour is not to be sought in sentimental sincerity, thematic innovation, or uniqueness of imagery, but above all in the craft by which he brings together conventional materials to produce a semantically knit poem. If the themes and motives are conventional, *discretio* guides the poet in putting them together so that they live a new life. It takes just a subtle *écart*,[2] an almost imperceptible deviation from convention, a *callida junctura* (to use Horace's prescription),[3] and those clichés sound as if newly created and become an integral part of the poem's texture. The complicity of the audience is made stronger by this subtle play because the commonplaces of the troubadour's *inventio* give life to a paradox: while they conventionalize individual expressions they also guarantee communication.[4] The poet must work with courtly *topoi* just as a plastic surgeon works with skin grafts: they must 'take' in a semantic unity, becoming indispensable conveyers of the poem's sense. When a troubadour reaches this perfect amalgamation of themes, motifs, and phonosymbolic and metrical features, his *discretio* has produced that ineffable elegance, that learned spontaneity which is often the enchanting quality of a Provençal poem. The disassembling, layer by layer, of Provençal poems by modern formalists has repeatedly shown the consummate mastery of the poetic matters of which a troubadour is capable. Thanks to this kind of originality, a troubadour never tires his audience, even if he sings of a lady who is predictably blonde, plump, witty, and rich, and even if she is predictably living far away, proud, and insensitive to his entreaties for love.

The previous two chapters have built a model of courtly love. It is now time to get inside that model, not to describe functions but to distinguish poetical voices, to have a closer look at some poets, at their themes, artistic craft, and learning, all of which give life to it. The ideal way to do so would be to write a series of chapters on individual poets; but space and energy do not permit it, and, besides, there are excellent studies on almost all major troubadours. A more modest approach, however, may produce satisfactory results. I have decided to focus on a figure of thought and speech called *adynaton*, that is, 'impossible.' Since this figure is present practically in all troubadour poetry, it allows a contrastive study of different poets and schools. The choice of this figure over others does not require many justifications since it emblematizes better than any other rhetorical device the troubadour's 'impossible' quest of love. The troubadours use adynata to signify their madness, their joy, their perseverance and loyalty, their despair and challenges – all major themes of the paradox of courtly love. In this survey we will see how *adynata* are a fixture in the code of courtly poetry, and how different *adynata* are used for different themes. They form a system which does not prevent a poet from using it with originality; but, at the same time, this system will allow some conclusions which have already been reached in studying the model: originality and respect for conventions coalesce in an ambiguous endeavour which ultimately celebrates courtliness.

The original occasion for studying the *adynata* was a perspicacious footnote by E.R. Curtius, who, while sketching the history of the *topos* 'the world upside down,' observed that Arnaut Daniel's *adynata* have a psychological function totally unknown in the classical tradition.[5] This observation is perspicacious and essentially correct; however, it does not consider Arnaut's immediate cultural context where *adynata* had been widely used with the same function. His originality is thus accentuated beyond the point at which it can be properly assessed. To do so, one must understand the way in which the troubadours use the *adynata* in order to see how Arnaut Daniel achieves his originality within the troubadour poetry code.

The use of *adynata* goes far back to Homer and to the Bible.[6] The name of this figure, however, came much later, and its definition is vague enough to make it quite difficult to propose a single formula for all types of *adynata*. Let us follow, for instance, a stylistic criterion[7] and define the *adynaton* as a figure formed by two correlative sentences (*cum/dum*; *citius/quam*; *antea/quam*), in which the first one states an impossible fact. How can such a definition absorb Juvenal's 'niger cycnus'[8] (black swan)? Let us further assume that the *adynaton* represents the failing of a natural law: how then is one to explain Plautus' 'aquam a pumice postulas' (*Persa*, 1. 41: You expect to get water from a pumice stone), where the implied assumption of a natural law underlines the futility of any attempt to break it? Thus, to the question 'quae est adynatos,' one should still answer with Fortunatianus: 'cum id in themate ponitur, quod sit contra rerum naturae fidem.'[9]

Within this definition it is possible to distinguish between *adynata* representing the impossibility of a natural phenomenon, and *adynata* which represent what we may call an *inanis opera*.

The first type might have as an emblem ἄνω ποταμῶν, the river which returns to its source. Many classical *impossibilia* belong to this family: dolphins that live in a forest while boars live in the sea; stars that change their course; wolves that mate with goats; and an entire series of phenomena which can take place only in a topsy-turvy world. In whatever context it may be used (anathema, oath, declaration of love or faith or hate are the most common ones), the *adynaton* always has an asseverating function which no hyperbole can equal.

As for the *inanis opera*, one can borrow a good definition from Erasmus: 'Quadrabit simpliciter in eos qui frustra moliuntur τὰ ἀδύνατα aut qui praepostere ibi quaerunt aliquid ubi ne sperare quidem possit'[10] [The *inanis opera* will be directly appropriate for those who uselessly struggle against impossible things or who absurdly expect to get something from them which is beyond hope]. The inane labour differs from the first type of *adynaton* in so far as the action can be pursued but never accomplished: it is an adynatic action and its performer is insane. Typical examples of this second kind of *adynaton* are Plautus's 'in aere piscari' and 'venari in mari' (*Asinaria*, l. 90 and l. 100: to fish in the air and to hunt in the sea), Terence's 'laterem lavare' (*Phormio*, l. 186: to wash a brick), Catullus's 'scribere in aqua' (LXX, ll. 3–4: to write on water), and Cicero's 'Penelopis telam retexere' (*Acad.* II, 94: to weave again Penelope's web).

The Latin authors of the Republican period made parsimonious use of *adynata*. A lesser restrain is shown by the authors of the Silver Age especially in their *controversiae* and *ecphrasis*[11] where *adynata*, oxymora, and paradoxes, together with all sorts of *kakozelia*, abound according to Quintilian.[12] Further stimulation for imaginative *impossibilia* came from the paradoxality of Christianism, and especially from the nature of Christ who is father to his own mother and older than time, as one is told in the *Laus Christi* attributed to Claudian.[13] The Carolingian poets continued this tradition to the point that an entire poem by Walfrid Strabo, *Similitudo impossibilium*[14] contains only *adynata*: an exercise that the Romance *fatrasies* and *disparates* will enjoy repeating. Understandably, the *adynata* became an indispensable ingredient in the *contemptus mundi* of the eleventh and twelfth centuries,[15] because the *adynaton* is the emblem of the topsy-turvy world. A cluster of *adynata* is found in the fifth meter of Alain de Lille's *De planctu Naturae*. It should be quoted, at least in part, because it deals with love:

> Pax odio fraudique fides, spes iuncta timori
>   Est amor, et mixtus cum ratione furor;
> Naufragium dulce, pondus leve, grata Caribdis
>   Incolumis langor, insaciata fames
> [...]

Tempestas grata, nox lucida, lux tenebrosa
    Mors vivens, moriens vita, suave malum
[...]
Dum furit iste furor, deponit Sylla furorem
    Et pius Eneas incipit esse Nero,
Fulminat ense Paris, Tideus mollescit amore
    Fit Nestor iuvenis, fit Melicerta senex[16]

[Love is peace united to hate, hope with fear, and fury mixed with reason: a sweet wreckage, a light burden, a grateful Charybdis, a safe and sound state of enervatedness, an insatiated hunger [...] A pleasant storm, a shiny night, a sweet evil [...] While this fury rages, Scylla lays down his wrath, and the pious Aeneas begins to be a Nero; Paris brandishes his sword, Tydeus is all soft in love, Nestor becomes young and Melicertes old ...].

'O, quam mira res est amor, quia tantis facit hominem fulgere virtutibus!' one would exclaim with Andreas Capellanus. Alanus's oxymora and *adynata* seem to echo the paradoxes of courtly love, which, in his day, had given a new version of the traditional 'amentia amoris.' But Alanus's condemnation of love had an illustrious precedent in a Provençal poet who warned his audience against the destructive power of love:

Pieger es que gualiana
    Amors que guespilha,
Cruzels cozens e baiana
    Calens e frezilha
Quar molt tratz mal e safrana
    Selhuy cui estrilha   [ed. Dejeanne, XXI, ll. 31–6]

[Worse still is love that deceives, that stings like a wasp, cruel, burning and treacherous, hot and freezing, because it treats badly and turns yellow the man whom it scourges].

This troubadour is Marcabru, the austere moralist who was acutely aware of the wrong direction taken by a world that goes backwards, 'a rebuzon.'[17] Marcabru saw that crime, adultery, self-interest, greed, and hypocrisy were taking the place of *proeza, mezura, joy,* and *joven* everywhere. In this topsy-turvy world, peasants claim to be courtly, and the righteous accuse themselves of sins they have not committed:

> Non sai que faire,
> Tant fort sui entrepres,
> Qu'entorn l'araire
> Si fant villan cortes,
> E 'l just pechaire
> De so qu'en lor non es   (ed. Dejeanne, XXXII, ll. 19–24)

[I do not know what to do, because I am so shocked by the fact that peasants around the plough pretend to be courtly, and the just ones (proclaim) themselves sinners of what is not in them (of a sin they have not committed)].

The pathos contained in this version is unknown to any author of *contemptus mundi* or to any poet who sang the death of *probitas*.[18] Marcabru reaches an intensity of expression through harsh language, through concrete reference to the contemporary world, through coarse sarcasm drenched with biblical overtones. He was certainly witnessing a profound change of customs brought about by the gradual transformation of castles into courts and by the rise of an urban civilization. These changes weakened feudal austerity and favoured a secularization of mores, a certain degree of moral laxitude, and a great concern for wealth and luxury. Marcabru interpreted this licentiousness as an expression of the courtly love which, in his day, had already become fashionable. Fathered by Ebles of Ventadorn, a poet about whom practically nothing is known,[19] this kind of love had singers like the Duke of Aquitania whose Janus-like[20] attitude towards love expressed itself in poems that were either obscene or spiritual, and like Jaufre Rudel, whose *amor de lonh* did not exclude an 'amor doussana dinz vergier e sotz cortina.'[21] In this early manifestation of courtly love, the presence of *fol'amor* is strongly felt: it is the phase which R. Nelli has called *chevaleresque*.[22] Marcabru (and a group of poets – Cercamon, Alegret, Marcoat – who belong to the same generation) is an implacable critic of this kind of love, which, under Ovidian elegances, corrupts society. He finds that it is dictated by sheer hypocrisy. Moreover, according to Marcabru, this love punishes those who preach it, is encouraged by venality which makes everyone a victim, and is a justification for lust and adultery which, universally practised, turn everyone into a cuckold.

Marcabru offers an antidote against this insidious way of loving.[23] He calls it – perhaps for the first time[24] – *fin'amors*: a new form of love which must be sung in *trobar naturaus* because it is a love which respects *Natura*, the twelfth-century goddess, the giver of cardinal virtues. This love which conforms to Natura is incompatible with any form of selfishness, be it lust or greed. In Nature there is no *frait cuidar*, no particularized form of interest: a leaf, for instance, grows in order to return life to a tree. Nature shows us that the true advantage for an individual is everyone's advantage, and this *entier cuidar* brings together the *utile* and the *honestum*. The courtly world should exorcise *amars*[25] (the *fol'amor* in Marcabru's language) which destroys society with its deceptive practices. It should instead pursue the *amor naturau*, which reinforces and celebrates that bond of mutual respect on which all societies are built. It is within this frame of thought that Marcabru, first among the troubadours, introduces the notion of *mezura*, the ideal of temperance which he identifies with courtliness itself. *Mezura* is achieved by living in full harmony with an individual's own nature – not just one's physical nature but the social status into which one is born. This social dimension of *mezura* is clearly stated in a strophe of the famous pastorela *L'autrier jost'una sebissa*,[26] where the shepardess rejects the *chevaleresque* love of a nobleman and condemns him for debasing the nobility of his status:

> Don, oc; mas segon dreitura
> Cerca fols sa follatura,
> Cortes cortez'aventura,
> E·il vilans ab la vilana;
> En tal loc fai sens fraitura
> On hom non garda mezura,
> So ditz la gens anciana   (ed. Dejeanne, XXX, ll. 78–84)

[Yes, Sir; but according to what is right the fool looks for foolishness, the courtly man for a courtly adventure, the peasant for a peasant girl. The old people say: judgment is missing where people do not respect *mezura*].

It is remarkable how similar Marcabru's ideas on the subject are to those of William of Conches. There may not be a direct connection between them, but they seem to share the cultural principles of the twelfth-century Renaissance.

Only in recent years have scholars begun to appreciate the extraordinary importance of Marcabru's role in shaping courtliness, in general, and courtly love, in particular. His understanding of *fin'amor* as an ennobling force, and of *mezura* as a social virtue, represents a turning-point in the history of courtly love. So powerful was his voice and so profound was his moral sense that the *chevaleresque* version of courtly love receded into a penumbra. The paradox in all of this is that Marcabru himself was not a poet of love. He was a moralist, a *cantor rectitudinis*, as Dante would say, who often felt the futility of his preaching:

> E s'ieu cug anar castian
> La lor folhia, quier mon dan;
> Pueys s'es pauc prezat si·n'azir,
> Semenan vau mos castiers
> De sobre·ls naturals rochiers
> Que no vey granar ni florir   (ed. Dejeanne XLI, ll. 25–30)

[And if I intend to keep correcting their foolishness, I seek my own harm. Since my outrages matter so little to them, I go sowing my sermons on real rocks which I do not see bear fruit or flower].

These are lines of pining lyricism in which the awareness of being a voice crying in the wilderness is expressed in a proverb-like *inanis opera*. Here, however, something new happens. The proverb – which still retains the *brevitas et figura* of the Ovidian 'arenae semina mandare' (*Her.* V, l. 115: to sow in the sand) or the Plautine 'verberare lapidem' (*Cucurculio*, l. 197: to flog a rock) – deviates from the tradition because its protagonist is the poet himself. The adynatic action is thus reduced to the lyrical *I*. The proverb becomes individualized and, conversely, the individual commits his experience to a timeless expression. The outcome of such a combination can only be an exemplary history that will be repeated, forever bearing the name of the poet. Even in this way, Marcabru begins a new chapter in troubadour tradition. Many poets followed him, all of them anxious to entrust their names and loves to the memory of generations to come.

The impact of Marcabru's teaching was profound and immediate. One of his greatest students,[27] Peire d'Alvernha, was already aware of belonging to a new generation of poets, a generation that practised a *novel trobar* versus the *vieill trobar*.[28] What characterizes this new wave of poetry is the notion of *fin'amor*, now enriched by the ethical aspirations preached by Marcabru. Peire d'Alvernha is a meditative, self-absorbed poet who clearly distinguishes love for a woman from love for God, although he brings a new spiritual dimension into the love of a creature of God. This spiritual nuance is also present in his notion of *mezura*, creating a model of the restless quietude so typical of the many troubadours who stress patience and hope as a sign of temperance. In his meditations, Peire discovers the paradoxicalness of his love. He epitomizes this in a line often imitated: 'Ses pechat fis penedenssa'[29] [I repented without having sinned], an *inanis opera* which has its subject in the first person.

Meditation can also bring exalted joy and confidence, which find expression in hyperboles of this type:

> per q'ieu mi pens: ia non te'n desrazics,
> quan mi conquis en loc on ilh me seis
> plus que se·m des Franssa lo reis Loics   (ed. Del Monte, VII, ll. 50–2)

> [So that I think: do not uproot yourself from the place where, when
> she conquered me, she crowned me (Del Monte's interpretation)
> more than if King Louis were to give me France].

This exaggeration is indeed meant as an *adynaton*, because the improbable is actually felt as impossible.

In his solitude Peire can also imagine, with a tinge of self-mockery,[30] that his far away lady sends him a message of love by means of a nightingale. Her hyperboles of love are not less engaging, but the more sincere they sound, the more impossible they are:

> Tostems mi fo d'agradatge,
> pos lo vi et ans que·l vis,
> e ges de plus ric linhatge
> non vueill autr'aver conquis;
>   mos cuidatz
>   es bos fatz;
> no·m pot far tortura
>   vens ni glatz
>   ni estatz
> ni cautz ni freidura   (ed. Del Monte, I, ll. 91–100)

[I always liked him since I saw him and before I saw him, and I would not have wanted to conquer another one of higher rank; my decision is well taken; no damage can I suffer from wind or ice or summer or heat or cold].

Peire is not exclusively a poet of love. Marcabru's heritage survives in his moralistic attitudes towards the contemporary world as well as in his feeling of impotence towards the *envers*:

S'als malvatz no fos tan grans guaucx,
avoleza ia no fora,
et es tant adubertz lo traucx
que sobre rocas laora,
selh cuy iais cors, e martelha   (ed. Del Monte, XV, ll. 25–9)

[If the wicked people would not enjoy vileness so much it would not exist any more; and the crowd of them is so ample that whoever has joyful (pure) heart, sows and hammers on the rock].[31]

The *inanis opera* is purposefully close to the one already seen in Marcabru.

Peire d'Alvernha's meditation on love heralded a new season in troubadour poetry. After William of Aquitania and Jaufre Rudel had introduced the great themes of courtly love, and after Marcabru had imposed his moral concerns on the poetry of love, it was necessary to think over past experiences and try to understand their profound meaning. The decisive steps in this direction were taken by Raimbaut d'Aurenga, who, like Peire, was a follower of Marcabru, not of his moralistic teaching but rather of his stylistic solution.

Although relatively neglected by the assiduous readers of Provençal lyrics, Raimbaut d'Aurenga is one of the greatest troubadours, perhaps second only to Arnaut Daniel in his artistic virtuosity, and to Marcabru in his historical role.[32] By and large, Raimbaut's artistic achievements gave such an electric jolt to troubadour poetry that they reoriented its goals. Moving away from Marcabru's penchant for sermonizing, Raimbaut focused only on the problem of love. Rather than singing about birds and landscapes,[33] and extenuating the drama of love in melancholic notes, as his predecessors had done, Raimbaut aims at grasping the essence of love.[34] Under this pressure of understanding Raimbaut reduces the key elements of courtly love to define them better, and he renders them more powerful in the process. For example, the lady is promoted from *midons* to a sort of goddess. In the poem *A mon vers dirai chansso* an idea appears which was never formulated by any previous troubadour:

> Dieus retenc lo cel el tro
> A sos ops ses compaigno,
> Ez es paraula certana,
> C'a mi donz laisset en patz
> C'a seignoriu vas totz latz,
> Qe·l mons totz li deu servir
> E sos volers obezir   (ed. Pattison, XXX, ll. 50–6)

[God reserved for himself the heaven and its throne without any partner for his work; and that is a certainty. So he left my lady in peace to have suzerainty everywhere else, for the whole world is to serve her and obey her desires].

This assertion[35] has no theological value, nor was it meant to have one. It seems dictated by Raimbaut's propensity for hyperbolic imagery. Yet these lines establish an analogy between God and the lady which was destined to have great consequences for much of medieval love poetry. They are also a statement of the courtly need to celebrate an autonomous and lay world, the self-sufficiency of the *honestum*, as it were. What matters at this point, however, is the realization that Raimbaut's lady is no longer the lady loved from afar, the lady secluded in a castle, inaccessible in her perfection. Raimbaut's lady is a universe or, better, the force which defines the universe for the poet, the geometric point towards which the whole universe gravitates. She is a source of energy which attracts and repels Raimbaut, whose mind is focused exclusively on her. Thus, Raimbaut brings to the point of an obsession the traditional notion of the lady's perfection and gives her an active role.

Concomitantly, the paradox of courtly love becomes more vivid and therefore more dramatic. With unmatched determination, Raimbaut anatomizes the contradictory elements of courtly love in an attempt to integrate them in a superior, rational understanding. Thus, the intellection of love's nature reveals the impossibility of ever separating joy from pain, sweetness from sorrow. The poet might temporarily overcome the paradox by choosing only one of the poles, but as soon as he finds respite in one haven, he is at once pulled into the opposite one. Sometimes the poet is euphoric because he thinks he has attained love, but then feelings of his inadequacy to sustain it arise and a rhythm of despair replaces notes of triumph. Raimbaut roams the immense universe of love alone, from its centre to the periphery, sometimes singing of pain, sometimes of joy, and very often striking a self-mocking tone which suggests a rational awareness of his existential pendulousness. Make no mistake though: it is not the plodding of a weeping, disarmed, and self-pitying lover, but rather the energetic walk of an aristocrat, proud and aware of beating untrodden paths, prone to boasting and – what can be more aristocratic? – to self-mockery.[36] The stylistic vigour of his verse conveys just such an impression, of a magnanimous lover. Raimbaut was conscious of the fact that a unique story should not be trivialized by a simple, popular style, but should be told in a precious, difficult, almost initiatory diction worthy of its uniqueness. This stylistic decision was of the utmost importance in the world of the troubadours because it prompted discussion on matters of art through which Occitan lyricism found a new awareness. Raimbaut perhaps was not the first poet to use the *trobar clus*, but he was certainly one of its major representatives and earliest defenders,[37] as evidenced by his debate with Giraut de Bornelh, who fostered the *trobar leu*.[38] Here Raimbaut states his aversion for commonplaces in poetry, for those motifs and stylistic clichés which become the stock of fools and peasants, because

>C'anc gran viutaz
>Non fon denhtatz:
>Per so prez'om mais aur que sal,
>E de tot chant es atretal   (ed. Pattison, XXXI, ll. 32-5)

[A thing of great vileness was never considered to have any worth: for that reason one esteems gold more than salt; and it is the same with any song].

The combination of Raimbaut's paradoxes, his aristocratic style and penchant for self-mockery and boasting, predictably results in some of the best *adynata* of troubadour lyrics. Indeed, among the figures of speech that Raimbaut uses to enhance his *trobar clus* and to dramatize his madness are oxymora, *adynata*, and their variants, the *inanis opera* and the *inaequalis pensatio*. Frequently, one finds verses of this tenor:

> Mos cors es clars
>   E s'esmaia!
> Aici vauc mestz grams-iauzens,
>   Plens e voigz de bel comens;
> Que l'una meitatz es gaia
>   E l'autra m'adorm Cossirs
> Ab voluntat mort'e viva   (ed. Pattison, IX, ll. 22–9)

[My heart is radiant and is dismayed! I am half sad and half joyous, full and void of fine undertakings, because one half is joyous, and grief numbs the other with a desire which is dead and alive at the same time].

These are the moments of paralysis in Raimbaut's madness, and nothing expresses them better than oxymora. As a matter of fact, in the oxymoron two elements oppose each other without creating a dialectical tension, thereby precluding the possibility of breaking the contradiction. They live in a contradictory but static continuity, dramatizing what we have called a restless immobility.

With the same frequency one finds *inaequales pensationes* of this kind:

> Mos volers cans
> Qe·m sal denan
> Me fai creire qe futz es pans   (ed. Pattison, XVI, ll. 33–5)

[My urgent desire runs before me (i.e., imagines happy solutions to my difficulties); it makes me believe that wood is bread].

One also needs *inanes operae* like the following, which reminds us of Plautus's 'piscari in aere':

> Mas ben grans talans afrena
> Mon cor, que ses aigua pesca   (ed. Pattison, V, ll. 50–1)

[But a truly great passion refrains my heart which fishes without water].

Both these variants of *impossibilia* represent the moment of mental confusion caused by love, and the poet uses them to express an indulgent self-mocking.

The most striking feature of Raimbaut's folly, however, is its energy. The restless immobility, the fictionalizing of himself as a fool, are only moments of pause in that state of permanent challenge against an irreducible antagonist which characterizes Raimbaut's madness. The more remote the possibility of reaching *joy* appears to him, the more determined he is to pursue it. After all, isn't his lady the greatest thing ever to live on this earth? And isn't Raimbaut the greatest lover ever? This love may seem like madness, but its uniqueness places it above all standards of judgment and redeems it from any negative connotation, and it is actually a profound cause of pride. Its impossibility offers a test of endurance for Raimbaut's will, which turns out to be as absolute as the joy he pursues. His fight is a titanic one with an aura of sublimity. From this poetical situation spring forth the most unforgettable of Raimbaut's *gaps* (boasts), which often take the form of *adynata*. It is enough to read these lines:

> E qui·s vol, corn, crit e flaug
>   D'amor, pos ieu cresc
> Sobre totz, c'als q'en fol pesc!   (ed. Pattison, XXI, ll. 22–4)

> [And whoever wishes to have trumpet, shout, of flute about love, may have it, since I rise above them all, for I fish differently from a fool!][39]

to understand how a device previously used for self-mockery is now utilized as a *gap* to declare the awareness of being different from all other lovers who do not rise above the vulgar swarm of crowing *fol'amadors*.

Raimbaut's adamantine love cannot be expressed with approximate hyperboles. Only *adynata* will do, and they must be of a certain type: 'Plus qe ja fenis fenics / Non er q'ieu non si' amics (IV, ll. 64–5: No more than the Phoenix was ever finished shall I ever cease being your friend!). This *adynaton* has not only the absoluteness of a physical law but also the preciousness of mythical imagery. Sometimes even the most conventional and simplest *adynaton* has the same effect, thanks to the *callida iunctura* of which Raimbaut is capable:

> Peire Rotgier, cum puosc sofrir
> Qez eu am assi ·solamens?
> Meravill me! Si viu de vens!   (VI, ll. 29–31)

[Peire Rogier, how can I bear to love in such a loneliness? I am astounded. I do live on wind!]

Here the classical 'vento vivere'[40] is reduced to the first person who can thus inscribe his own history on an unalterable adage, but a person, also, who puzzles his readers by injecting a note of irony into a *gap*.

Since Raimbaut understood the *adynata* as *gap*, it became possible for him to conceive his greatest *gap* by realizing an *adynaton*. In the troubadour world this meant reaching the joy of love. This conception is carried out in the poem *Ar resplan la flors enversa*, which Pattison considers the last of Raimbaut's poems. Although one should avoid viewing the troubadours' works as *canzonieri* – that is, as reconstructions of a psychological history, in the manner of Petrarch's *canzoniere*[41] – it is still appealing to imagine this poem closing Raimbaut's sentimental quest with a victory. Since it is an exceptionally beautiful work, one of the greatest achievements of troubadour craft, it is worthwhile to reproduce it in its entirety:

> I
> Ar resplan la flors enversa
> Pels trencans rancx e pels tertres,
> Cals flors? Neus, gels e conglapis
> Que cotz e destrenh e trenca;
> Don vey morz quils, critz, brays, siscles
> En fuelhs, en rams e en giscles.
> Mas mi ten vert e jauzen Joys
> Er quan vey secx los dolens croys.
> II
> Quar enaissi m'o enverse
> Que bel plan mi semblon tertre,
> E tenc per flor lo conglapi,
> E·l cautz m'es vis que·l freit trenque,
> E·l tro mi son chant e siscle,
> E paro·m fulhat li giscle.
> Aissi·m suy ferm lassatz en joy
> Que re non vey que·m sia croy –
> III
> Mas una gen fad'enversa
> (Cum s'eron noirit en tertres)

Que·m fan pro pieigz que conglapis;
Q'us quecx ab sa lengua trenca
E·n parla bas et ab siscles;
E no y val bastos ni giscles
Ni menassas; – ans lur es joys
Quan fan so don hom los clam croys.

IV

Qu'ar en baizan no·us enverse
No m'o tolon pla ni tertre,
Dona, ni gel ni conglapi,
Mas non-poder trop en trenque.
Dona, per cuy chant e siscle,
Vostre belh huelh mi son giscle
Que·m castion si·l cor ab joy
Qu'ieu no·us aus aver talan croy.

V

Anat ai cum cauz'enversa
Sercan rancx e vals e tertres,
Marritz cum selh que conglapis
Cocha e mazelh'e trenca:
Que no·m conquis chans ni siscles
Plus que folhs clercx conquer giscles.
Mas ar – Dieu lau – m'alberga Joys
Malgrat dels fals lauzengiers croys.

VI

Mos vers an – qu'aissi l'enverse,
Que no·l tenhon bosc ni tertre –
Lai on hom non sen conglapi,
Ni a freitz poder que y trenque.
A midons lo chant e·l siscle,
Clar, qu'el cor l'en intro·l giscle,
Selh que sap gen chantar ab joy
Que no tanh a chantador croy.

VII

Doussa dona, Amors e Joys
Nos ajosten malgrat dels croys.

VIII

Jocglar, granren ai meynhs de joy
Quer no·us vey, en fas semblan croy

[Now the upside-down flower shines through the sharp cliffs and hills. What flower? Snow, ice, and frost which burns and torments and cuts; so that I see dead the calls, the cries, the songs and the warbling among the leaves, the branches and twigs. But joy keeps me green and happy now when I see that grievous evil men are withered.

Because I turn things upside down for myself in a way that hills seem beautiful plains to me, and I take the frost for a flower; and it appears to me that heat breaks the cold, and the thunder is songs and warblings for me, and the twigs seem covered with foliage. I am so firmly bound in joy that I do not see a thing which seems bad to me –

Except stupid upside-down people (as if they were reared in the hills) who do me much more harm than frost: each one of them cuts with his tongue and speaks low and with whisperings. And no stick nor whip nor threats are of any avail; on the contrary, they rejoice when they do things for which people call them ill-bred.

Neither plains nor hills, my lady, ice nor frost can prevent me from laying you back and kissing you. But an excessive powerlessness holds me back from it. Lady, for whom I sing and warble, your beautiful eyes are the whips which flog my heart with joy that I do not dare to have a base desire towards you.

I have gone like an upside-down thing searching rocks and valleys and hills, distressed like one whom frost afflicts and kills and breaks; for neither song nor warbling conquered me any more than a whip conquers a foolish student. But now – I praise God – joy gives me hospitality in spite of the false and evil slanderers.

Let my poem go – for so I put it in verses that neither wood nor hill may hold it – there where man feels no frost, and cold has no power to harm. Let it be sung and warbled to my lady, clearly so that its shoots will enter her heart, by someone who can sing graciously and joyfully, since it is not fitting for a vile singer.

Sweet lady, let love and joy unite us in spite of the ill-bred ones.

Jocglar, I have much less joy, because I do not see you and I show a sad countenance].

The most obvious feature of this poem is also a dazzling one. Raimbaut uses eight rhyme words which recur in every stanza in the same position, their only alternance being a different grammatical form:

enversa / enverse, tertres / tertre, etc., one time an adjective, another time a noun or verb. Through this unusual scheme every stanza becomes integrated both musically and thematically in the song as a whole. Arnaut Daniel undoubtedly found in this poem the model for his *sestina*.

The first part of the opening stanza (ll. 1–6) can be considered a *Natureingang*, which to a fine scholar like Scheludko appeared quite elementary.[42] And, indeed, it would seem so, especially when compared with the more elaborate forms which usually begin with a *lanquan* or *can* that introduce a complex temporal sentence. Raimbaut's *Natureingang*, however, is not at all simple; it is disconcerting. The opening *ar*, so typical of Raimbaut's beginnings,[43] has an abruptness that plunges us *in medias res*, into a present in which everything is suspended and controlled, as if an intellectual fulguration had taken place. The verb *resplan*, with its meaning and in its present tense, reinforces this effect. The subject follows it, but is delayed and emphasized by a strong caesura. It is a 'reversed' flower, an image with a powerful effect of estrangement, which neutralizes the bright intensity of the verb and transforms it into a light of death over a harsh landscape.

The first rhyme word has an iconic value and sets the theme developed throughout the poem; it is the theme of turning the world upside down. The next rhyme word is the first obvious linguistic sign of this operation because it is formed by two syllables which are, to a degree, reversed: *TER-TRES*. Reading the first two lines one is struck by a sense of musical *continuum* created by the syllables formed by a labial + liquid, *res PLAn-FLOrs*; by the alliterations of *TREncans-TERTRES* and *treNCANS-rANCS*, by the repetition of *PELS* and the arsis on the syllable *LA* in *respLAn LA*. On closer scrutiny, however, that musical continuity is upset and even denied by a systematic inversion of syllable notes which support the song's theme. The initial *ar*, if corrected into *ER* (as it should be, both on the evidence of the critical apparatus, and on the authority of Appel's edition), would contain the same letters as the following *REsplan*, but their order is reversed. Then a syllable of *RESplan* appears as the anagram of another, of *envERSsa*. In the second line, besides the inversions of *TREncans-TER-TRE*, we also have *trenCANS-rANCS*. Akin to these palindrome-like devices are some vocalic apophonies which also enhance the alliterative quality of the text. Such are *RESplan-flORS-envERSA; resplAN-ENversa*. These musical effects,[44] pursued throughout the entire poem, give an overview of an immobile and stupefied nature, which is subsumed under the emblem of the 'reversed flower.'

The *Adynata* 99

The arresting effect of this scenery of a dead landscape illuminated by a magic flower is soon overcome by a question which may be ironic or exclamative: 'Cals flors?' Here one perceives an echo of the previous apophonies and inversions. The answer is a staccato (in classical rhetoric it would be called an *articulus*),[45] which further fragments and immobilizes that landscape, for its components and their predicates are mostly monosyllables, as if they were intentionally syllabicated prosodemes.[46] It should be noticed that the *rapportatio*[47] of lines two and three creates the oxymoron which recalls the classical 'icy fire.'[48] None the less, this still life, burned by snow and frost, magically immobilized by the strange light of the 'reversed flower,' does not affect the poet because joy keeps him green, especially now that he sees how the churls are disappointed. Thus, the last two lines, which introduce the poet as being in sharp contrast with the surrounding world, complete the theme of the *Natureingang* in a traditional fashion. Except for the theme, however, there is nothing traditional about it, and obviously nothing 'elementary.' Indeed, another insight into the complexity of this strophe, and of the whole poem, comes from its dominating image, the reversed flower, which must be interpreted as a lily, the Plinian *flos resupinus*. We have thus a very difficult and rare type of metaphor called *transumptio* (Quintilian, VIII, 6, 38), because the reversed flower is the lily and the lily means summertime.[49] Suddenly a net of symbolic allusions and thematic correspondences becomes really 'resplendant' as the similarity / opposition between the snow and the lily becomes clear. It is also clear that from the first line Raimbaut anticipates the theme, which then appears in the last two lines. He is so taken by joy that he mistakes snow for lilies! This time, though, the poet is not a fool but a crafty magician who controls the metamorphosis of the world. Moreover, the whiteness of the lily anticipates the notion of the poet's purity before his lady.

The following two strophes elaborate on the themes set in the previous one – namely, the poet's joy, which produces the turning of the world upside down, and the plague of the churls. The second stanza presents a series of *inaequales pensationes* which mean euphoria rather than bewilderment. The third stanza populates the harsh landscape with a breed of people over whom the poet has no power because they are already 'una gen fad'enversa.'

In the middle of the poem we learn the cause of the joy after having seen its effects; thus, even in the *dispositio*, Raimbaut adopts an *ordo artificialis*, a sort of inversion of the logical line of the argument. The conquest of the present is announced again by an opening *ar*. The impossible is won: the poet can 'reverse' his lady and kiss her. The whole world, as wide as it can be ('pla ni tertre'), as hostile as it can be ('gel ni conglapis'), becomes the desired bed. But there a miracle takes place: the poet cannot consummate his love because of a *no-poder*. Time stops. Raimbaut is under the spell of his lady's eyes, and his fascination with her purifies his heart! I do not know of any other dramatization of *mezura* that can rival this one where the poet, with two beautiful oxymora (*belh huelh / giscle, castion / ab joy*), can express at once the paralysis of contemplation and the joy of renunciation.

From this situation of attained joy, Raimbaut re-envisions those tormented days in which he was an *enverse*. To the new Raimbaut who 'reverses' all things, the past search and bewilderment look, in retrospect, like an epic quest endured with absolute dedication. An *adynaton* ('plus que folhs clercx conquer giscle') again stresses the epic persistence of the poet, who from extreme despair has risen to the purest joy, completely 'reversing' his situation.

Now the entire world is far away and a full song is born. The poet *in-verses* it, puts it into verses because the upside-down world must be fixed forever in unalterable verses. The poem must go to the lady, source of the analgesic joy which nourishes 'reversed flowers.'

Time moves again, and with the conclusion comes another great surprise. The poem has indeed two conclusions – a very happy one and a very sad one. This unique case of poetic closure in what are probably the last lines written by Raimbaut is like an epitaph which contains the essence of Raimbaut's cyclothimia. He has sustained throughout the whole poem a metaphor indicating joy, but the last couplet dissolves the illusion and introduces a melancholic note. The lady, called by her *senhal* Jocglar,[50] again acquires a historical but distant presence. Yet we are sure now that Raimbaut's love, as sung in this poem, is purely noetic, wholly intellectually apprehended. The *flors enversa* does not, however, lose its colour or appear less intriguing to us because this creation is the real victory of the poet.

Commenting on this poem, Pattison observes: 'One of the effects of love is to make the lover insane or at least so befuddled that he takes everything for its contrary – frost for flower, hills for plains, etc.'[51] Such a generic observation suggests that this poem is based on a *topos*. As a matter of fact, Pattison recalls two other places[52] where Raimbaut takes heat for cold and rain for sunshine. He also quotes the following lines from a poem by Bernart de Ventadorn:

> Tant ai mo cor ple de joya,
>   tot me desnatura.
> Flor blancha, vermelh'e groya
>   me par la frejura,
> c'ab lo ven et ab la ploya
>   me creis l'aventura,
> per que mos chans mont'e poya
>   e mos pretz melhura.
> Tan ai al cor d'amor,
>   de joi e de doussor,
> per que·l gels me sembla flor
>   e la neus verdura   (ed. Lazar, IV, ll. 1–12)

[My heart is so full of joy that it transforms everything for me. The frost seems to me a white, vermillion, and yellow flower; and with the wind and the rain my happiness increases, so that my singing strives for higher notes, and my prestige is increased. I am so much in love and full of joy and sweetness that the ice seems to me a flower and the snow greenery].[53]

The resemblance between this poem and Raimbaut's is obvious, but also extrinsic. Bernart goes like a *res enaurada* – as Cercamon[54] would say – lost in reverie, seeing the metamorphosis of nature in a dreamy vision. Not so in Raimbaut's poem, where the metamorphosis of nature is the result of a controlled process. Raimbaut is not at all a spectator in an upside-down world. Instead, he is the one who turns it upside down, realizing once again the most comprehensive of all *adynata*, without ever losing the awareness of his operation, without ever being *desnaturatz*.

The stylistic torment of the composition is an unmistakable sign of the 'impossibility' of the operation that Raimbaut undertakes and achieves.[55] Indeed, concluding all lines with a prescribed word seems a challenge to good sense. These rhyme words are obstacles, as difficult as the nature they describe. But they are audaciously challenged so that every line-end sounds like a victory cry which becomes more exalted as the poem progresses. The first rhyme word, *enversa*, could be the emblem of Raimbaut's success: turning the world upside down means realizing an *adynaton*, and, in Raimbaut's case, writing one of the more beautiful *gaps*[56] ever created by a troubadour.

Raimbaut learned from Marcabru's moralistic poems how to 'personalize' the *adynata*, but he used them in love songs. His poetic success was such that he was soon imitated. The first poet to do so was a troubadour of the stature of Giraut de Bornelh, the poet whom Dante called 'cantor rectitudinis' (*De vulgari eloquentia*, II, 2) perhaps because Giraut was a tireless preceptor of the ideals of courtliness and courtly love. In one of his poems, famous also because Dante quoted it in the *De vulgari eloquentia* (II, 5), Raimbaut d'Aurenga is mentioned by the *senhal* 'Linhaure.' The poem, *Er'auziretz enchabalitz chantars*, presents a situation of repentance: the poet regrets having claimed, on some occasion, to be worthy of his lady. Blaming this mistake on his *folia*, Giraut says: 'tenia·l drech per envers, / tan er'en amar esmers!' (ed. Kolsen, XXX, ll. 15–16: I used to take the right for its opposite. So much was I immersed in love!). This is an *inaequalis pensatio* in Raimbaut's mould. Sure enough, towards the end of the poem, the name Linhaure occurs and confirms this suspicion of imitation:

> E cudatz setz m'enoi ni dejunars
> Ni·m tenha dan? No fai, que·l dolz pensars
> M'aduri' ab una micha
> San e let al chap de l'an! –
> Fols, c'as dich? Pauc t'en creiran
> De so c'anc vers no parec! –
> Si fara be, si l'enquers,
> Mos Linhaure lai part Lers   (ll. 57–64)

[Do you imagine that thirst tortures me and hunger harms me? Not at all; for the sweet thought will keep me healthy and happy until the end of the year with just a crumb. – Fool, what did you say? Very few will believe that which never seemed to be true. – Yes, if you ask him, my Linhaure, who lives beyond Lers, he will believe it].

Only Linhaure can believe that it is possible to live for one year on a crumb: Linhaure, who lives on wind!

The relationship between the two troubadours was much stronger than this instance suggests. The debate between them, a debate in which Raimbaut defends the style of *trobar clus* against the *trobar leu* newly adopted by Giraut, is well known. Also well known is the *planh* Giraut wrote on the death of the Count of Orange, one of the most moving tributes of gratitude (*S'anc jorn agui joi ni solatz*, ed. Kolsen, LXXVI) for his artistic teaching.[57] It is thus possible that Raimbaut inspired some personalized *inanes operae* such as the following:

> Pero, pos enfolei,
> Torn ferir en la palha
> Don esper que·l gras salha (XLIV, ll. 28–30)

[But, I am so mad, that I hit again the chaff hoping to see grain coming out of it].

It is also likely that the theme of *foldatz*, so frequently treated by Giraut, found its inspiration in Raimbaut's poems. Indeed, one can consider Raimbaut's *Escotatz, mas no say que s'es* the model for Guiraut's *Un sonet fatz malvatz e bo*. We should quote this poem, at least partially, because it is composed almost entirely of oxymora or what may better be termed *inanes operae*, or even *inaequales pensationes*, which dramatize the madness of the poet:

> Un sonet fatz malvatz e bo
> e re no sai de cal razo
> ni de cui ni com ni per que
> ni re no sai don me sove
> e farai lo, pos no·l sai far,
> e chan lo qui no·l sap chantar!
>
> Mal ai, c'anc om plus sas no fo,
> e tenh malvatz ome per pro,
> e don assatz, can non ai re,
> e volh mal celui que·m vol be;
> tan sui fis amics ses amar
> c'ancse·m pert qui·m vol gazanhar.
> . . .
>
> Detorn me vai e deviro
> foldatz, que mais sai de Cato.
> Devas la coa·lh vir lo fre,
> s'altre plus fols no m'en rete;
> c'aital sen me fi ensenhar
> al prim qu'era·m fai foleiar (LIII, ll. 1–11, 19–24)

[I am composing a song which is bad and good, and I do now know the what, whom, how, and why of it;[58] nor do I know anything that I can remember; and I will do it, since I do not know how, and let it be sung by him who knows not how to sing it.

I do not feel well, although there was never a healthier man, and I take a churl for a worthy person, and I give a lot when I have nothing, and I hate the one who loves me; I am loyal without loving so that he who wants to win me always ends up losing me....

Madness surrounds me, yet I know more than Cato. I turn the brake towards the tail, unless someone more foolish than I restrains me; at the beginning wisdom made me so wise and now makes me crazy].

The poem goes on for a while in the same mechanical way, using a repertory of images – the same heuristic, as it were – as the content of the poem itself. We are far from the poetical imagination of a Raimbaut; we are closer to the world of nonsense poems, the *sottie*.[59] But it is important to remember that, however frigidly, this poem by Giraut dramatizes the paradox of courtly love.

The model of Raimbaut was present more often than not in the poems of Peire Vidal. According to his old biographer, Peire Vidal 'fo dels plus fols homes que mais fossen'[60] [was one of the craziest men who ever lived]. *Fol* here could be rendered as 'crazy,' 'bizarre,' 'boastful,' 'versatile,' or even 'aggressive,' for all these attributes qualify the multifarious aspects of his poetry.[61] Peire Vidal certainly capitalizes on his folia, finding either tones of self-mockery or – with a marked predilection – tones of *gap*. In this bipolarity, he resembles Raimbaut, and like Raimbaut he can brag about realizing impossible deeds. In the poem *Pos tornatz sui em Proensa*, celebrated for its *razo* (which contains the beautiful legend of the 'stolen kiss'), there is a series of *impossibilia expleta*. The poet sings his return to Provence, whence he had been exiled for having kissed the wife of his patron, En Barral, while she was asleep. Now the lady wants to give a kiss to Peire, in order to donate to him what had previously been stolen. Peire immediately transcribes this event as the fulfilment of an *adynaton*:

> E sel que long'atendensa
> Blasma, fai gran falhizo;
> Qu'er an Artus li Breto
> On avion lur plevensa.

Et ieu per lonc esperar
Ai conquist ab gran doussor
Lo bais que forsa d'amor
Me fetz a ma domn'emblar,
Qu'eras lo·m denh'autreiar (ed. Avalle XL, ll. 10–18)

[Whoever scoffs at a lengthy waiting makes a big mistake, for now the Bretons have an Arthur in whom they had their trust. And I, by long waiting, have won with a great sweetness the kiss which the force of love caused me to steal from my lady who now is kind enough to give it to me].

Peire alludes here to the legendary hope the Bretons had for the return of King Arthur, long dead. Peire's return is compared to the King's second coming. If there is no historical allusion (and very likely there is not),[62] these lines create the atmosphere of a fulfilled parousia in which the following *adynata* are natural corollaries:

E poiran s'en conortar
E mi tug l'autr'amador,
Qu'ab sobresforciu labor
Trac de neu freida fuec clar
Et aigua doussa de mar.

Ses pechat pris penedensa
E ses tort fait quis perdo
E trais de nien gen do
Et ai d'ira benvolensa
E gaug entier de plorar
E d'amar doussa sabor
E sui arditz per paor
E sai perden gazanhar
E, quan sui vencutz, sobrar.

Estiers non agra guirensa,
Mas quar sap que vencutz so,
Sec ma domn'aital razo
Que vol que vencutz la vensa (ll. 23–40)

[In my example all other lovers can find consolation, because by my very intense work I can extract from cold snow a bright fire and fresh water from the sea.

> I did penance without having sinned, and asked for pardon without having committed a crime, and I got a kind gift out of nothing and sympathy out of annoyance, and full joy out of tears and a sweet taste out of bitterness; I am daring out of fear, and I know how to win when I am beaten, and to survive when I am vanquished.
>
> In no other way I would be safe; but because my lady knows that I am vanquished, she reasons thus: that I, the vanquished one must win her over].

Drawing fire from snow;[63] repenting over no fault, winning while being vanquished – these form an amalgam of fulfilled *adynata*, of paradoxes, of useless works which turn out to be fruitful: in sum, a world turned upside down, in the best of Raimbaut's tradition. In these lines Peire Vidal brings to fruition one of his *ricas folias* in the exultation of an unforgettable *gap*. And again in the finest manner of Raimbaut, this *gap* is a monument to the *I*, the person who performs all those *impossibilia*, who may like to dazzle his spectators with his theatrical postures but who also proves that love overcomes any obstacle.

The greatest *gap* Raimbaut could have written, however, was to count among his followers a poet like Arnaut Daniel. It would have been a paradoxical *gap* because Arnaut was to steal from him the glory of the supreme laurel. Some, of course, may dispute the assertion that Arnaut Daniel was the greatest of the troubadours. Bernart de Ventadorn, for instance, could claim this primacy, and the assessment may very well depend on individual taste for one style or another. In any case, the signs of admiration for Arnaut, even in his day, were frequent. Dante held him in the highest esteem and said so on several occasions. Arnaut is the last character Dante meets in *Purgatory* before entering the earthly paradise, undoubtedly a significant position. Moreover, Arnaut is unique among the characters of the *Divine Comedy* because he speaks in his own language, in Provençal. The first *terzina* of his address to Dante evokes notes which are familiar to any reader of Arnaut:

> Tan m'abellis vostre cortes deman,
> qu'ieu no me puesc ni voill a vos cobrire
> Ieu sui Arnaut que plor e vau chantan.[64]   (*Purgatory*, XXVI, ll. 140–2)

The oxymoron *plor/chan* contains the essence of Arnaut's poetic life.[65]

The author of the *vida* tells us that Arnaut 'amet una auta domna [...] mas no fo cregut que la domna li fezes plaiser en dreit d'amor'[66] [He loved a noble lady ... but it was not believed that she ever pleased him according to the law of love]. Independently of any historical confirmation, we have here a mythographic interpretation of Arnaut's poetry dominated by a constant awareness of the impossibility of ever fulfilling his love. This consciousness, however, does not extinguish love. On the contrary, it reinforces love by purifying it, bringing it close to a sort of love for love, love in search of itself: love which is potentially transformable into a myth.

The prevailing poetic tone which accompanies this noetic love is retiring and pensive. The remoteness of any concrete referent demands a difficult language, free from any prosaic solutions, worthy of the love which dictates it, so that a perfect love transpires in a perfectly fashioned language.[67] It is as if Arnaut were writing for himself, so that his language is primarily an instrument for understanding the absoluteness of his love. The profuse neologisms in his verses are elements of a private code which records the perceptions of a love that is so new that it requires a novel vocabulary. Even his obsessive use of monosyllables seems to transcribe every beat, perceived through a most careful and intimate auscultation. Arnaut's language, in sum, generates images while producing self-knowledge. This combination creates the most transparent *adynata*.

Arnaut's meditations on the nature of his love never lead to rebellion. Arnaut is truly magnanimous as he accepts with dignity and pride his destiny as a lover. He knows that the only possibility of victory over love is given precisely by the poetry which defines it. It is a paradoxical victory, because *obediensa* to love dictates the words for its own definitions.

> Obri e lim
> mos de valor
> ab art d'Amor
> don no ai cor que·m tueilla,
> anz, si be·m fail,
> la sec a trail
> on plus vas mi s'orgueilla   (ed. Perugi, II, ll. 12–18)

[I fashion and file words of great value with the art of Love from which I have no wish to escape; on the contrary: although it is unjust towards me, I follow its track the more it shows haughtiness towards me].

Actually, the behaviour of those lovers who curse their love can be viewed as paradoxical:

> Petit val orgoil d'amador
> c'ades trebucha so seignor
> del luoc auzor
> bas el terrail
> per tal trebail
> que de Joi lo despueilla (ll. 19–24)

[It is of no avail the pride of a lover who keeps laying low his lord from his highest place down to the ground through such a suffering that it deprives him of Joy].

Arnaut cannot be confused with this breed of self-harming lovers, because his heart does not harbour any malicious thoughts:

> Er ai fam d'Amor don badail
> e no sec mesura ni tail:
> sols m'o egail
> que anc n'ovim
> del temps Caim
> amador menz acueilla
> cor trizador
> ni baudador,
> per que mos jois capdueilla (ll. 46–54)

[Now I am hungry for Love and I yawn because of it, so that I do not follow *mesura* nor rule; but I set this situation right because it was never heard, from Cain on, of a lover with a less treacherous and deceitful heart than mine; and this is why my joy is at its highest peak].

This hyperbole has a tinge of *gap*, which comes from perceiving as unique the poet's existential situation. This explains Arnaut's tendency to mythicize his love, which dictates *adynata* of this kind:

> qu'il m'es plus fin'e eu lei sers
> que Talent'e Meleagre (ed. Perugi, XI, ll. 31–2)

[because she is more loyal to me and I am more faithful to her than Atlanta and Meleagre were (to each other)]

and:

> No foi mariz
> ni no presi destautas
> al prim qu'intrei el chastel dinz los decs
> lai on midon stai, de cui ai tal fam
> que anc non ac lo neps sain Guilliem (XII, ll. 9–13)

[I was not confused and I did not take the wrong way the first time I entered the castle within the boundaries where my lady lives of whom I have more hunger than the nephew of St William did].[68]

Here Arnaut's *gap* and the *adynaton* result from comparing himself with and being superior to mythical-literary characters exemplary in their deeds. We shall return to this type of *adynata* in a while.

Just like any troubadour, however, Arnaut is aware that his love is unattainable. Thus, the result is a conscious madness which stresses both the irrevocability and the gratuitousness of Arnaut's commitment. This situation, rather than causing tears or inciting rebellion as in other troubadours, produces negative *gaps*, which are *adynata* drenched with melancholic considerations. This is the real trademark of Arnaut. Let us read, for instance, the song *Ab gai so conde e leri*.

The poet begins by presenting himself at work, polishing his words because love moves him. Actually, Arnaut is an instrument through which the superior force of love manifests itself because, when there is singing, there is also love. And when there is love there is hope and trepidation. Arnaut remembers the thousands of masses (hyperbole) he has heard and all the candles he has lit to obtain from God the grace of being loved by the lady against whom he has no defence ('no·m val escrima'). When he thinks of her blonde hair and her beautiful, slender, and fresh body, he loves her more than he could love any person who would give him the lost city of Lucerna (*adynaton*). He grows in his love ('meillur e esmeri') and can tell it in clear letters: he belongs to her from foot to head ('seus soi del pe tro el cima'), and the love that rains into his breast keeps him warm in the cold winter.

The poet is so overwhelmed by his own loving that he may not be able to contain it:

> Tan l'am de cor e la queri
> c'a trop-voler cuit la·m toli,
> s'om ren per ben amar pert:
> que·l sis cors sobretrasima
> lo meu totz e no s'esaura;
> tant ai de ver fait renuo
> c'obrador n'ai e taverna   (ed. Perugi, X, ll. 22–8)

[So heartily I love and desire her that I am afraid to lose her for wanting her too much, if indeed it is possible to lose anything by loving it perfectly. Her heart rises above mine without vanishing into the air. My stock of feelings is grown so much that I can keep a store and a shop of them].

Arnaut would rather become rich with her love than become emperor or pope (*adynaton*). Love burns and consumes him and, unless she kisses him before New Year's day, he will die. The immediacy of this deadline suggests the urgency of Arnaut's desire as well as the unlikelihood of her granting him a kiss. But this awareness does not make him desist from loving her:

> Ges per·l maltrait qu'eu·n soferi
> de ben amar no·m destoli
> si tot me ten en desert,
> c'a si·m fas lo son e·l rima:
> peiz trai aman c'om que laura,
> c'anc plus non amet d'un uo
> sel de Monclin Odierna   (ll. 36–42)

[Yet, in spite of the harm I get from it, I do not renounce perfect loving – although it keeps me without the price – and I am inspired by her for my song and my rhyme. By loving I suffer more than a peasant, and Monclin's love for Odierna compared to mine is worth peanuts (literally: less than one egg)].

From the understanding of this *folia* springs the famous *tornada* analysed by E.R. Curtius:

> Eu son Arnauz c'amas l'aura
> e chas la lebr'a lo buo
> e nadi contra siberna (ll. 43–5)

[I am Arnaut who heaps up air, and hunts the hare with an ox, and swims against the stream].

It is a softly ironic *gap* which sums up the existential 'doing' of the poet. Out of three *inanes operae*[69] he constructs the most beautiful ethopoeia of himself, clearly depicting his delirium of immobility, the presence of an action notwithstanding. Here is Arnaut's destiny, the quintessence of his love, which he entrusts to formulas of proven inalterability, formulas that bear the seal of his unmistakable signature ('Eu son Arnauz'). The process of self-mythification gets underway, as one can readily see, with the change of subject from the first to the third person, though both are named Arnaut. Is it a sign of detachment which then creates better possibilities for irony? Perhaps; but also it is a way for Arnaut himself to define a living myth.

The *tornada* became famous: it reappeared in the *vida*,[70] and the Monje de Montaudon[71] used it to prepare a literary portrait of the poet. The same Arnaut considered it a self-portrait, an *impresa* in which he could recognize the essence of his love life. It became a point of reference for following the vicissitudes of the *folia*. Song number fourteen begins with a reference to this *tornada*:

> Amors e jois e liocs e temps
> mi fan tornar lo sen en derc
> d'aquel joi c'avia l'autr'an
> can chassava lebre a bou (ed. Perugi, ll. 1–4)

[Love and joy and place and time have altered[72] my mind from the state of joy in which I found myself yesteryear when I used to hunt the hare with the ox].

It is an occasion for a palinode or, more to the point, for showing another path walked by Arnaut in his closed lyrical space: while the *so conde e leri* opens as a song of joy and slowly progresses into a melancholic note of self-mockery, this song follows the opposite route, from sadness to strong self-exaltation. The euphoria of hope is the source of energy here. The poet *knows* that he will conquer his lady if he respects the rules of the road of love. And he is on his way:

> Contramon vau e no m'encreis,
> car gen mi fai cujar mos cucs:
> cor, vai sus! ben ai si·t sofers:
> sec tan qu'en lieis cui encobi no·t pecs   (ll. 45–8)

[I am going up on a steep slope and I am not impeded by pride because my brains are thinking well. Go up, my heart; I will gain if you are patient: I am following the one with whom I fell in love; so do not make any mistake towards her].

This paraenesis to obey the imperative of love is followed by an *adynaton* in the classical mould[73] which contains the message of the poem:

> Anz er plus vils aus non es fers
> c'Arnauz desam leis on esfer manz necs   (ll. 49–50)

[In fact, gold will be less noble than iron before Arnaut quits loving that lady in whom I make sense of my mumblings].

It is an oath which binds him forever – given the adynatic quality of the formula – to his own destiny of perfect lover.

How could it be otherwise if one perceives the Medusa-like power of Arnaut's lady and the strong swelling of the poet's heart?

> Nuillz jausimenz no·m fora breus ni corz
> de lei, cui prec c'o vueilla devinar,
> que ja per mi non o sabra esteirs
> si·l cors ses dins no·s presenta defors:
> que ges Roines per aiga que l'engrueis
> non a tal briu c'al cor plus larga doz
> no·m faz'estanc Amors, can la remire   (ed. Perugi, XV, ll. 22–8)

[No enjoyment coming from her would be brief or skimpy, and I hope that she would please imagine it because otherwise she will never know, unless my heart shows her its wounds. The Rhone, for

however much water swells it, has not so much power as love does
in my heart, for it turns it into a pool when I contemplate her].

Sometimes this devotion proves Arnaut right, because in his fate of love-suffering there are moments of pauses and gratification. When this happens, the world is turned upside down:

> Anz que sim resto de branchas
> sec ni despoillan de fueilla
> fas, que Amors m'o comanda,
> breu chanzo de raiso lonia
> cui gen m'aduz de las ars de sa scola:
> tan sei que·l cors fas restar de suberna
> e mos buos es per plus correnz que lebres (ed. Perugi, XVI, ll. 1–7)

[Before the tree-tops remain dry in their branches and without their foliage, I compose – because love orders me so – a short song on a long topic which it (i.e., love) proposes to me from the arts of its schools: I am so good that I can stop the course of a stream, and my ox is by far faster than the hare].

The ox and the hare (the turtle and the Achilles of Arnaut's mythopoetic world) reverse their respective natures here, and Arnaut is caught up with joy! In this beautiful poem, Arnaut reaches an authentic intimacy with his two accomplices: with Love, whose advice he humbly obeys, and with his heart, whose promptings he likewise follows. Love orders him not to distract himself from his lady and to be green (i.e., loyal and youthful) with her like the laurel or the juniper. Arnaut should not be like the violet which withers and changes colour as soon as the weather turns cold. What do past labours matter, now that Arnaut has reached the pure joy of having his heart always next to his lady: 'You, my heart, never depart from her, no matter where I may be' ['cors, on qu'eu an de lei no·t loing ni·t sebres,' l. 28). A sort of *ensenhamen* follows a mixture of jussive and exhortatory speech which Arnaut addresses to his heart, asking it only to praise her without ever claiming any rights. The pure joy which nourishes itself on pure contemplation has been attained. Arnaut can take leave of his readers and write his envoy:

> Seus es Arnautz del sim tro en la sola:
> eu ses lei no voil aver Luderna
> ni·l seignoriu del reing on cor Ebres (ll. 43–5)

> [Arnaut is hers from head to foot (lit. sole). Without her I would not want to have Lucerna or the lordship of the kingdom where the Ebro runs].

These last *adynata*, which, paradoxically, reinforce the truth, could indeed seal Arnaut's testament. By now the poet as well as his readers know that Arnaut has attained the eternity of myth, as emphasized by the treatment of himself in the third person. The last image, however, is that of an Arnaut portrayed in the best of literary tradition from head to foot rather than 'del pe tro a·l coma' (from foot to head), as he said in a previous poem (IX, l. 34). One may read in this iconic inversion a sign that Arnaut has finally turned the world upside down, just as joy touches upon him. A careful reader will catch in this line an echo of Arnaut's great teacher, Raimbaut d'Aurenga, who declared his belonging to his lady *del suc entro la sabata* (from the pate to the shoe, ed. Pattison, XXXVII, l. 66). The reader will inevitably compare the master and the pupil. Arnaut's joy is intimate and discrete; it shuns the theatricality of the Raimbaut of the *flors enversa*. Arnaut's conquest of joy presupposes a tactic meditated in silence; Raimbaut's volition leans entirely on the vitality of his instinct. Thus, they have different ways of enjoying their conquests, different ways of going from one point to its opposite in the closed space of love.

Arnaut's *adynata* had numerous and direct imitations. His 'inane venari' in particular struck the imagination of his fellow poets, so that we have several variations on this motif, including its reduction to the first person. We find it, for instance, in the poetry of Elias Cairel, who also recalls Raimbaut's 'flors enversa':[74]

> Mas mon cor trop fol quar cassa
> so qu'ieu non crei qu'aconsega (ed. Jaeschke, II, ll. 13–14)

> [But my heart is too crazy because it hunts what I do not believe it can attain].

The same motif is used by Guilhem Magret:

> Aissi cum fan volpilh encaussador,
> encaus soven so qu'ieu non aus atendre,

e cug penre ab la perditz l'austor;
e combat so dont no me puesc defendre   (ed. Naudieth, II, ll. 11–14)

[Just like the timid hunters do, I often pursue what I hope not to reach; and I want to catch the hawk with the partridge; and fight something against which I cannot defend myself].

Aimeric de Peguilhan, in a *partimen* answering Guilhem de Berguedan's question on whether it is better to love while remaining unloved or not to love while being loved, remembers the fruitlessness of the hunt:

Non sui, q'en loc de gauch pren la dolor;
Mas bos respieitz m'aiud'a sofertar,
Per qu'eu vuoill mais ses consegre enchaussar
Que conseguir so don non fos pagatz,
Car mil d'autres val us bens desiratz   (ed. Shepard and Chambers, XIX, ll. 31–5)

[I am not because, instead of joy, I take pain; but good expectation helps me to endure, since I would rather pursue without attaining than to attain that with which I would not be pleased. Indeed, a desired good is worth a thousand others].[75]

It is possible that, under the suggestion of Arnaut's model, Raimon de Miraval devised this *inanis opera*:

Per un joy que m'alezera
Estau en bon'aventura;
E quar a totz jorns esmera
La belh'on mos cors s'atura,
E si tot me desmezura,
Ges de lieys no parc m'espera
Ans combat ab queirs de cera
Bastimens de peira dura   (ed. Topsfield, I, ll. 17–24)

[Because of a joy which gives me respite, I live in happiness. And since the beautiful one on which my heart rests becomes every day more refined, and although she does not treat me well, my hopes never depart from her; on the contrary, I attack rampart of hard stone with arrows of wax].

Not much different from the above *inanis opera* is one by Daude de Pradas, which is found in the *tornada* (in true Arnaut's style) of the poem *En un sonet guay e leuger*:

> De mon mal ayp conosc, en ver,
> c'a fer freg i bati e martelh (ed. Schutz, XI, p. 49)

[To my own harm, I recognize in truth that I worked and hammered on a cold iron].

In Daude's lines, there is perhaps an echo of 'bat fer freg' ('I hammer on cold iron') found in a poem attributed to Jaufre Rudel (ed. Jeanroy, VII, ll. 33–4).

So far we have seen complex adynatic formulas which express both the inanity of the poet's endurance and the absoluteness of his dedication. The most remarkable feature common to the numerous examples cited is the 'personalization' of a classical *adynaton*, accomplished by giving a first-person subject to an *impossible*. We shall return shortly to this way of writing about the madness of love.

Along with such highly personal and complex formulas, troubadour language contains a few types of *adynata* expressed either by a coded word or by a proverb or proverbial allusion. To convey the sense of the inanity of a long wait, the troubadours use three such adynatic formulas. The first is the word *faidia*, which ethymologically means 'fatigue,' but which also means 'vain hopes,' depending on the context. Here is one example from Folquet de Marselha:

> Sitot me soi a tart aperceubutz,
> aissi cum cel qu'a tot perdut e jura
> que mais non joc, a gran bonaventura
> m'o dei tener car me sui conogutz
> del gran engan qu'Amors vas mi fazia,
> c'ab bel semblan m'a tengut en fadia
> mais de detz ans, a lei de mal deutor
> c'ades promet mas re no pagaria (ed. Stroński, XI, ll. 1–8)

[Although I have realized it too late – just like the one who has gambled away everything and swears never to play again – I should consider it as great luck because I have realized that love was deceiving me, since with a good appearance he has kept me vainly waiting for more than ten years, like a bad debtor who always promises but never delivers].

Folquet emphasizes the *faidia* by placing it in rhyme and by creating an ample syntactic construction which gravitates towards this key word. The main themes of the strophe also converge on *faidia*: illusion (*joc, bel semblan*) and disappointment (*tot perdut, gran engan*). Moreover, both themes are stressed by temporal expressions (*a tart, mais de detz ans*) and by the verb *jura*.[76]

The second adynatic formula is the proverbial *esperansa bretona*, the hope the Bretons had to see King Arthur come back to his throne although he had already died. We have found this same expression in the poetry of Peire Vidal. It seems, though, that the first one to use it was Bernart de Ventadorn, in his poem *La dousa votz ai aizida*:

>Mout l'avia gen servida
>tro ac vas mi cor volatge;
>e pus ilh no·m'es cobida,
>mout sui fols, si mais la ser.
>Servirs c'om no gazardona,
>et esperansa bretona
>fai de senhor escuder
>per costum e per uzatge   (ed. Lazar, XXXIV, ll. 33-40)

[I served her very nobly before she showed me her fickle heart; and since she is not destined for me, I am truly mad if I ever serve her. Serving without recompense, and the 'Bretons' hope' by use and custom (i.e., if customarily used) turn a knight into an esquire].

This strophe is a variation of the theme of hope and disappointment treated in the poem. The reference to the 'cor volatge' points to the subject of this alternation; the allusion to the Bretons' hope clearly indicates what the outcome of the alternation will be.

This hope for the 'second coming' of King Arthur occurs very often.[77] Gaucelm Faidit, for instance, closes a poem (ed. Mouzat, II) woven with the fidelity/hope theme by realizing that he may be affected by 'l'esperansa del Breto.' Guilhem de Montanhagol also uses this theme ('atendemen de Breto' ed. Ricketts, XIV, ll. 42-3, but this poem is a *sirventes*), as does Giraut de Bornelh (ed. Kolsen, LXVII, l. 30), and many other poets.

The third formula expressing the inanity of the troubadour's endeavour is *obra d'aragna,* 'a spider's work.' Modern readers in general consider this expression the equivalent of 'spider's web,' with the transparent meaning of 'weak, fragile work.' But it is possible to see in it an Ovidian echo: an allusion to the 'opus Arachnis,'[78] the weaving which Arachne undertook in her competition with Minerva. Arachne won the contest, but her 'opus' was destroyed by the goddess. The 'obra d'aragna' would then suggest 'impossibility of a real victory' rather than the inadequacy of the poet's power. It is, thus, an expression similar to the 'esperanza bretona,' as proven by these lines of Peire Vidal's:

Fach ai l'obra de l'aranha
e la muza del Breto   (ed. Avalle, X, ll. 17–8)

[I have done 'l'obra de l'aranha' and the vain awaiting of the Bretons].[79]

By and large this proverbial allusion seems to be the least frequent way of expressing inane hope.[80] The other two examples, which are found in the work of Jausbert de Puycibot (ed. Shepard, IV, l. 50) and of Lucchetto Gattilusio (ed. Boni, V, l. 9), are both in *sirventes.* One explanation may be that this expression has to compete with the related metaphor *fil d'aranha* ('spider's thread') which refers to the fragility (not the inanity!) of the troubadour's undertaking.[81]

Foolish hopes, useless waiting, vain attempts – one knows, though, that a troubadour is never deterred by these perceptions. As a matter of fact, he finds in them an occasion to renew his commitment to love forever and to proclaim over and over again the uniqueness of his love. This averring attitude creates the ground for another series of *adynata,* which can be called 'asseverating *adynata.*'

This type of *adynaton* is formally a comparison, having the structure of *plus ... que* or *mas ... que.* The second term of the comparison is a character representing the paradigm of the lover in a remote or recent literary tradition: a character who loved unto the limits of all human possibilities. The first term is depicted by the troubadour himself who, by overcoming those limits, realizes an *impossibile.*

The first example that comes to mind is by Bernart de Ventadorn in his famous *Tout ai mon cor ple de joya,* already mentioned and compared with Raimbaut's *Ar resplan la flors enversa,* because of their similar theme of turning the world upside down under the euphoria of the joy of love. It is in this context that one reads:

> Plus trac pena d'amor
> de Tristan l'amador,
> que·n sofri manhta dolor
> per Izeut la blonda. (ed. Lazar, IV, ll. 45–8)

[I have more pain of love than had Tristan the lover, who experienced so much pain for Isolde the blonde].

This is technically a hyperbole, but in fact it is an *adynaton*, because it is not possible to suffer more than Tristan[82] did: his sorrows are written in the *historia*, and have attained the exemplarity of myth.

Another example is one from Raimon Jordan's *Quan la neus chai e gibron li verjan*:

> Qu'eu·l servirai oimais, cossi que m'an,
> o serai li leials e ses engan
> melhs qu'Elena no fo al frair' Ector,
> e, s'a leis platz, mon servir no·m soan
> qu'anc non amet Hero tan Leander (ed. Kjellman, XI, ll. 26–30)

[I will serve her from now on, however it may go, and I will be to her more loyal and without deception than Helen was to Hector's brother (i.e., Paris); and if she likes not to disdain my service, I will love her more than Hero ever loved Leander].

Finally, here is one more example to show that, besides the heroes drawn from the Ovidian and Arthurian tradition, the troubadours often turn to the Bible. It occurs in Peire Vidal's poem *Be·m pac d'ivern e d'estiu*:

> Am la mais per San Raphel
> Que Jacobs no fetz Rachel (ed. Avalle, XXXVI, ll. 49–50)

[I love her more – by St Raphael – than Jacob loved Rachel].

Adynata of this type are the most copious ones in the stock of troubadour *inventio*. That repertoire is a whole universe populated by mythical couples: Thisbe and Pyramus, Flore and Blanchefleur, Landric and

Aya, Aude and Roland, Narcissus and his shadow, Sara and Abraham – heroes who, ultimately, show that 'Amor omnia vincit' or, as Bernart de Ventadorn renders this Virgilian maxim, 'Amor vens tota chauza' (ed. Lazar XXVI, l. 37).[83] If nothing else, true love earns fame and the solidarity of every authentic lover! Later troubadours, in particular Peire Ramon de Tolosa, Elias de Barjols, Lanfranc Cigalo, Pistoleta, Peire Bremon Ricas Novos, and Rambertius, sought it.

It is time to come to some conclusions and see whether such a variety of *adynata* can be systematized in a model. The *adynaton* is a rhetorical device which 'takes' in one of the four following themes which pervade the poetry of the troubadours:

1 The poet declares that in no situation will he ever desist from loving his lady. In this case, the *adynata* are of the type one finds in Strabo's *similitudo impossibilium*: 'gold will be less noble than iron;' 'the Phoenix will die before ...' etc.
2 The poet perceives how his love is entangled in a net of paradoxes. His *adynata*, then, are more like *inanes operae* or *inaequales pensationes*: 'living on wind,' 'waiting for the return of King Arthur,' 'hunting a hare with an ox,' etc. They represent in a deictic way the theme of the poet's foolishness.
3 The poet has attained *joy*. He can then use the type of *adynata* which are actually *impossibilia expleta*, like 'I am warmed up by snow,' 'I draw fresh water from the sea,' and the like. This kind of *adynaton* sustains the theme of the world turned upside down.
4 The poet is a moralist and the whole world seems topsy-turvy to him. The poems containing these messages are often *sirventes* or political songs, but sometimes they are aimed at those who would spoil courtliness. In this case, the *adynata* can be one of the two types already seen: if they refer to the poet, they are *inanes operae* (e.g., Marcabru, Peire d'Alvernha, Gavaudan); if they refer to the world, they fit into the mould of the *impossibilia expleta*. In both cases they sustain the theme of the *contemptus mundi*.[84]

The first three themes dramatize in various forms the *folia* of the troubadour, marking well the extremes within which the vicissitudes of his love move. They also convey the same idea of the poet as a great soul, a magnanimous man, both in suffering for love and in devoting himself to it. From this viewpoint, the fourth theme also belongs with the other ones: the poet is a man of high moral integrity even though his voice might sound like a *vox clamantis in deserto*.

A classification and some general conclusions are possible at the formal level as well. There are three ways of expressing the adynatic notion – 1/a proverb that the poet appropriates to his own vital experience; 2/a coded word or proverbial allusion; 3/a comparison between the poet and a mythical or historical character whom the literary tradition has made into archetypal lover, loyal servant, foolish hero, or whatever the case may be – and the poet transcends the limits set by such models.

The first kind of *adynaton* is used almost exclusively by Marcabru, Peire d'Alvernha, Raimbaud d'Aurenga, Arnaut Daniel, Elias Cairel, Gavaudan, and a few others. This succession of names suggests a hypothesis – namely, that the proverb-*adynaton* meets some profound poetic needs of the *trobar clus* style.[85] Moreover, among the poets of this style, the *adynata* present the morphological peculiarity of having a first-person subject. Another important trait is that these *adynata* are drawn, by and large, from the classical tradition. Of the poets mentioned above, only Arnaut Daniel[86] uses the names of archetypal lovers with an adynatic meaning; even then the names of Atalanta and Meleagre, of Monclin and Odierna, and of the 'nebot Sain Guillem' are unique in the whole troubadour *corpus*.[87] As far as I know, no poet of *trobar clus* uses the ready-made meaning of *faidia, esperansa bretona*, and the like.

The common denominator of all these features is a principle inherent to the poetics of the *trobar clus*. Leaving aside the question of whether the main characteristic of the *trobar clus* is its gradual unfolding of different levels of meaning, there is no doubt that the most obvious feature of this kind of composition is its stylistic preciosity, which always reveals an anxiety for distinction. A follower of the *trobar clus* approaches the old clichés and the established themes with the great aims of drawing new meaning from them, even if this requires a degree of violence imposed on language or some daring metrical solutions. He looks for a new twist of a conventionalized expression, for a rare or unusual meaning of a word, for a difficult rhyme, for words that will turn out to be *hapax legomenon*, for an unpredictable melodic effect – in sum, for an expressiveness of high and hitherto unknown intensity. Conventional language becomes a point of departure rather than the final goal, as with the poets of the plain style. The ambiguity of the *trobar clus* lies, to a great extent, in this attitude of adhesion-estrangement to convention.

The finished product looks more like a monument to the poet than to convention, and its linguistic texture points to the uniqueness of the poet's love.

It is by this tendency to mythopoetical singularization that the proverb-*adynata* of classical extraction can be clearly understood. They are the simplest ones and the most remote in literary tradition. One can say of them what Rabanus Maurus said about letters (grammata): 'sola carent fato, mortemque repellunt'[88] [only they lack of destiny and repel death]. Reduced by time to their essentiality – and therefore less susceptible to further erosion – those proverbs offer an unrivalled basis for the troubadour's process of mythification. Just by adding an *I* to them, the poet can be sure that his story of love will live as long as those proverbs will live – that is, forever.

The *trobar leu* followers could not accept the strongly individualizing proverb-*adynata*. Actually, they would have sounded out of tune in a conventional context. It is not by accident that Bernart de Ventadorn, the purest representative of the *trobar leu*, shunned such *adynata*. Bernart knows, for instance, the *inanis opera* of repenting before sinning (as Peire d'Alvernha does), but the referent is a third person: 'Qui vid anc mais penedensa / faire denan lo pechat?' (ed. Lazar, XLIV, ll. 31–2: Who ever saw anyone repent before the sin?).

The *trobar leu* wound up prevailing over the *trobar clus*. The courtly paideia, with its notion of *mezura*, gradually muffled and phased out the highly original expression of love and preferred a more conventional language. Courtliness taught every troubadour to live up to the ideal of the perfect lover with all the sorrows, joys, hopes, and lapses that accompany such a 'profession.' It was only a question of how to define that ideal. Was Arnaut Daniel's desire of living up to the myth of himself preferable to Bernart's conforming to the literary myths of the Tristans and the Pyramuses? As things turned out, the plain style prevailed, and literature proved to be truer than life! Indeed, looking behind the drama of love, behind the *folia* of love which the *adynata* hypostasize, one sees that the deepest aspiration of courtliness was not to create lovers who could displace the Tristans from their archetypical status, but rather to promote lovers capable of matching those perfect prototypes. Some lines of Bernart de Ventadorn define this aspiration better than any other manifesto could. In his poem *Can vei la lauzeta mover*, Bernart describes, with enchanting simplicity, the joy experienced by a lark which moves its wings in the rays of the sun until it is overcome by sweetness and lets itself fall. Bernart compares this joy to the elation he felt when he first saw his lady's eyes:

> Anc non agui de me poder
> ni no fui meus de l'or'en sai
> que·m laisset en sos olhs vezer
> en un miralh que mout me plai.
> Miralhs, pus me mirei en te,
> m'an mort li sospir de preon,
> c'aissi·m perdei com perdet se
> lo bels Narcisus en la fon (ed. Lazar, XXXI, ll. 17–24)

[I never had control over myself, nor was I in my own power from the moment when she allowed me to look into her eyes, into a mirror that pleases me greatly. Mirror, after I looked at myself into you, my deep sighs have killed me, for I lost myself as the beautiful Narcissus lost himself in the fountain].

The lark's ecstasy and the poet's rapture have an equal intensity. Bernart and Narcissus experience the same 'cupio dissolvi': myth and life coincide as the courtly *paideia* requires! This is a real *gap*, the most authentic way of living up to an ideal.

Conclusion

Year 1289. Almost two centuries earlier the dawn of a splendid cultural phenomenon was marked by a few poems of love by a troubadour. That day was coming to a close, and at this sunset a man called Matfre Ermengaud, not a troubadour but a troubadours' admirer, set for himself the task of preserving their heritage. Not an easy task, to be sure, especially considering the fact that the sponsor had neither poetic ambition nor poetic vein whatsoever. He was very likely a lawyer, a profession not at all incompatible with the world of the troubadour, at least with its penchant for casuistry, subtle debates on questions of love and love's laws. But Matfre was not ready to get entangled in any particular debate and waste his energies to settle, one by one, all the minute and often fictitious questions debated in many *partimen* and *tenzos*. His ambitions aimed at a much higher level, a level from which he could embrace the whole of courtly poetry in order to settle once and for all its constant debate between erotic desire and spiritual elevation. In Matfre's intentions his verdict was not intended to condemn courtly love, as Andreas Capellanus did, but rather to reorient its energies.

Matfre entitled his work *Breviari d'Amor*, perhaps borrowing the technical term *breviarium* from the tradition of studies of Roman and Canon law. Indeed, a legal model seems to be the basis for the opening part of his work where a distinction is made between *dreit naturaus* and *dreit de gens*, which echoes the distinction between divine and human law found at the outset of the *Decretum Gratiani*. It takes more than 35,000 lines for Matfre to develop all the implications and articulations of the two rights which provide the main grandiose structures of this lengthy encyclopedia. It is not possible here to follow all the ramifications (Matfre, in fact, envisions this universe as a tree of love, *arbre d'amor*, having its roots in God, and having as many branches and leaves as there are natural and social orders, vices and virtues) of this encyclopedia, one of the longest in any medieval vernacular. But it should be pointed out, however cursorily, the cultural achievement represented by the *Breviari* with its opening of the troubadour culture to the great trends of thirteenth-century encyclopedism. At the same time, one should stress that, within that context, the *Breviari* represents the unique case of an encyclopedia written from a special angle, *a parte amoris* as it were, and with the precise purpose of intervening in a problem which was neither taxonomy nor hermeneutics (the traditional problems of encyclopedias), but rather troubadour love. The combination of this double undertaking allows Matfre to put troubadour love in a large context, in a universal and providential design. Love is given a metaphysical justification because all the universe is held together by love, and it is through love that all living species are preserved. The troubadours never looked for a metaphysical basis for their love since they perceived it as the beginning and the end of all, *causa efficiens* and *causa finalis* at the same time. Now Matfre finds the strongest justification for erotic love against those who consider it the root of all evil; but, as we shall see, it is a costly justification whose price will be the loss of *mezura*.

Matfre focuses on troubadour love only in the last 7,000 lines of his encyclopedia. It is not an appendix but rather the culmination of a long discourse which offers the philosophical and religious background against which one must see courtly love. Matfre becomes here the man of a court of law, abandoning the descriptive or moralistic mode followed in surveying the order of this universe, and introducing the troubadours to talk directly about their love. Thus, this part, like the dialogues of the *De Amore*, takes the form of a vast *dragmaticon* with the only difference being that in Andreas's work, all the talk is done by *personae*, whereas in Matfre's encyclopedia the speakers are historical poets of courtly love. But before putting the witnesses on the stand, Matfre warns his listeners that they will hear talk for and against love and that therefore such statements should be carefully evaluated because discourses on love tend to disguise poisonous ideas as wisdom.

The first people to take the stand are those who see love as a source of suffering. To counter such accusations Matfre invokes the authority of the troubadours and makes a dossier of verses taken from their poetry (precious materials for editorial purposes) proving that love is a source of joy and moral perfection. But then other texts by the same troubadours and by new ones present the accusation that love sometimes takes refuge in poor people, and not aristocratic ones. Matfre takes love's defence, still quoting troubadour poems, by saying that the defendant loves whomever he loves and prefers *coratge* to beauty, and good lovers to riches. Then comes a graver accusation, well documented with troubadours' texts: love makes its followers crazy. Matfre relies again on new texts to prove that madness becomes wisdom if love is pursued with loyalty and courtliness. Lovers decide to make war to love; but Matfre reminds them that love is too powerful to be won. As a last accusation lovers complain about women. Matfre understands now that courtliness has vanished when women are blamed. Women, however, break the impasse and ask our encyclopedist to teach them how to be courteous. Matfre offers them a piece of literature taken from the *ensenhamen* by Garin lo Brun. Once the ladies are well indoctrinated in courtliness so that nobody can complain any more about them, men ask Matfre to give them a remedy against love so that they can follow it without becoming mad, desperate, and hateful of women. This was precisely the moment Matfre was waiting for. To live in peace and enjoyment with love, its followers must look at his tree of love where they can learn to distinguish good from bad and learn those virtues which they must practise in order to be perfect and happy lovers. These virtues are *largueza* (generosity), *ardimen* (fortitude), *cortesia*, *domney* (gallantry), *allegria* (cherfulness), *retenemen* (reserve or discretion), *ensenhamen* (learning or wisdom), *proeza*, and ... marriage! Marriage? Yes; and in order not to leave any doubt on this unusual virtue, Matfre dwells on how a man has to behave with his wife, why he must try to control his jealousy, etc.

How far we have come from that restless immobility we have seen in troubadours' dramas! When in the background of such plotless dramas there is a marriage it is always that of the lady with a *gilos*, an added obstacle to the fulfilment of love and another splendid occasion to show *mezura*. But troubadours never spoke of marriage, because such a happy ending in many other circumstances would have meant the sad ending of poetry, of a mythopoetic exercise, to say the least. Why, then, does Matfre propose a solution so contrary to everything courtly love stood for? In a way his proposal is not surprising. The pattern within which he operates is rather well known: first came the great season of the Greek tragedy and then came the great season of Greek philosophy which interpreted the former; first came the French Revolution and then came the philosophers who interpreted its historical meaning. The same here: first came courtly love and then came its interpreters. The fact that Matfre could write a *breviari* already shows that he could avail himself of a *corpus* of poetry which was well defined and somewhat immobile: historians are a bit like anatomists who work on dead bodies in order to understand the mechanisms of movement and life. It was possible for Matfre, in that condition of a distant observer, to isolate some main themes in troubadours' poetry and reduce their quest for love to a model. For him that quest was not going anywhere because it was paralysed by what we have called the cyclothymia of courtly lovers who, being at times deliriously happy and at others possessed by despair, live on a perennial psychological see-saw. The cycle, in Matfre's mind, could be broken only by marriage. To this end he begins by considering love the indispensable force of the universe, then he tames the ladies to become more accessible and courteous, and finally he coaches the men to be virtuous in the courtly manner; when all these conditions are met, marriage is the next logical step, because in marriage love finds not only that fulfilment intensely hoped for by lovers, but also the fulfillment of that universal law which requires every species to perpetuate itself.

Thus, at the sunset of the splendid day of troubadour poetry we hear a voice not so different from the one we heard at noon. Andreas Capellanus, like Matfre, was aware that erotic love was a natural drive indispensable for preserving mankind; but, just like Matfre, Andreas wanted erotic love to be contained within the rules prescribed by the sacrament of marriage. Matfre's solution was bourgeois rather than clerical in tone, a fact that somehow proves the success of courtly culture. Matfre shows great admiration for the troubadours and finds them confused rather than hypocritical, as Andreas did, and that is why he seems to be offering a cure for courtly love rather than a condemnation of it; but still the level of incomprehension is high. Interestingly enough, Matfre ignores *mezura*, and his neglect of this courtly virtue is more surprising than that by Andreas, considering that the author of the *Breviari* had a much broader field of observation. But maybe we should measure the success of mezura precisely through this silence. The troubadours, after all, do not mention *mezura* often enough to catch the attention of their listeners; but they practise it, finding a consubstantiation of eros and moral beauty which, to outsiders, might seem ambiguous, but which for them was the ultimate expression of elegance and self-control. They sang of suffering, of dreaming, of desiring, of remembrances, of conquests, and their listeners believed them, because, as Pessoa said, poets are good at pretending. The poets, however, did not intend to deceive anybody by pretending; they rather aspired to dominate language because it is the instrument with which myths are made. The troubadours celebrated one myth at base: a lover capable of controlling his natural instinct, not through any form of mortification or abstinence, but through poetry, through a refined and original expression which sounds like a confession but is in fact an elegant composition in which a symbiosis of nature and culture is objectified. In this sense the troubadours' greatest merit and contribution to our civilization is having created a *vulgaris eloquentia*, to be the first *vulgares eloquentes*, as Dante would say; and as such they were *viri boni dicendi periti* (Quintilian, *Inst. orat.* XII, 1). There was a fundamental difference between the old and the new *eloquentia*, because for the troubadour the *bonitas*, the moral goodness, was not the background or the presupposition that gave credibility to his discourse, but the very object of his discourse, the point to be demonstrated; and their only persuasive argument was to prove that they loved as intensely as possible, actually even to the point of impossibility, because love is the source of moral goodness, and because, where there is true love, there are the appropriate words to express it. The mesure of success in this demonstration was having *mezura*, that complex interaction of eros and culture by which a personal and unique love is celebrated as common patrimony, as a personal tribute to courtliness. *Mezura* is almost an ineffable notion, irreducible to logical terms. The gravest mistake one can make is to analyse it by disassembling its components and establishing how much is eros and how much is spiritual beauty, because then, almost by magic, one of the two would prevail and completely hide the other. When that happens, it seems to me that the world of the troubadour loses much of its enchanting ambiguity.

Notes

INTRODUCTION

1 Zumthor 1963, 282
2 Ibid, 205–17
3 Frank 1942. Frank's interpretation has been upheld, though with some variations, by other scholars such as D. Zorzi (1955); D.W. Robertson (1952); Y. Lefèvre (1973); I. Kasten (1986, 76–87).
4 Spitzer 1944
5 See, for instance, Ferrante 1980 and Kendrick 1988.
6 This concept is put forth by P. Zumthor (1972, 73–5).
7 *Libro de natura de amore* (Mantua 1525)
8 *De l'amour* (1822), ch. 51
9 'Wie gedachte er dann der Troubadours, die nichts mehr fürchten als erhört zu sein.' *Die Aufzeichnungen des Malte Laurids Brigge*, in *Sämtliche Werke*, vol. 6 (Frankfurt: Insel 1966), 941
10 Spitzer 1944, 12

THE AMBIGUITY OF COURTLY LOVE IN ANDREAS CAPELLANUS'S MODEL

1 For a survey of these various theses see Moore 1979, and especially Boase 1977.
2 This sceptical attitude was already present in Robertson 1952–3 and 1962, and in Donaldson 1965; but it had its explicit manifesto, as it were, in a booklet edited by F.X. Newman (1968) containing essays by D.W. Robertson and J.F. Benton, who firmly oppose the notion of courtly love. Such a negative stand provoked fine rejoinders by J. Frappier (1972), who defended the historicity of courtly love, and F.L. Utley (1972).

3 See, for instance, J. Frappier 1959 and 1973: 'l'expression "d'amour courtois," si employé aujourd'hui, manque d'authenticité. A peu près ignoré au Moyen Age (on n'en a guère signalé qu'un seul example dans la poésie des troubadours – courtez'amors – chez Peire d'Alvernhe dont l'activité littéraire s'étend entre 1138 et 1180) elle appartient à la terminologie de la critique moderne. Elle ne semble pas antérieure à Gaston Paris' (p. 4). In another study, Frappier (1971) analyses the terminology used by a few Romantic historians of courtly love (from Sismondi to Fauriel) and concludes again that the expression 'courtly love' is not used before 1883. Frappier, however, does not rely on this argument to prove that courtly love never existed. See also Reiss 1979; Calin 1980; J. Ferrante 1980, who bring together several medieval instances of 'courtez'amors' and point out how often the notion of love and courtliness occur in combination. See also Cherchi 1989 with the finding of the definition and ample explanation of 'amor cortese o onesto,' applied to medieval poetry, in a 1553 'lezione' at the Accademia Fiorentina by Benedetto Varchi. But the best defence for the label 'courtly love' is provided by R. Schnell (1989).
4 Paris 1883; this expression occurs on p. 519.
5 Marrou 1947 and 1971. The latter is one of the best treatments of the subject, and the author defends the uniqueness of courtly love.
6 Dronke 1965–6
7 Cf. Zumthor 1963.
8 For all these different types of poetry celebrating both *amicitia spiritualis* and carnal desire, the best surveys still remain those by H. Brinkmann (1925, 1926). Some indications on erotic poetry can be found in Bruno 1977, and in Schnell 1985. On obscenity in troubadours' poems, see Bec 1981 and Lazar 1989.
9 For this theme see R. Schnell 1989.
10 These lines are taken from *Farai chansoneta nueva* whose attribution to Guilhem IX of Aquitaine is highly debated (see, on the negative side, Monteverdi 1955; Pollman 1962, pp. 349–54; Mölk 1968; Pasero in his edition of 1973; and Pfister 1976; in favour of the authenticity, see Camproux 1968–9; de Riquer 1975; Jensen, 1983, p. 240; and Tavera 1986). Guilhem uses the word *obediensa* several times, but its meaning does not always seem to be the same. It appears twice in the song *Poz vezem de novel florir*:

> Ja no sera nuils hom ben fis
> contr'amor, si non l'es aclis,
> et als estranhs et als vezis
> non es consens,

et a totz sels d'aicels aizis
obediens.

Obediensa deu portar
a maintas gens, qui vol amar;
e cove li que sapcha far
faitz avinens
e que·s gart en cort de parlar
vilanamens (ed. Pasero, VII, ll. 25–36)

[No one will be ever-devoted to love if he is not submissive to it, and if he is not obliging to strangers and to his closest ones, and if he does not offer his services to all those belonging to his group. He who wants to love must have *obediensa* towards many people; and it is becoming to him to be able to accomplish beautiful deeds, and to avoid talking in a gross way at the court].

Whatever the exact meaning of *obediensa* may be in this passage (see several of the possibilities in Pasero's commentary) it is to be excluded that it means 'obedience to a lover.' R. Bezzola (1944–63, vol. II, p. 302) perceives in these lines an echo of Ovid's *Ars am.*, II, ll. 250–60; but Ovid's *obsequitas* is to be practised only towards the lover's servants and is, therefore, another strategy of conquest. Guilhem's *obediensa* is akin to the one we will see in Andreas Capellanus (see n. 28 below). The other instance in which Guilhem uses the word obedienz is in the first stanza of what is considered his last poem, *Pos de chantar m'es pres talenz* (ed. Pasero, XI); but here its meaning does not seem to be that of 'servant of love.' Roncaglia (1964) interprets it in a strictly legal and feudal sense.

11 For the frequency and the meaning of these terms see Cropp 1975. This work takes into consideration only the troubadours of the twelfth century.
12 On the history and meaning of this word see Hackett 1971; Cropp 1975, pp. 285–94; and Paden 1975.
13 On the Christian background of the notion of *obediensa* see Bezzola 1944–63, vol. II, p. 302. The problem had been previously treated by D. Scheludko (1940, pp. 194–6), who gathers many quotations from the Patristic tradition and especially from the *Regula Benedicti*; but none of these quotations seems to be pertinent to the idea of troubadours' *obediensa*.
14 See Köhler 1964b (and also Mancini 1987), who defines Guilhem's and troubadours' *obediensa* as the supreme law assuring stability to the courtly world. This may be true for the feudal form of obedience; but, when it

132 Notes to pages 9–11

comes to love, it is quite clear that *obediensa* can upset the social hierarchy. As we shall see, Andreas Capellanus found this notion quite disturbing. Köhler's idea of *obediensa* is close to that of reverentia, which, to use Dante's definition, is a 'confessione di debita subiezione per manifesto segno' (*Convivio*, IV, 8, 11). Troubadour *obediensa* contains an element of reverence for the beloved, but it does not exclude – in fact it encourages – the striving to *paritas*, often by denying any limiting value to a 'clear sign of superiority' based on social status. The best study to date on this concept is Kasten 1986, pp. 53–64.

15 See Favati 1970 and 1975. Favati could have found another model of 'descending' love in the classical notion of friendship: 'Maximum est in amicitia, superiorem parem esse inferiori' (Cicero, *De amicitia*, 69: 'The highest thing in friendship is for a superior person to be equal to his inferior'), a model which supports the idea that much of medieval love is basically *amicitia*. For the theories of love in the Middle Ages see the succinct but insightful survey by J. Chydenius (1970) and R. Schnell's more thorough treatment (1985).

16 See Pollmann 1966, pp. 218–19. The problem of the relation between the troubadours and the Arabic culture is an old and vexing one (see Giffen 1971), but has been somewhat dormant in recent years. M.R. Menocal (1987) tries to rally attention on the subject.

17 The idea that the Duque of Aquitaine created once and for all the key elements of *fin'amor* has its most recent sponsor in Y. Lefèvre (1981). According to him the song *Molt jauzens mi prenc en amar* contains 'la première énumeration des qualités de ce que les troubadours et les trouvères appeleront par la suite la fin'amor, en développant mille et une variations sur ces qualités sans rien leur ajouter de fondamental, comme si l' "amour courtoios" avait été defini une fois pour toutes par la voix du comte de Poitiers, duc d'Aquitaine' (p. 298). But the 'spiritual' interpretation of the poem given by Lefèvre is not thoroughly convincing; Pasero's explanation of Guilhem's 'courtly materialism' as the thematic key to this song is much more persuasive.

18 Andreas is a victim of a critical paradox well defined by G. Vinay (1951): 'È questa strana situazione fatta ad uno scrittore ridotto a immagine della sua età, mentre egli è stato il prisma attraverso il quale quell'età abbiamo veduto' (p. 205). The same methodological concern is expressed by J.F. Benton (1961): 'Andreas' book is not a source of unambiguous historical evidence, but is itself to be interpreted in the light of what we know about medieval society and literature' (p. 581).

19 By P. Dronke (1963, p. 59)

20 For a first introduction to the critical bibliography on Andreas, see Schlösser 1960, and the book review by B.H. Wind (1964). Updatings are to be found in Schnell 1982, Karnein 1985, and Monson 1988.
21 The fact that no troubadour ever mentions Andreas should not be a surprise. The troubadours, by and large, very seldom mention any contemporary Latin authors even though they were familiar with some of their work (see Pirot 1972); Andreas does not seem to have enjoyed any special consideration. Much more problematic is the silence on Andreas's part concerning the troubadours; but it is not at all out of line with the extreme poverty of historical allusions in his treatise, and with the twelfth-century Latin texts tradition where the quotation of or even allusions to vernacular texts are extremely rare. Moreover, one should not forget that Andreas was working on a model of courtly love and, to that end, did not need to use explicit historical references. Ultimately Andreas's knowledge of troubadour poetry must be proven by the themes he uses in his work.
22 The only sure date concerning the publication of *De Amore* is the *terminus ante quem*, the year 1238, when the treatise is referred to by Albertanus of Brescia in his *Liber de amore et dilectione Dei et proximi*. All the other elements of chronology are less certain. They have been studied in detail by P. Rajna (1889), whose conclusions – placing the composition of the treatise between 1186 and 1196 – are widely accepted.
23 The strongest evidence is presented by A. Karnein (1985, pp. 21–39), with exhaustive bibliographical information. It is virtually certain that Andreas worked at Troyes more or less at the time that Chrétien de Troyes was conducting his own polemic against courtly love. It is important to remember that Chrétien was familiar with troubadour poets, as proven by L. Rossi (1987); it is important because it offers some indirect support to the thesis that Andreas was familiar with the world of the troubadours.
24 The strongest piece of evidence is the mention of Eleanor of Aquitaine (bk. II, ch. 7), but it is not a decisive one. Perhaps the best way of settling this problem is that presented by J.J. Parry in the introductory study to his translation of *De Amore*'s (1941): 'Although Andreas' book was almost certainly intended to portray conditions at Queen Eleanor's court at Poitiers between 1170 and 1174, the actual writing must have taken place some years later when Marie de France was at Troyes ruling as regent for her son after her husband's death' (p. 21).
25 For some of these differences see P. Zumthor (1972, pp. 470 ff.).
26 The troubadours knew quite early the Arthurian theme of the 'esperensa bretona' as well as the Tristan legend (see Pirot 1972, pp. 435–539). However,

the poetry of the troubadours had an audience in the North (see McCash 1979, also Raupach and Raupach 1979, who study the manuscript tradition of Provençal lyrics in northern France where, by the end of the twelfth century, troubadours' poems were being copied in some interested circles. See also the already-mentioned Rossi 1987).

27 In this long tradition that associates Andreas with the troubadours one should mention, only as a sample of its duration, Zonta 1908; Denomy 1945 and 1947; and Schlösser 1960. These studies, among others, have attempted to see the northern trouvères (who, in any case, echo the troubadours) as the models for Andreas's treatise (see Dragonetti 1959).

28 Andreas Capellanus, *De Amore*, ed. by Trojel 1892, p. 106. All quotations are taken from this edition. There is an excellent English translation of Andreas's text by P.G. Walsh (1982), which supersedes that by J.J. Parry (1941), which, however, remains important for its commentary. I have consulted both translations but decided to provide my own in order to adhere as closely as possible to the text for the sake of my argument, even if this has often meant a loss of elegance.

29 In another passage (bk. I, ch. 4) Andreas talks about *obedientia*: 'obsequia cunctis amorosus multa consuevit decenter parare' (p. 10: a man in love becomes accustomed to serve everyone gently); but, in this instance, it does not exactly mean *obediensa* to the lady. However, as seen in n. 9 above, Andreas's phrase cannot be traced back to Ovid (*Ars Am.*, II, ll. 250 ff.) who talks only about a lover being obsequious to the lady's servants. Instead, Andreas's sentence has a lot in common with many passages of troubadour lyric (see many instances culled by D. Scheludko [1934, especially p. 136, n. 1]). One example taken from Bernart de Ventadorn may show this similarity: 'per leis es razos e mezura / qu'eu serva tota creatura' (ed. Lazar, XIII, ll. 41–2: It is just and becoming that for it [i.e., Love] I serve all creatures).

30 See Sakari 1949, p. 185. The theme is touched upon in stanza 3 of this woman poet's only known poem.

31 See, for example, Viscardi [1948] 1970: 'Ed è proprio Guglielmo di Montanhagol (+1258) quegli che trova la formula nuova: amore è fonte di castità. L'amore che il Montanhagol celebra è remoto da ogni passione ed esclude nel modo più assoluto l'accensione dei sensi. È un amore che non comporta attentati alla purezza, nemmeno nel segreto pensiero, né minaccia l'onore della dama' (p. 375). Less purity but not less seriousness is detected by L.T. Topsfield (1975): 'Montanhagol's idea of castitatz is probabily very close to that of Thomas Aquinas in his *Summa Theologica*' (p. 248). Along the same line, see Ricketts 1966.

32 Nelli 1963, pp. 181–2. See also Akehurst (1973), who raises some objections to Nelli's study (pp. 145 f.).
33 Besides the examples quoted here, others from Raimbaut de Vaqueiras and Guilhem de Montanhagol are quoted by M. de Riquer (1975, p. 93). Another example can be seen in the poem *Aissi cum a sas faissos* attributed to Guilhem de Sant Leidier but almost certainly written by a later author (see A. Sakari's edition of 1956, pp. 164 ff.). More examples, from Giraut de Bornelh, Raimbaut d'Aurenga, and Daude de Pradas, can be found in Cropp 1975, pp. 356–7. Not all these examples, where the terms *assag* or *assai* or *esai* appear, represent an irrefutable proof of such a 'test of love.' A systematic canvassing of troubadour poetry would undoubtedly provide further evidence. See, for example, Guilhem Ademar (ed. Almqvist, IX, sl. 4).
34 See Sakari 1971.
35 Other occurrences are quoted by G.M. Cropp (1975, pp. 372–8).
36 *Faitz* is etymologically related to many similar expressions found in Romance languages, all derived from the well-known Latin expression *facere in re venerea*. In Provençal we find *faire az alcuna* ('to make it with someone'), *faire, fag, faitz*, etc.; in Spanish *hacerlo*; in Old French *le faire, affaire*, etc.; in Old Italian *afare* (see Avalle 1977, p. 75). Also the troubadours use *merce* as a synonym of *faitz* (see Deroy 1971).
37 Indicated by Shepard and Chambers in their 1950 edition of Aimeric de Peguilhan, p. 186. The text of this *partimen* can be seen in Schultz-Gora 1888, p. 25; and most recently in A. Riege 1991, pp. 292–306, with an important commentary. The same problem is discussed in the exchange of *coblas* between Pujol and Poestat, edited by A. Jeanroy in 1921.
38 A series of similarities between *De Amore* and Raimon de Miraval's poems has been pointed out by L.T. Topsfield (1956, p. 40). However, the themes and motifs compared here are too general, and they appear in the poems of many troubadours preceding Andreas. Raimon de Miraval's activity spanned the period 1191–1220. This fact can create some problems: if there are similarities between Andreas and Raimon they do not constitute (although they do not exclude) proof of filiation since they both could have drawn their themes from earlier troubadours. A much more cogent document tying Andreas to the world of the troubadours is the famous question raised by the lady in the last dialogue, whether the higher part of the body is preferable to the lower one. The same question appears in a *partimen* debated between Sifre and Mir Bernart, who are otherwise unknown to us (the text was published by A. Kolsen in 1939). This problem is too rare to think of a mere coincidence; but given that the *partimen*

seems to have been composed later than *De Amore*, its source could be Andreas, unless we conceive of another source common to both but lost to us.

There is another puzzling correspondence between Andreas's treatise and the allegorical poem by Guiraut de Calanso *A leis cui am de cor e de saber*, written before 1202. It is the details of the description of the *Palace of Love*, which explicit similarities in these texts. But such resemblance also raises a question. Guiraut talks about *Quatre gras* (v. 29) or 'four steps' of love, and he mentions them again in his *ensenhamen Fadet joglar* (*los catre gras*, v. 218). This represents a significant deviation from the traditional *quinque lineae amoris* of Ovidian memory, which are recalled by, among others, Alanus de Insulis in this order: 'visus et alloquium, contactum et oscula, factum' (P.L. 210, p. 1222), that is, 'sight and talk, contact and kisses, factum [the *faitz* of the troubadours].' This deviation also appears in *De Amore* where Andreas speaks about four stages of love: 'Ab antiquo sunt gradus in amore constituti distincti. Primus in spei datione consistit, secundus in osculi exhibitione, tertius in amplexus fruitione, quartus in totius personae concessione finitur' (p. 32: From antiquity four distinct steps in love have been established. The first consists in giving hopes; the second in granting a kiss; the third in the enjoyment of an embrace; and the fourth is completed in the concession of the whole person). As one can see Andreas deviates from the ancient tradition he mentions, and not only in the number of stages of love but in the description of the first two as well. Unfortunately Guiraut de Calanso does not mention what the four stages are, so it is impossible to establish for sure whether they are the same ones mentioned by Andreas. Moreover, Andreas does not mention the four stages of love in the description of the Palace of Love, as does Guiraut. However, the coincidence of the four stages versus the five of the ancient tradition makes plausible the supposition of a relation between the two authors. In any case it should be remembered that, among the troubadours, there seems to exist a tradition of the stages of love that differs from the ancient one as does Andreas's (see, for instance, Sansone 1980). On this problem in general, see Jung 1971, pp. 147 f. On the poem of Guiraut see Pirot 1972, pp. 197–261 and 563–95; Jones 1978; and Capusso 1987. On the *quinque lineae amoris* see Friedman 1965-6. For the unlikely possibility that Guiraut's four steps of love echo St Bernard's four levels of love, see Gilson 1947, pp. 200 f. For another explanation see also Monson 1984.

39 Edited by S. Battaglia in 1948. Actually Battaglia publishes integrally only one of these two translations. The second one was published by G. Ruffini

in 1980; here *probitas* is usually rendered with *senno*. For some insights on the subject of *probitas* see Favati 1945, and above all Topsfield 1979.
40 Cf. G.S. Burgess (1970), who surveys only Old French texts; see also Cropp 1975, pp. 88–93.
41 See the few examples that G.M. Cropp (1975, p. 89) culls from non-lyrical texts; all these examples, however, could bear a different interpretation.
42 This text, taken from a treatise on penance, was published by De Lollis in 1891, and partially reproduced by C. Appel (1902, pp. 185–7), from which I quote. Here is the translation of the passage: 'For this reason Boethius, a great Doctor who in the Holy Church is called monsignor Saint Sever, says: "magna nobis, ubi dissimulare non velimus, indicta *probitas* necessitas, cum agamus coram occulis iudicis cuncta cernentis," that is: "We need great *proeça* where we do not want to pretend, since we know and we are sure that all of our actions are present in the eyes of our judge who sees it all."
43 Edited by M. Eusebi in 1969. This *ensenhamen*, with 347 lines, is one of the shortest of this genre.
44 These lines echo Virgil's 'Parcere subiectis et debellare superbos' (*Aen.*, VI, 853), a line often repeated in rhetorical treatises and in moral-political works. Echoes of this Virgilian line are frequent among the troubadours, especially in connection with the notion of *orgolh*; for example: Bertrand de Born (ed. Stimming, XXIV, ll. 33–5); Guilhem de Cabestanh (ed. Långfors, III, ll. 48–9); Jausbert de Puycibot (ed. Shepard, VI, ll. 12–26; XI, ll. 3–6). But the extent to which Virgil's influence on the troubadours was a direct one is not clear. The problem is discussed by A. Roncaglia (1985) and L. Rossi (1989).
45 Pertinent materials – from Seneca's 'animus facit nobilem' (*Epist.* 44, 5) to Matthew of Vendôme and to Dante – are to be found in Curtius 1953, pp. 179 f.; for this *topos* in troubadour poetry, see Wettstein 1945, pp. 49 f.
46 See, for example, Köhler 1955–6 and 1960 for very interesting observations on *proeza*, even if somewhat schematized within a sociological frame.
47 Book IX, ch. VII, fol. 104 of the 1492 Venice edition
48 *Liber Canonis*, book III, fen. I, tractatus IV, ch. XXIV, fol. 190^v of the 1507 Venice edition
49 Cf., for example, C. Buridant's 1974 edition of Andreas, pp. 207 f.
50 Cf., for example, Robertson 1952–3, and Karnein 1985, pp. 59–71. Karnein is well acquainted with the 'medical' interpretation of Andreas's definition of love – an interpretation first presented by B. Nardi (1942 and 1959) and repeated by P. Cherchi (1979) and R. Schnell (1982). Karnein, however, refutes this interpretation in favour of a 'moral' one along the

lines proposed by Robertson. But then how can one explain the frequent physiological elements appearing in *De Amore*? For a friendly discussion between Karnein and myself, see Cherchi 1985, pp. 28–9. On the subject of love and medicine, an ample bibliography can be found in Wack 1990.

51 The studies on the 'disease of love' have increased in recent years, but one should still consult Crohns 1905, and Lowes 1913–14. On the recent side, see Nardi, 1942 pp. 6 ff., and 1959; important for what they say about Andreas's definition of love are Busse 1975; Ciavolella 1976; and Agamben 1977, pp. 5–35, 73–155.

52 On p. 335: 'nam ex ipso Veneris opere, ut physicalis monstrat auctoritas, corporis plurimum potentia minoratur, sed propter amorem corpus minoris cibi et potus assumptione nutritur, et ideo non immerito debet esse potentiae brevioris' [as a matter of fact, as physicians tell us, the body's power is greatly weakened by the mere venerial act; but because of love the body takes in a lesser portion of food and drink, so that there is a further reason for the body's strength to be reduced]. On p. 337: 'in dictis quibusdam physicalibus' [in the words of some physicians]. Thus Andreas admittedly relies on medical authorities. The quotation from Johannicius appears on p. 336; it is, however, an indirect quotation taken from William of Conches' *Philosophia mundi*, as proven by Z.P. Zuddy (1965). It is interesting to notice that the troubadours often talk about the 'disease of love'; such is the case in Guilhem IX (ed. Pasero, IV, ll. 19–21), Jaufre Rudel (ed. Jeanroy, III, ll. 55–6), Raimbaut d'Aurenga (ed. Pattison, V, ll. 22–8) and many others. To the troubadours, however, this disease is just a metaphor, without any 'physiological' elements. How could they have seen love as a physical disease!

53 L. Landouzy and R. Pépin, eds., 1911. Some similarities between this treatise (written ca. 1238) and *De Amore* have been shown by A. Viscardi (1970 [1948], p. 783).

54 The term *joven* has been widely studied, beginning with A.J. Denomy (1949), who attempts to prove the Arabic origin of this notion; whereas both G. Duby (1964), and E. Köhler (1966), study its sociological aspects.

55 Some of these effects are frequently mentioned by the troubadours. As an example, see these lines from Guilhem IX:

> Per son joi pot malaus sanar,
> e per sa ira sas morir,
> e savis hom enfolezir,
> e belhs hom sa beutat mudar,
> e·l plus cortes vilaneiar,
> e·l totz vilas encortezir   (ed. Pasero, IX, ll. 25–30)

[For her joy a sick person can recover; and for her disdain a healthy man can die; and a wise man can become crazy, and a handsome man can lose his beauty; and the most elegant man can turn into a peasant, and a real peasant can become courtly].

The general theme of these paradoxes is the 'topsy-turvy world' as we shall see in the chapter on the adynata.

56 See n. 44, above. The conservative aspect of Andreas's ideology is underlined by G. Duby (1980, pp. 338–46).

57 P. 52: 'Since we all descend from the same log, Adam.' This image is a conventional one, and it also appears in the poetry of the troubadours, for example: in the *partimen* between Lo Dalfi d'Alvernhe and Perdigon (ed. Chaytor, XI, l. 23); in the last line of Guilhem's IX *Farai chansoneta nueva* (ed. Pasero, VIII, l. 34); and in Raimon Jordan (ed. Kjellman, I, l. 35). Some indications on Andreas's ideas of nobility are to be found in Simonelli 1966. For the general problem of the notion of nobility in the Middle Ages see Corti 1959. It may be opportune to remember that Andreas was not the only 'Latin' author to notice the centrality – and to some extent the originality – of the ideas of the troubadours concerning nobility. At least another anonymous author of the second half of the fourteenth century uses troubadours' texts in his *Liber de nobilitate animi* (see Thomas 1929, and Anglade 1929).

58 P. 183: 'This Love is known to be of such a virtue that the origin of all moral goodness derives from it.'

59 Cf. P. Demats 1970, especially pp. 227–33. In my opinion Demats's essay offers the best explanation of the 'contradictions' contained in *De Amore*. G. Vinay (1951) also provides good insights; however, Vinay takes great pains to cover up Andreas's contradictions and confuses his thoughts with those of his characters.

60 See Robertson 1962, pp. 391–448. This truly remarkable essay shows how much humour went into the composition of *De Amore*. One could accept most of Robertson's analysis of Andreas's treatise except for its main thesis – namely, that Andreas did write against *concupiscentia* and not against 'courtly love,' the latter being a notion lacking in historical foundation. After Robertson's reading of *De Amore*, Andreas's wit received much attention from different angles: see Cherniss 1975; Paepe 1966; Kertesz 1971; Butturff 1974; Ruiz-Domenec 1980; and Schnell 1982. Andreas's wit has been seen as obscene by B. Bowden (1979), who reads words like *poena* (*pena* in medieval spelling), *solatia*, *cunctus* (paleographically close to *cunnus*), *languor*, *mors* (meaning ejaculation), and many others as obscene puns. Along this line proceeds H. Silvestre (1980) who, accepting Bowden's

suggestion that *probitas* may mean 'erection,' counts all the occurrences of this word (130 of them!) in *De Amore* and relates it to the French *bita*, a word meaning 'virile member,' but recorded only from the fourteenth century on. More obscene puns are discovered by B. Roy (1985). My only comment on these sotadic interpretations is: 'omnia munda mundis' (St Paul, *Ad Titum*, I, 15). Indispensable for its bibliographical information and acute observation on the problem of Andreas's humour is Monson 1988 in which Andreas's humour and contradictions between the two parts of the book are said to depend on his inconsistency as an author.

61 As an example one may recall the concluding words of the *plebeia* to the *nobilior*: 'Et quantumcunque quisque bonum operetur in orbe quo ad aeternae beatitudinis praemia capienda sibi valere non potest, nisi ex caritatis illud procedat affectu. Eadem igitur ratione, quantumcunque actibus propriis et operibus studeam regi servire amoris, si illud non ex cordis affectione procedat et ex actu derivetur amandi, ad amoris mihi praemia valere non potest. Ergo quoadusque me radius non pertinget amoris, mei non potestis amoris largitate potiri.' [p. 123: No matter how much good a man does in this world, it will not enable him to attain the reward of eternal beatitude, unless it moves from the feeling of *charitas*. For the same reason, no matter how much I apply myself to serve the King of Love with my deeds and my work, they cannot be of any help in attaining the reward of love unless they spring from the heart's affection and from the act of loving itself. Thus, as long as Love's ray does not touch me, you cannot win the gift of my love]. The same idea is expressed by Andreas (the author, that is) by the end of his third book: 'Amor praeterea ratione alia satis videtur odibilis, quia saepius inaequalia pondera portat et eam semper cogit amare, quam nulla posset homo sollicitudine obtinere, quia mutuum illa non sentit amorem, quum amoris non instigetur aculeis. Non est ergo illius arbitrium eligendum, qui te cogit instanter illud toto mentis ingenio postulare, quod ipse idem tibi facit penitus denegari. Nam, si amor iustus vellet moderator haberi, id solum ad amandum cogeret amatores, quod statim vel post dignos labores eos mutua vice diligeret; quod quum non faciat, merito videtur eius militia recusanda' [p. 357: For yet another reason Love seems loathsome: because more often than not it carries uneven weights, always forcing a man to love a woman whom he cannot win regardless of whatever means and sollicitous courtship, because she does not feel reciprocal love since she has not been compelled by the stings of love. Therefore you should not decide to follow the whims of Love who presses you to ask, with all of your mental powers, for what it itself has caused to be completely denied to you. Indeed if Love wanted

Notes to page 39   141

to be considered a just ruler, it would have people fall in love only with those persons who would reciprocate, either immediately or after worthwhile pains. But since Love does not do so, it seems proper to reject its services].

The idea that love cannot be requited if the darts of love do not intervene was quite common among the troubadours. See, for example, Bernart de Ventadorn:

> En agradar et en voler
> es l'amors de dos fis amans.
> Nula res no i pot pro tener
> si·lh voluntatz no es egaus   (ed. Lazar, II, ll. 29–32)

[Love between two fine lovers consists in their mutual pleasure and desire. Nothing can benefit it if they do not have an equal desire]

or Arnaut de Maruelh:

> conquisa non er per mi estiers,
> si fin'Amors, que·i a mon cor assis,
> lo sieu ric cor per forssa non languis   (ed. Johnston, XV, ll. 12–14)

[she will never be conquered by me otherwise unless fin'Amor, which has placed my heart in her, does not soften her noble heart by force].

The troubadours, however, were not discouraged by this truth; in fact, they were challenged by it in the hope of inspiring love in their reluctant ladies.

62 On Andreas's 'courts of love' – which for a long while were considered to have had an historical existence – the book by R. Schnell (1982) is fundamental; it not only surveys the vast literature on this theme, but points out for the first time Andreas's expertise in Canonical as well as in Roman law. Schnell indicates the sources of many of Andreas's *iudicia amoris* and demonstrates how his legal expertise pervades the whole *De Amore*.

63 Among the most recent supporters of this thesis one should mention Schlösser 1960; Taiana 1977; I. Singer 1973 (on p. 1290 he speaks of *De Amore* as a work 'of dramatic ambivalence, as itself a dialogue between two aspects of the medieval soul, two ways of life brilliantly elaborated and dialectically confronted with one another'); and Singer 1984. Many

of the interpretations of this tenor, and of that indicated in the following notes, find their support in the famous syntagm 'duplex sententia' (p. 358) used by Andreas in the closing paragraph of his treatise when he seems to give a clue for the contradictions of his own work. This support, however, comes from a questionable way of translating the word *duplex* which does not necessarily mean 'contradictory' or 'conflicting,' but could simply mean 'double': indeed, the Italian translator of the fourteenth century renders with 'scienza doppia' (Battaglia's edition of 1947, p. 417), that is, the same lesson given in two different versions. Moreover, Andreas's sentence should be seen in its context, which makes clear – so, at least, it seems to me – that the chaplain condemns the type of love defended by his characters in the first part of his book.

64 This idea was first proposed by H. Grabmann (1932) and fully accepted by A.J. Denomy (1946). There are, however, some difficulties with Andreas's Averroism. One of them is certainly this: if one accepts the dating of *De Amore* in the decade 1186–96, then Andreas's Averroism would be *ante literam*, since Averrois was translated into Latin at a later date. If one goes back to the condemnation by Bishop Tempier and to the prologue to the syllabus of the 219 condemned books, one can see that the condemning of Andreas falls under a different category from the purely philosophical texts. According to R. Hissette (1977) 'l'evêque ne condamne pas seulement les erreurs doctrinales professés par certain maître de la faculté des arts, mais aussi la dépravation des moeurs qui sévit dans les milieux universitaire. Il confirme donc que des profonds désordres moraux et disciplinaires allaient de pair avec les troubles doctrinaux auquels le syllabus a tenté de porter remède' (p. 16). All the instances of Averroism provided by Denomy are proven wrong by Hissette (pp. 256, 261, 245, 247–9, 304), who concludes: 'en dépit de resemblances doctrinales évidentes, les exposés du *De amore* sont depourvus du caractère radical qui affecte les 8 propositions y référés [...] On sera donc prudent avant de considérer André le Chapelain comme l'inspirateur direct de l'une on de l'autre proposition du syllabus' (p. 315). R. Hissette (1983) has returned to the subject, arguing with H. Silvestre (1982).

65 See, for example, Palumbo 1969, where one finds an excellent bibliographical survey of Andreas criticism.

66 Kelly 1968

67 'Si voluisset Deus sine crimine actus fornicationis exerceri, sine causa pracepisset, matrimonia celebrari, quum magis per illum modum quam per matrimonia Dei posset populus multiplicari' (p. 315: If God wished

the act of fornication to be practised without fault, he would have had no reason to order marriages to be celebrated, since God's people could multiply faster in this way than by marrying).
68 Wechssler 1909; Casella 1938; Briffault 1945; Lazar 1964
69 On the reception of *De Amore*, Karnein 1985 is fundamental.

MEZURA

1 *Convivio* II,10. On Dante's notion of courtliness see Vallone 1950.
2 Perhaps the same identity was meant in the opening lines of Daude de Pradas's *Romanz* on the four cardinal virtues:

> Honestatz es e cortesia
> Pessar tal re que bona sia (ed. Stickney)

[It is *honestatz* and courtliness to think of things which are good].

Daude de Pradas, however, may be using a synonymic dittology, whereas Dante clearly establishes an identity between onestade and cortesia.
3 *Convivio*, IV, 6
4 Quoted by M. Pohlenz (1934, p. 4)
5 On Cicero's influence through the Middle Ages see Nelson 1933, although this study is somewhat outdated. For St Ambrose's adaptation of Cicero, Thamin 1895 is still a classic, but see also Madec 1974. On St Augustine, see Holte 1962. On the presence of the *honestum* in grammar teaching, Delhaye 1958 is indispensable.
6 The best edition of this work is that of J. Holmberg (1929), which has an important introduction, an excellent commentary, and an appendix containing medieval translations into French and German. This edition, however, has not put to rest some problems concerning this work, especially that of its authorship. The candidacy of Hildebert of Lavardin (Migne, *PL*, CLXXI, prints the treatise under his name) now abandoned, it remains that of Walter of Châtillon although William of Conches remains the strongest competitor. A survey of these attributions is provided in Delhaye 1949 and 1950, which prompted the reaction of R.A. Gautier (1951), defending the candidacy of Walter of Châtillon. Delhaye (1953) replied in favour of Guillaume, but Gautier (1953) stood his ground. Guillaume's authorship remains the most plausible.
7 Migne, *PL*, CLXXVIII, 1646
8 It is useless to try to cite relevant sources for such a vast problem. One can get an idea of the richness of the debates involving the relation between

cardinal and theological virtues just leafing through the six volumes of the collected studies of a specialist on the subject, O. Lottin (1942–60).
9 Cf. Paré, Brunet, and Tremblay 1922.
10 Ehrismann 1919
11 The text of Curtius's contention is available in English (Curtius 1953, pp. 519–40).
12 As refutations of Curtius's thesis, see Neumann 1951 and 1952–3; and Rocher 1964. These articles, including Curtius's and Ehrismann's, are reprinted in Eifler 1970, a critical anthology on medieval 'chivalric virtue-system' in which no mention is made of the troubadours' concern for *honestum*. See also Jaeger 1985, p. 174 and passim (this work focuses on the origins of courtliness in Germany).
13 The notion of 'human perfection' is stated at the beginning of Hildebert's work:

> Quatuor eximias virtutum proprietates
>   Complures docti disseruere viri;
> Quarum se formis si mens humana coaptet,
>   Perfectum faciet integra vita virum.
> Officiis igitur propriis descripsimus illas
>   Fiat ut his apte morigeratus homo. (*PL*, CLXXI, 1055–6)

[Many wise men have discussed the excellent proprieties of the four virtues. If man's mind would conform itself to them, a perfect life would make of him a perfect man. Therefore we describe them here according to their respective duties, so that man can properly comply with them].

14 See B.L. Whorf (1956), for whom language is not merely 'a reproducing instrument for voicing ideas, but rather is itself the shaper of ideas, the program and guide for the individual's mental activity' (p. 12).
15 For the twelfth-century discussions on the virtue of magnanimity see Gauthier 1951, especially pp. 251–94.
16 P. 41 of J. Holmberg's 1929 ed.
17 The concept of *mensura* as harmony and proportion was a fundamental one in the medieval world. See De Bruyne 1946 and the two volumes of *Miscellanea Mediaevalia* (1983) devoted to 'Mensura: Mass, Zahl, Zahlensymbolik in Mittelalter' where, however, no reference to Provençal *mezura* is made. It is important to remember that Provençal has its correspondences in Old French *mezure* and Old German *maze*; but it would be misleading

to interpret them all as having exactly the same meaning, for the *mezure* of the knight has different nuances from the *mezura* of the troubadours.

18 An excellent study on the *ensenhamen* and related genres (*novas, salut d'amor*, allegories of love, etc.) is that by D.A. Monson (1981). G.E. Sansone (1977) offers a good anthology of *ensenhamens*. What is missing so far is a study of the relation that may have existed between these Provençal texts and the medieval Latin didactic tradition. There are many reasons to suspect that the correspondences between the two traditions are overwhelming. And didactic elements are found in *summas*, sermons, allegorical poems, and so forth (see, for some indication related to the notion of temperance, Hermanns 1913). By seeing the *ensenhamens* against the Latin background, the historical understanding of the origins of the courtly world might be enhanced.

19 Ed. Dejeanne, XV, l. 19. It is interesting to notice that Marcabru was the first troubadour to use the word *mezura*. It is equally interesting to realize that he always uses it in a moralistic context, in poems which portray the ideal of courtly ethics where *mezura* plays a major role. One can never appreciate enough the impact that Marcabru's moral poetry had in shaping courtliness and courtly poetry.

20 From the poem *Si tot non es enquistz* (ed. W. Bernhardt), a sort of *ensenhamen* resembling a scholastic dissertation on the key words of the courtly vocabulary (cf. Monson 1981, pp. 115 f.)

21 Di Capua 1959, vol. II, pp. 252–347 (the chapter concerning *discretio* on pp. 289–314). Important material on this subject can be found in Gillmeister 1972.

22 A.H. Schutz (1958) is the only one, as far as I know, who has attempted to shed light on this terminology concerning wisdom; but his attempt could bear some improvement, as one can infer from his simplistic conclusion: 'In short, *sen* is good sense, judgement; *saber*, wisdom of higher kind, in which learning could be a component; *sciensa* is a scientific knowledge of demonstrable character; *conoissensa*, the ability to discriminate' (p. 514). Not much is added by Serper 1986.

23 E. Stroński, XII, l. 41. There is practically no major study on troubadour poetry which does not touch upon the concept of *mezura*; however, there are not many essays which deal specifically with this subject. Besides Hermanns 1913 (which, in any case, mentions only one troubadour, Daude de Pradas, [p. 27, n. 10]), see Wettstein 1945, Margoni 1965, and Dembowski 1986. The last cited provides a computerized list of instances in which the word mezura appears. From this inquiry it seems that the word is used

less frequently than one would expect, given the importance of the concept it contains; however, the same can be said for many historical phenomena, such as Mannerism or Baroque, or even with other concepts of troubadour poetry such as the very same word *cortez'amor*, as we saw in the previous chapter. The ideal of *mezura* is present every time a troubadour sings in public about his love, as we hope to demonstrate.

24 F. Diez 1883: 'Man kännte sich diese ganze Literatur als das Werk eines Dichters denken, nur in verschiedenen Stimmungen hervorgebracht' (p. 107).
25 I borrow this notion from Jaeger 1945.
26 This aspect has been thoroughly studied by S. Thiolier-Méjean (1978).
27 An excellent article on this aspect of troubadour's poetry is that by R. Warning (1979), whose *Rezeptionästhetik* finds an ideal testing ground in a literature such as the Provençal, so strongly conditioned by audience expectations.
28 For the models and the rules to be followed in these physical portraits see Faral 1962 [1924], pp. 79–82; but one finds important material in Renier 1885. See also, for comparative and contextual purposes, Colby 1965 and Georgi 1969.
29 The conventional nature of these portraits can also be proven *e contrario*, that is, with portraits of ugly and old women, who, as one can imagine, have no representative in troubadour lyrics but do exist in the world of the troubadours, in novels (cf. the anonymous *Jaufre*, ed. Breuer, ll. 5192–221), in *pastorelas*, and in *sirventes*. The archetype of such description is Matthew of Vendôme's Beroe (*Ars versificatoria*, 58, in Faral 1962 [1924], pp. 130–2).
30 *De Amore*, pp. 15 and 348
31 See Press (1970); Paden 1975.
32 See, on this subject, Sutherland 1961.
33 The classical origins of this theme have been indicated by A. Roncaglia (1952). The theme has been studied by G. Contini (1957). For other bibliographical information see Avalle's commentary to Peire Vidal's poem.
34 *De Trinitate* X, 1, 1 (see Cherchi 1972b). In talking about this love *ex auditu* St Augustine perhaps had in mind authors such as Ovid (*Heroides* XVI, ll. 17 ff.), Propertius (I, 6, l. 27), Cicero (*De amicitia*, 28). The presence of this theme in the classical tradition makes it unlikely that Jaufre had to borrow it from the Arabs, as L. Ecker (1934, pp. 70–81) believed. An ample bibliography on the critical literature surrounding the theme of *amor de lonh* is provided by R.T. Pickens in his 1978 edition, and by M. Allegretto (1979). See also G. Wolf and R. Rosenstein's edition of 1983, pp. 95–124, and G. Chiarini 1985, pp. 85–116; and his edition (1985) of Jaufre's.

35 The *amor de lonh* theme is quite frequent among the troubadours (see many instances cited in Moore 1914) who never thought of allegorizing it, as many modern critics have done.
36 On the ironic elements ensuing this situation see, in general, Gaunt 1989.
37 This is a notion used by P. Bec (1968). See also Bec 1971, and the vast work by G. Lavis (1972) where twenty-four troubadours are studied.
38 A. Limentani 1977
39 A situation similar to that of this *serena* occurs in the medieval Latin poem on Pyramus and Thisbe (edited by P. Lehman [1927, pp. 35–46]) where both lovers complain about the long wait for the night:

> Tempora cum noctis sint pacta, queruntur amantes,
>   sol quod ad occasum non properanter eat.
> 'Heu, nox tarda venit, que nos coniungere debet!
>   Et querimur tardum sideris esse iubar.
> Devotis precibus te nos, o Phebe, rogamus,
>   ut cito quadrupedes precipitare velis ...   (ll. 135–40)

[Having agreed to meet at night time, the lovers complain that the sun does not set faster. 'Alas! the night which is supposed to bring us together comes slowly; and we bewail that the stars' light is being delayed. We beg you, Apollos, that you might want plunge your horses ...'].

This anxious waiting for the night to come – a theme which may go back to Ovid *Metam.* IV, l. 91 and IV, ll. 197–9 – is not uncommon in Romance poetry: see, for example, the Old French poem *Pyramus et Thisbé* (ed. C. de Boer, Paris 1921, ll. 596–601), and Chrétien de Troye's *Le Chevalier de la charrette* (ed. M. Roques, ll. 4533–41).

40 Weinrich 1971
41 Greimas 1970, p. 203
42 The word *stage* should be more than a metaphor since troubadours' poems were indeed sung in public. This fact has vast implications for various aspects of those poems, from their composition to their textual transmission. The critical literature on the 'orality' component in troubadour poems is rather vast. For our purposes, it is sufficient to mention only Nichols 1991 because it shows that erotic elements in troubadour poems were enhanced by their public performance.
43 For the different manifestations of madness in the troubadours see Akehurst 1978 and chapter 3 of this book.

44 Surely psychoanalytic interpretations of *fin'amor* are not lacking. R. Barthes, J. Lacan, L. Irigaray, to mention the most illustrious names, are representatives of this approach (for a bibliography and a brilliant refutation of their readings see Mancini 1984, pp. 9–31). For a more historical approach to medieval narcissism see Goldin 1967; Frappier 1976; Köhler 1964a; Poirion 1970; Picone 1977; and Knoespel 1985.

45 They are all found on p. 94 of Nemesius's *Premmon Physicon*, ed. by C. Burkhard (1917). Nemesius of Emesa wrote this work towards the end of the fourth century. Besides the translation by Alfanus (d. 1084) there were several others, the most influential of which was that by Burgundius of Pisa (d. 1195). The ample circulation of this work (cf. Morani 1981) may justify our quotations in the context of a study on Andreas, who, as we have learned, was curious about 'medical' literature. The troubadours did not speak about the disease of love; the inquiry by R. Rohr (1990) relies mostly on late literature (Matfre Ermengaud's *Breviari d'Amor*), and even so there is not much 'medical' attention to the problem of love.

46 On this subject see Bundy 1927, especially ch. 9; Wolfson 1935; and Klubertanz 1952, especially chs 3 and 4.

47 In order to understand this difference, one can say that the *vis imaginativa* combines images in a way that may not have a correspondence in reality (from the most common metaphor to the *adynata*), whereas the *vis cogitativa*, which is an embryo of intelligence, *feels*, as it were, the possible or the impossible: in other words, it nourishes the hope and the despair.

48 *Liber de anima*, IV I, ll. 79–88: 'Deinde aliquando diiudicamus de sensibilibus per intentiones quas non sentimus, aut ideo in natura sua non sunt sensibiles ullo modo, aut quia sunt sensibiles sed nos non sentimus in hora iudicii. Sed quae non sunt sensibiles ex natura sua sunt sicut inimicitia et malitia et quae a se diffugiunt quam apprehendit ovis de forma lupi et omnino intentio quae facit eam fugere ab illo, et concordia quam apprehendit de sua socia et omnino intentio qua gratulatur cum illa: sunt res quas apprehendit anima sensibilis ita quod sensus non doceat eam aliquid de his; ergo virtus qua haec apprehenduntur est alia virtus et vocatur aestimativa' (vol. 2, pp. 6–7) [Then sometimes we judge about sensible things because by their nature they are not sensible in any way, or because they are sensible but we do not sense them at the moment of judgment. But things which are not sensible by their nature are things like enmity, malice, and mutual adversion: this is what a sheep apprehends concerning the form of the wolf; and it is absolutely this intentio that makes her escape from him. Such is also the concord which the sheep apprehends concerning her mate and what causes the latter to like her. There are, thus,

things that the sensible soul apprehends even if the external senses have taught nothing about them. Therefore the power by which these things are apprehended is a different power (virtus, called estimative power)].

49 For a bibliography on the 'lover's malady' see n. 59 of chapter 1. The etiology of the disease of love is essentially the same in all medical treatises: the memory repeatedly provides to the *cogitativa* the image which the *aestimativa* found so delightful. The subsequent cogitation is intense, and because of it the heart increases its beats and pumps 'vital spirits' or nervous energy, to the brain in order to sustain the cogitation. But since the spirits are rushed, they become warmer than normal, thus altering the body's temperature; consequently, the melancholic, or black, humour prevails over the other humours, which can bring on a melancholic condition that, in severe cases, even produces death.

50 'Sometimes, indeed, a man can be in love without ever seeing the object of his love; but that love which urges one with fury has its origin in the eyesight.' These lines are taken from the sonnet *Amor è uno desio che ven dal core* (ed. G. Contini 1960, vol. 1, p. 90). In this sonnet, Giacomo da Lentini answers a question on the nature of love asked by Jacopo Mostacci. His answer is strictly scientific, drawn from the medical literature. The first to notice the similarities between the thesis of this sonnet and Andreas's definition of love was B. Nardi (1942, p. 15 f.)

51 Among the most recent essays on this subject are Desmond 1982, Kay 1985, and Monson 1987.

52 *Paradox sur le comédien.* Some passages of this work could have been written for any troubadour – one example: 'S'irrite, s'indigne, se désespère, présent à mes yeux l'image réelle, porte a mon oreille et à mon coeur l'accent vrai de la passion qui l'agite au point qu'il m'entraine, que je m'ignore moi-même, que ce n'est plus ni Brizard, ni Le Kain, mais Agamennon que je vois, mais Néron que j'entends ... etc., d'abandonner à l'art tous les autres instants ... je pense que peut-être alors il en est de la nature comme de l'esclave qui apprend à se mouvoir librement sous la chaîne: l'habitude de la porter lui en dérobe le poids et la contrainte' (ed. P. Vernière 1965, p. 369). On this paradox see also the enlightening chapter 'Spontaneity and Convention' in Hauser 1982, pp. 18–39. But one should not forget that the actor's paradox had first been pointed out by St Augustine in a way very similar to that of Diderot: 'Quia scilicet aliud est falsum esse velle, aliud verum esse non posse. Itaque ipsa opera hominum, velut comoedias aut tragoedias aut mimos, et id genus alia, possumus operibus pictorum fictorumque coniungere. Tam enim verus esse pictus homo non potest, quamvis in speciem hominis tendat, quam

illa quae scripta sunt in libris comicorum. Neque enim falsa esse volunt, aut ullo appetitu suo falsa sunt, sed quadam necessitate quantum fingentis arbitrium sequi potuerunt. At vero in scena Roscius voluntate falsa Hecuba erat, natura vera homo; sed illa voluntate etiam verus tragoedus, eo videlicet quo implebat institutum: falsus autem Priamum assimilabat, sed ipse non erat. Ex quo iam nascitur quiddam mirabile, quod tamen ita se habere nemo ambigit' (*Soliloquia*, II, 10). In this context one should read Spence 1988, where the analysis of troubadour as 'orators' in the line of Augustinian rhetoric bears some similarity with our idea of the troubadour as an actor whose rhetoric is controlled by the audience and by the poet.

53 Here is the original text by this Portuguese poet, one of the greatest of this century:

O poeta é um fingidor.
Finge tão completamente
Que chega a fingir que é dor
A dor que deveras sente.

54 For an insight into the role of Natura in the civilization of the twelfth century see Chenu 1957; Gregory 1955; Wetherbee 1972; Economou 1972; and, in particular, on Natura and the troubadours, Kaehne 1983, pt. 2, pp. 210–27. See also Frank 1988.

55 One should not forget that intense contacts existed between William IX and the school of Chartres; this relation is relevant to our argument in so far as it ties more concretely the troubadours' culture to the new learning and the new ethics of Chartres (cf. Bezzola 1944–60, vol. 2, pp. 255–62).

56 *Don Quijote*, pt. 2, ch. 9: 'en todos los días de mi vida no he visto a la sin par Dulcinea, ni jamás los umbrales de su palacio, y que sí lo estoy enamorado de oídas y de la gran fama que tiene de hermosa y discreta' (ed. J. García Soriano and J. Morales, Madrid 1960, p. 1069).

57 Part II, ch. 32 (transl. by R. Smith, 1932, p. 283

THE *ADYNATA*

1 An attempt to define and distinguish these different styles is that by L.M. Paterson (1975). For further bibliographical indications see n. 85.

2 For this notion of *écart*, which allows the passage from the paradigmatic to the syntagmatic level, see P. Zumthor (1963), who borrows it from P. Valéry. The understanding of the texture of courtly poetry owes a

great deal to the seminal ideas of P. Zumthor, R. Guiette (1960), and R. Dragonetti (1960).
3 *Ars poetica*, ll. 47–8: 'Dixeris egregie notum si callida verbum Reddiderit iunctura novum' (You will egregiously express yourself if a skilful construction will give a new twist to a common word).
4 The notion of literary *topoi*, as established by E.R. Curtius (1953 [1948]), has won many followers. An idea of the impact Curtius's method has had on both the theoretical and the historical areas can be drawn from the anthologies of P. Jehn (1972) and M.L. Baeumer (1973). It is a common assumption – one which is held throughout this book – that the poetry of the troubadours is made up of clichés. This, however, should not allow us to ignore the views recently proposed by J. Gruber (1983), who maintains that one of the motivating forces behind troubadour lyrics is an intertextual operation and that therefore many poems must be read as interpretations of previous ones by the same poets or by other poets with the aim of lifting (the *Aufhebung* of Hegelian brand) their sense to a higher spiritual level. Thus the poetry of the troubadours should not be labelled as 'Poesie der Gemeinplätze' but as 'hermeneutische Lyrik.' The study of the reception within the world of the troubadours, presented with some variations by M.L. Meneghetti (1984) and S. Kay (1987, 1991), is quite stimulating in so far as it offers a series of new insights into troubadour poetry: for one thing it ensues that the troubadour tradition is less static than other traditions such as that of the northern *trouvères*; it sheds new light on the ambiguity (hence the possibility of or the need for interpretation) of troubadour poetry; and it sheds new light on the notion of subjectivity (the point of view of the interpreter), on the problem of 'sincerity,' and on the relation between the troubadour and his audience. Undoubtably this line of investigation will rally many scholars. For our typological purposes, it offers an indirect support to the fact that troubadour poetry is particularly prone to use *topoi*: every interpretation (can one call it rewriting?) implies a degree of 'appropriation' of the material interpreted; if this is the zero degree, that is, a theme, a motif in its neutral form, we can call it a *topos*.
5 Curtius 1953 [1948], pp. 94–8; the reference to Arnaut Daniel is on p. 97, n. 27.
6 The studies on the *adynata* and the 'world upside down' theme are numerous and include (in a chronological order) Demling 1898; Pirrone 1914; De Cavazzani Sentieri 1919; Coon 1928; Canter 1930; Schultz-Gora 1932; Fucilla 1936; Dutoit 1936; Cocchiara 1963; Cherchi 1971; Babcock 1972; and Angeli 1978. For the frequence of *adynata* in periods other than medieval, also see Colie 1966 and Genette 1966, the first ch.: 'L'univers réversible.'

7 This is precisely what O. Schultz-Gora (1932) does.
8 *Sat.* VI, l. 165
9 *Ars rhetorica* (ed. L. Calboli Montefusco), I, 4. According to Fortunatianus's definition (the first one ever as far as I can ascertain) the *adynaton* belongs to the mode of argumentation called *asystata*, that is, arguments which are 'inconsistent' ('non consistunt') or incongruent. Fortunatianus's entire passage reads as follows: 'Quae est adynatos? cum id in themate ponitur, quod sit contra naturae fidem, ut si infans accusetur adulteri, quod cum uxore cubarit aliena' [What is an *adynaton*? When one brings up a fact which is against normal credibility, like, for instance, an infant being accused of adultery because he was in bed with someone else's wife].
10 *Adagia*, 1603, p 182. The definition appears in the *adagium* 'in aere piscari, venari in mari.' Among the thousands of proverbial expressions Erasmus collects are many classical 'inanes operae.' Akin to the inane endeavours are what Erasmus calls 'inaequales pensationes,' that is, 'error non in re sed in scientia' [an error not in a thing itself but the way in which one perceives it]. Under this label Erasmus catalogues many sayings such as 'pilos pro lana,' 'umbra pro corpore,' 'pro malo cane suem,' etc. These types of confusions inevitably lead to 'inane' undertakings, and they presuppose a state of madness, as we shall see among the troubadours.
11 Cf. Norden 1918, pp. 285 f.
12 *Inst. orat.* 8: 73 f. 'Cacozelia' may be rendered as 'unsuccessful striving towards a strong rhetorical effect.' It is, essentially, a hyperbole in bad taste. See Jocelyn 1979.
13 In *MGH, Auctores Antiquissimi*, vol. 10, p. 411. On the Christian paradoxality see Leclercq 1963.
14 *MGH, Poetae Aevi Carolini*, vol. 2, p. 392
15 For a bibliography on this genre see Lazzari 1965 and Bultot 1963–5.
16 Ed. by N.M. Häring (1978). The lines quoted belong to the *metrum quintum* – respectively 1–4, 9–11, and 25–8 on pp. 842–4.
17 From the poem *Aujatz de chan, com enans'e meillura* (ed. A. Roncaglia 1957), l. 16
18 I am thinking, for instance, of a poem by Walter of Châtillon which has remarkable thematic similarities with Marcabru's compositions:

>Ecce torpet probitas
>virtus sepelitur;
>fit iam parca largitas
>parcitas largitur
>verum dicit falsitas
>veritas mentitur.

Notes to pages 86–7   153

> Regnat avaritia
> regnant et avari;
> mente quivis anxia
> nititur ditari
> cum sit summa gloria
> censu gloriari ...   (ed. K. Strecker 1929, p. 180)

[Now probity languishes, virtue is buried, generosity becomes stingy, falsity tells the truth, and truth lies. Avarice reigns, and so do avaricious people; everyone is anxious to become rich, and the greatest ambition is to have glory in wealth].

19 A good *mise au point* of the discussion on this troubadour – to whom some scholars have recently attributed a few poems – can be found in M. de Riquer 1975, vol. 1, pp. 142–7.
20 See Rajna 1928.
21 'A sweet love in a bower or behind a curtain' (ed. Jeanroy, II, ll. 12–13)
22 Nelli 1963
23 Marcabru is one of the better-studied troubadours, yet we still do not have a good edition of his poems (Dejeanne's appeared in 1909 and is certainly praiseworthy, but it could be greatly improved), and no comprehensive studies on him have appeared since Appel 1923 and Errante 1948, the latter having a very specific focus. For a bibliography on Marcabru see Pirot 1967 and Taylor 1977, pp. 89–99. Excellent studies of Marcabru's 'trobar naturau' are those by A. Roncaglia (1969), and L.E. Topsfield (1975, pp. 70–107). See also Lawner 1973 and Gaunt 1990.
24 According to G.M. Cropp (1975, p. 38), Cercamon was the first to use the expression *fin'amors*. This is possible, especially if we believe the *vida* which tells us that Cercamon was Marcabru's teacher rather than the other way around. The question is not settled in an incontrovertible way. Recently the problem has been revived by V. Tortoreto (1976), who maintains that Marcabru followed Cercamon's teachings. See also the edition by Wolf and Rosenstein 1983. Surely the two poets were contemporaries and they were both kin to moralistic poetry. It is difficult, if not impossible, to establish the paternity of the successful expression *fin'amor*, but it seems clear that it was coined with a strong ethical connotation.
25 *Amors* and *amars* (bitterness) often go together, forming one of the most fortunate puns of Provençal and French poetry, and later even of Italian poetry. Marcabru gives *Amors* the meaning of 'venal, sexual love' (e.g., ed. Dejeanne, XXVII, ll. 13–16); but there is no question that he is also creating a pun. This pun is also used by Cercamon, perhaps even before

Marcabru: 'Amors es douza a l'intrar E amara al departir' (ed. Tortoreto IV, ll. 6–7: love is sweet at the beginning and bitter at the end). It is a classical pun as proven by E. Paratore (1965), who, however, misses capital texts in the history of the *topos*, such as the *Rhetorica ad Herennium* (VII, 14, 21), Quintilian's *Institutiones* (IX, 3, 69), St Augustine's *Sermo* 295, and Fulgentius's *De aetatibus mundi* (ed. R. Helm, p. 143, ll. 10–14). Closer to the troubadours' times the pun is still alive and well, as proven by the following passage from a letter by Hildebert of Lavardin: 'Inter amorem huius mundi et amorem Dei haec est differentia, quod huius mundi amor in principio dulcis esse videtur, sed finem habet amarum; amor vero Dei ab amaritudine incipit, sed ultima eius dulcedine plena sunt' (Migne, *PL*, CLXXI, p. 206: Between love of this world and love of God there is this difference: love of this world at the beginning seems sweet but its ending is bitter; whereas love of God begins with bitterness but its results are full of sweetness). The similarity this passage bears to the lines of Cercamon quoted above shows once again how close, indeed dependent, the troubadours are upon their medieval Latin masters. And even when it is not possible to establish for sure such a dependence (e.g., an expression such as 'to sow on sand' used by Marcabru could have its origin in a proverb rather than in one specific author) the fact that similar expressions have a literary dignity because authors have used them paves the way to expressions previously unrecorded.

26 For the study of this *pastorela* see Köhler 1952 and Olson 1976.

27 Among these students deserving mention is Bernart Marti, who seems to imitate his master in these verses depicting a topsy-turvy world:

> A, senhors, qui so cuges
> Del segle qu'aissi baysses?
> Lo dreyt torna daus l'envers.   (ed. Hopffner, II, ll. 1–3)

> [Oh, gentlemen, who would have thought that the world would fall this low? What is right turns into its opposite].

28 The best treatment of Peire's notion of love, besides A. Del Monte's 1955 introduction to his edition and the commentary to the poems, is to be found in Topsfield 1975, pp. 159–91.

29 Ed. Del Monte, III, l. 33. This paradox became quite common: see, for example, Bernart de Ventadorn (ed. Lazar, XLIV, ll. 31–2); Folquet de Marselha (ed. Stroński, XIII, l. 27); Peire Vidal (ed. Avalle, XL, l. 28). A variation on this theme is that of the undeserved punishment, of which one

example, found in a poem attributed to Berenguer de Palol, may suffice: 'Assi quom hom que senhor ochaizona Ses tort' (ed. Beretta-Spampinato I, ll. 1–2: like a man accused by his lord without having committed any wrong).

30 For this aspect and others related to irony see the chapter S. Gaunt (1989, pp. 97–120) dedicates to Peire d'Alvernha.
31 The inane attempt at sowing on a sterile terrain appears also in a *sirventes* by Gavaudan (ed. Guida, VIII, ll. 41–4), a late follower of Marcabru's style. Probably these *inanes operae* have their model in Isaiah XXXII: 20 and Matthew VII: 26.
32 The most thorough studies on Raimbaut d'Aurenga, besides W. Pattison's 1952 introduction to his edition, are Appel 1928; Topsfield 1975, pp. 137–58; and a lucid article on Raimbaut's historical position, conception of love, and stylistic solution, by M. Picone (1977). See also Serper 1986a and Vuijlsteke 1981 and 1991. For a sociological perspective see Milone 1979 and 1983.
33 See, for instance:

> Non chant per auzel ni per flor
> Ni per neu ni per gelada,
> Ni neis per freich ni per calor
> Ni per reverdir de prada;
> Ni per nuill autr'e sbaudimen
> Non chan ni non fui chantaire,
> Mas per midonz, en cui m'enten,
> Car es del mon la bellaire (ed. Pattison, XXVII, ll. 1–8)

[I do not sing either for birds or for flowers or for snow or for frost, or even for cold or for heat, or for meadows which grow green; I do not sing nor was I ever a singer except that for my lady to whom I aspire because she is the most beautiful in the world].

34 Cf. Scheludko 1937.
35 This assertion is not unique in Raimbaut's poetry; cf. another instance: 'c'adonx cug tener Dieu, o lieis don me volh temer' (XXII, ll. 15–16, which Pattison translates as: then I feel as if I possessed God, or her concerning whom I wish to hide my thought).
36 For a variety of aspects of Raimbaut's humour and irony and boastfulness, see the chapter S. Gaunt (1989, pp. 21–44) dedicates to him.
37 For a detailed analysis of Raimbaut's uses of style – be it the *ric* or *prim* or *clus* – see Paterson 1975.

38 Raimbaut's text is *Era·m platz, Giraut de Bornelh,* which is analysed in all discussions concerning the *trobar clus*; see, in particular, Mölk 1968, pp. 116–37, and Roncaglia 1968, pp. 125–50.
39 On the image of 'fishing fools,' see Paden 1986.
40 See Erasmus 1603, p. 179.
41 A statement as strong as the one just made should be softened in view of recent studies (Gruber 1983, Meneghetti 1984, and Kay 1991) that highlight frequent cases of troubadours referring (in an implicit or explicit way) to previous poems of their own, which indicates awareness of a historical (chronological) and psychological change.
42 Scheludko 1935–7, pp. 302–5. For the technique of opening a poem by a description of nature see Ross 1954, Press 1961, Picarel 1970, Rieger 1983, and Ghil 1986.
43 Eight of Raimbaut's thirty-nine poems begin with this temporal adverb.
44 Roncaglia (1975), in reviewing P. Zumthor's essay on the paragrams in troubadour lyrics (in *Romanic Review* 65, pp. 1–12), uses some of my ideas (Cherchi 1971) on this poem and expands some of my observations into a detailed phonic analysis from which I have freely drawn. His analysis goes beyond the first two lines to the whole poem, and it is worth reporting some of his results: 'nel terzo (i.e. verse) cALS...gELS, FLORS... conGLapis; nel quarto desTRENh e TRENca; con replicazioni, alliterazioni, omofonie ed anafonie fittissime e con particolare insistenza su trasposizioni seriali (5 morZ QUILS SISCLes, 18 eRON NOiRit, 21 BAS et AB Siscles con 22 BAStos, 23 meNASsas ANS, 43 SERCAN RANCS, 38 clERCS conQUER, 39 LAu m·ALberga con 40 fALS LAuzengiers, 41 VERS aN... eNVERSe 48 TANH a CHANTador.'
45 'Articulus dicitur cum singula verba intervallis distinguuntur caesa oratione' (*Rhet. ad Herennium* IV, 19, 26). This definition is rendered as follows by H. Caplan for his Loeb edition: 'It is called articulus when single words are set apart by intervals in staccato speech' (p. 295).
46 The *versus monosyllabici* (e.g., 'Don vey morz quils, critz, brays, siscles') are often used in the *trobar prim* of Arnaut Daniel, but they are quite frequent in Raimbaut's poetry. This type of verse had its model in medieval Latin poetry; see, for instance, these lines by Eugenius Vulgarius (quoted by D. Norberg 1958, p. 59): 'Si sol est, et lux est, at sol est: igitur lux / Si non sol, non lux est, at lux est: igitur sol.' For other examples see E.R. Curtius (1953, pp. 284 f.), who points out in Ausonius the primeval source of this device.
47 The series of three subjects (*neus gels e conglapis*) and the three respective verbs (*cotz e destrenh etrenca*), distributed, as they are, on two different

lines, present a case of *versus rapportati* (see Norberg 1958, p. 60). This example prompts another observation – namely, that Raimbaut often uses a sequence of three elements, be they nouns, verbs, or adjectives; besides the example discussed here, see those in ll. 6 and 36. According to B. Spaggiari (1977, p. 270 ff.) such ternary sequences are typical of the trobar clus.

48 For the study of this *topos*, especially in the Petrarchan tradition, see Forster 1969.
49 For the identification of the 'flors enversa' with the lily see Cherchi 1972.
50 According to the *vida* (ed. Boutière-Schutz-Cluzel, 1964, p. 401), Raimbaut 'amet longa sason una domna de Proensa, que avia nom madonna Maria de Vertfuoil, et apellava la "son joglar" en sas chansos' (he loved for along time a lady from Provence whose name was Maria de Vertfuoil, and he used to call her 'his minstrel' in his poems). A. Sakari (1949) has identified this lady with the *trobairitz* Azalais de Porcairagues.
51 In his edition, p. 202
52 They are ll. 24–5 and 61–6 of the poem XVIII, *Aissi mou*; but actually only the latter place presents an *inaequale pensatio*:

> Era·m plou
> Qe·m fara sou
> Trichan ses datz;
> Et, en breu,
> vei cazer neu.
> Anz est estatz   (ll. 61–6)

[Now it is raining on me! It could be the sun for me without great deception; and, in a short time, I see snow falling. In fact it is summer].

53 One could still quote from Bernart:

> Prat me semblon vert e vermelh
> aissi com el doutz tems de mai;
> si·m te fin'amors conhd' e gai:
> neus m'es flors blanch'e vermelha   (ed. Lazar V, ll. 9–13)

[The meadows are to me green and vermillion as in the sweet time of May; fin'amor keeps me so youthful and gay that snow seems to me a white and red flower].

The last lines quoted offer an indirect proof of the fact that Raimbaut d' Aurenga's 'flors enversa' is not the 'opposite of a flower' (that is, snow) but, rather, is literally an 'inverted flower.' The *topos* of the contrast between the lover's feeling and landscape is indeed a 'common place' among the troubadours, and it is not used exclusively in the *Natureingang*. This *topos*, too, may have medieval Latin roots. I find an example in the *Epistulae duorum amantium* (ed. E. Könsgen 1974, epist. n. 18): 'Quamvis sit hiems in tempore, estuat tamen pectus meum amoris fervore' (Although it is winter, my heart is seething because of the heat of love). Another example is given in a strophe of the melancholic anonymous poem *De ramis cadunt folia*:

> Modo frigescit quid quid est
> > sed solus ego caleo;
> immo sic mihi cordi est
> > quod ardeo
> hic ignis tamen virgo est
> > qua langueo

[Now everything becomes cold, but I alone am hot. Indeed, I am in such a state that, in my heart, I am burning; but this fire is a maiden for whom I yearn].

It is interesting to remember that this text (taken from Vecchi 1958, p. 170) originates from the workshop of St Martial of Limoges, a centre that had a great importance in the development of troubadour music. This text is a *tropus conductus* which presents a rhythmic form that is transposed in many Provençal poems, such as Marcabru's *Lo vers comens quan vei del fau*.

54 Ed. Tortoreto, IV, ll. 14–15: 'Qe per lei plaing, plor e sospir, / E vau cum res enaurada' (For her I complain, cry and sigh, and go as a person who has lost his mind).

55 For other readings of this poem, see Renzi 1976, Shapiro 1984, and Planche 1986. Not as pertinent as the title seems to suggest, and in general disappointing, is Roubaud 1986.

56 On Raimbaut's *gap* see Fechner 1964, pp. 28 f.

57 The basic study on Giraut still remains Kolsen 1894. Important are also Salverda de Grave 1938, Panvini 1949, and Sharman 1983. On the relation between Giraut and Raimbaut, see Serper 1974.

58 It is probable, considering Giraut's schooling, that in this passage he had in mind the *loci* of the *inventio* which were epitomized in a medieval

mnemonic hexameter: 'quis, quid, ubi, quibus auxiliis, cur, quomodo, quando' (in Faral 1962 [1924], p. 150).

59 Kolsen classifies this poem as a riddle; so does M. de Riquer (1975, p. 499). Technically it is a *sirventes* (cf. the edition of R. Verity Sharman [1989], which, regrettably, came to my attention when this research was completed) made of *coblas reversas*, a type of composition of which the *Leys d'Amor* (ed. Anglade, book 2, pp. 152 and 153) gives two examples:

> Tu sentes greu freg en calor
> E caut arden en gran frejor;
> Le freytz te fay tot jorn suzar
> E·l cautz glatir e tremolar;
> Volontiers en dol totas horas
> Rizes et en alegrier ploras;
> En los boscz pescas los peyssos
> Et en la mar cassas leos

[You feel great cold in the heat and burning heat in a great cold. The cold always makes you sweat, and the warmth makes you chatter and tremble. Gladly, at all times, you laugh while in pain, and cry while happy. You fish fishes in the woods and hunt lions in the sea]

and this other *cobla*:

> Reumpli lo vi del tonel
> Et am lo pa talha·l cotel;
> Uebri la clau am la saralha
> E·l dalh am l'erba del prat dalha;
> Am los singlars los lebriers cassa
> Et am lo tonel fier la massa;
> Ten am la balesta lo croc
> Et ard am la lenha lo foc

[Fill up the wine with the barrel, and cut the knife with the bread; with the lock open the key, and with the grass saw the scythe; with the boar hunt the greyhounds, and with the barrel hit the hammer; hold the hook with the arbalest, and with the wood burn the fire].

Indeed a 'reversed world'! These examples, however late, show that the Occitanian world cultivated genres similar to the *fratras*, the *fratrasie*, the *sottie,* the *disparates,* which are all types of nonsense poetry where *adynata,* oxymora, *inanes operae,* and *inaequales pensationes* grow almost by parthenogenesis and create a surreal world. On these genres, but with no reference to the Provençal realm, see Arnaud 1942; Porter 1960; Zumthor 1963, pp. 161–4, and 1975, pp. 68–88; Goth 1967; Kellermann 1968; Angeli 1978. For the *disparate,* which is the Spanish version of the nonsense poetry, see Chevalier and Jammes 1962, which has a good bibliography.

60 Ed. Avalle, p. 9
61 See Battaglia 1933; Sutherland 1961, pp. 98–100; and Musso 1971.
62 Is it likely that Peire alludes here to the birth of the son of the Count Geoffrey of Brittany, called Arthur (1187)? It is not impossible, but it is unlikely: the context suggests an *impossibile expletum,* as noticed by I. Frank (1952, p. 169 n. 39), who sees in this supposed allusion the result of a pure coincidence and explains Peire's line as follows: 'J'ai enfin obtenu le fruit de ma patience obstinée, semblable à l'attente des Bretons, car le baiser que j'ai volé jadis m'est accordé à présent de plein droit.' Cf. also Avalle's commentary on p. 367.
63 It was actually possible to draw fire from snow by compressing it until it formed a lens which could then be used for lighting a fire. Avalle, commenting upon this passage and a similar one (XXXVIII, ll. 30–1), illustrates the history of this scientific notion from Seneca and Pliny down to Marbod of Rennes. Yet the context would suggest once again that Peire uses the image to convey the idea of impossibility, to coin an *adynaton* which could have some classical antecedent (see, for example, Lucretius, *De rerum natura* III, ll. 622–3). The best proof is given by the line: 'aigua doussa de mar,' which is clearly an *adynaton* for which it is possible to find a classical parallel in Seneca's *Hercules Oeteus,* l. 1583: 'fretum dulci resonabit unda' (the sea will resound with a wave of fresh water).
64 Ed. Petrocchi: 'Your courtly request pleases me so much that I cannot and I do not want to hide from you. I am Arnaut who cries and keeps singing.' This terzina is interesting not only for the etopeya of Arnaut but also for the echoes of troubadour poetry. The first line echoes Folquet de Marselha's 'Tant m'abellis l'amoros pessamens'; the first emistich of the third line echoes a line of Arnaut himself: 'Eu sui Arnaut'; and the second emistic echoes – if I am not wrong – Raimbaut d'Aurenga's 'En ploran serai chantaire' (ed. Pattison IX, l. 9: I shall sing shedding tears). Dante, however, never mentions Raimbaut in his work; but it seems unlikely that he did not know his poetry. For the reputation Arnaut enjoyed – from the Monge de Montaudon to Petrarch – sufficient indications are given by M. de Riquer 1975, p. 605 ff.

65 General and recent studies on Arnaut Daniel include Del Monte 1953, pp. 73–96; G.L. Toja's 1960 introduction to his edition, with an exhaustive bibliographical survey; Hoepffner 1955, pp. 94–9; and Topsfield 1975, pp. 195–218. Useful is also the introduction by J.J. Wilhelm 1981 to his edition. Since Arnaut was the 'miglior fabbro del parlar materno,' there are many studies devoted to his language. It will suffice to cite here Paterson 1975, pp. 186–206. Also Arnaut is the inventor of the *sestina* and, predictably, there are several studies on this aspect of Arnaut's production; for a bibliography on it see Taylor 1977, pp. 52–4.
66 Ed. Boutière, Schutz, and Cluzel 1964, p. 59
67 This concept is repeatedly stated by Arnaut, as it can be seen just in one example: ' ... Amors mi asauta / qui·ls moz ab lo son acorda. (ed. Perugi VIII, ll. 8–9: Love assaults me, love which makes words harmonize with the music). Arnaut is the first poet in vernacular who clearly identifies love not just with poetry but with artistic perfection. This was a fundamental acquisition for medieval love poetry. Perhaps Dante held Arnaut in the highest esteem because of such identification, which proves that outside the universe of love there is no real poetry. See, on this problem, Paterson 1975, pp. 187–90; and Picone 1979, pp. 32–9.
68 The allusion to the nephew of St William has been clarified by G.L. Toja (1959), and summarized in his edition (p. 306). The Vivien alluded to here is a character in the *chanson de geste* of the Guillaume cycle. His figure was proverbial for the hunger and thirst he suffered during a siege.
69 All these *adynata* seem to have a classical origin. The first one has its correspondent in Horace (*Ars poetica*, l. 230): 'dum vitat humum, nubes et inania captat' (while avoiding smoke, he snatches clouds and other empty things). The second may go back to Ovid (*Rem. Am.*, l. 122): 'Pugnat in adversas ire natator aquas' (The swimmer fights to make his way against the current). The third apparently has no classical parallel (cf. Toja's edition, p. 111); but I found one in Erasmus (p. 069) who attributes it to Plutarch: 'bove venari leporem,' that is, to hunt a hare with an ox). See, on this last *adynaton*, Spaggiari 1982.
70 Boutière, Schutz, and Cluzel 1964, p. 59
71 In his poem *Pois Peire d'Alvernh'a chantat* (ed. Klein, I, ll. 3–8). There are two recent editions of this poem; one is by M.J. Routledge (1969) and another by N. Scarone (1975).
72 I follow here Perugi's translation rather than Toja's, which reads: 'ho rimesso la mia mente a posto'; but this translation does not make sense in the poem's context.
73 See Curtius 1953, p. 97, n. 27.

74 In the poem *Abril* (ed. Jaeschke, I, l. 12)
75 The same image is also in XX, l. 32: 'Quar encaus so qu'ieu no vuelh cosseguir' (for I pursue what I do not want to attain), a line that is very closely reminiscent of Rilke's thought that 'the troubadours feared nothing more than seeing their desires fulfilled' (see Introduction, n. 9).
76 For a list of occurrences of this key word, see Cnyrim 1888, nn. 311–13; but this collection is far from being a complete or even a satisfactory list. Several new examples could be added. One is in a poem by Cadenet:

> Jes eu, dompna, no·us repren,
> Pero ben dic qu'es vertatz
> Que dompna reigna mieills assatz
> Que·l seu acorra breumen,
> Que cill que long temps lo ten en faidia   (ed. Zemp XXV, ll. 45–9)

[Far be it from me, my lady, to blame you; yet I tell what is the truth: the lady who gives succour to her lover quickly behaves much better than she who keeps him for a long time in a vain hope].

Another example comes from Arnaut de Maruelh: 'mais val belha fadia / qu'us dos dezavinens (ed. Johnston XIII, ll. 39–40: a fruitless waiting is worth more than an unliked gift [i.e. from another lady]). This motif was repeated almost *verbatim* by Berenguer de Palol (ed. Beretta Spampinato, IX, ll. 21–2: 'n'am mais la belha fadia / Qu'el don d'autra no faria': I love more the beautiful and vain waiting than I would the gift from another woman). Another instance appears in Daude de Pradas: 'qu'el beill semblan e il doutz sospir / no son messatge de fadia' (ed. Schutz I, ll. 27–8: because her beautiful looks and sweet sighs are not messengers of vain hope). Very likely a systematic canvassing of the troubadour *corpus* would provide many more examples. It should be noticed that all the examples quoted above emphasize the word *fadia* by always using it in rhyme, even when it is a verb rather than a noun, as it happens to be in a poem by Berenguer de Palaol: 'E ja Dieus amia no·m do / s'en lieys mos cors se fadia' (ed. Beretta Spampinato VII, ll. 18–19: 'And God should not grant me a lover if my heart hopes in vain for her).
77 A list in Cnyrim 1888, nn. 965–77. See also M. de Riquer's 1971 edition of Guilhem de Berguedan, vol. 2, p. 242.
78 The story of Arachne is narrated in *Metam.* VI, ll. 5–145, and the word *opus* occurs a few times, e.g., in l. 82: 'operis Victoria finis' (Victory crowns Arachne's completed work); and in ll. 129–30: 'Non illud Pallas, non illud

carpere Livor Possit opus' (Not Pallas, nor Envy itself could find [a flaw] in that work) I think that even Dante (*Purgatory* XII, ll. 43–5) uses *opera* in an allusion related to Arachne's episode having Ovidian *opus* in mind, and his usage could offer an indirect support to the interpretation proposed here. If indeed this phrase has Ovid as its model, then the expression 'obra d'aranha' should be spelled with a capital letter: 'obra d'Aragna.' Ovid's influence on the troubadours is well canvassed by Schrötter 1908, and more recently, focusing on rhetorical strategies rather than on motifs and themes, L. Cahoon 1989.

79 Avalle's commentary on this passage – after recalling two more similar instances in Peire's work – glosses 'obra d'aranha' by saying that 'sta ad indicare inconsistenza e vanità.'

80 See Cnyrim 1888, nn. 484–8, where Lucchetto's passage is missing.

81 See some examples in Cnyrim 1888, nn. 487–88.

82 On the legend of Tristan among the troubadours, see Payen 1984, with the essential bibliography, and, more pertinently for Bernart de Ventadorn, Monson 1991. For an example see Pouz de Capduoill (ed. Napolski, XXIII, 15).

83 The Virgilian expression 'Amor vincit omnia' comes from *Ecl.* X, l. 69. Bernart's version is quoted in an interesting book by E. Kohler (1935, p. 23). The military and war imagery found in the poetry of the troubadours is worthy of a more ample study than the one done in Kohler's book, which focuses primarily on German poetry. This imagery is often derived from the classical tradition. On this subject also see Spies 1931. Some indications on the 'Kriegsdienst' are given by W. Schrötter (1908, pp. 85–9). On Virgil's influence on the troubadours, see Roncaglia 1985 and Rossi 1989.

84 The use of *adynata* in moral and satyrical poetry is well documented in Thiolier-Méjean 1978. Since our present inquiry is limited to love poetry (the only exception being Marcabru and his followers, who, in any case, deal with courtly love), it is easy to see why some poets like Peire Cardinal – whose religious-moral poetry presents long chains of *adynata* resembling the medieval *contemptus mundi* – are not taken into consideration.

85 Throughout these pages I have been using the label *trobar clus* in a broad way, meaning a style which is not *leu* and as such it may also include other styles, like *trobar ric, prim, brau*, etc. The bibliography on the subject is vast. For an orientation, besides L.M. Paterson (1975), who makes the greatest effort in distinguishing among all these styles, see Del Monte 1953, Frappier 1963, Pollmann 1965, Mölk 1968, Roncaglia 1969, Köhler 1970, and a sensible *mise au point* of the whole problem in Di Girolamo 1983. The idea that the difference of styles is due in great part to the

author's desire to control and protect his own text against the modifications inevitably brought upon by its *mouvance* or transmission (mostly oral) is sponsored by A.E. Van Vleck (1991) (the *trobar clus*, for instance, is more impervious to alterations).

86 Actually Raimbaut d'Aurenga once used the name of Tristan (ed. Pattison, XXVII, ll. 29 and 37) but without any adynatic meaning. In another poem (IV, l. 24) there is an allusion to the 'bretols' but it is very unlikely that Raimbaut is referring to the 'esperansa bretona' (cf. Pattison's commentary on this line).

87 This fact can easily be checked, thanks to F.M. Chambers (1971). Arnaut uses the names of Paris and Helen once:

> tal m'abelis
> don eu ai plus de joia
> non ac Paris
> de Lena, sel de Troia.

[Such is (the lady) I like that I get more joy from it than Paris got from Helen; yes that Paris of Troy.]

But these lines (45–8) appear in a stanza of doubtful authenticity (see Perugi's ed. III, 3 str., n. 6).

88 It is line 9 of the poem *Lex pia cumque dei latum dominans regit orbem* , *MGH, Poetae Aevi Carolini*, vol. 2, p. 186. The proverbs, as it is well known, enjoyed a special function in medieval poetry which was duly acknowledged in the *artes dictandi* and in the *artes poetriae*. The *adynata* taking the form of a proverb perform a similar function.

Bibliography

ABBREVIATIONS

Archiv	Archiv für das Studium der Neueren Sprachen und Literaturen
CCM	Cahiers de Civilisation Médiévale (X^e–XIIe Siècles)
CN	Cultura Neolatina
MGH	Monumenta Germaniae Historica
Mittelalterbilder	Mittelalterbilder aus neuer Perspektive. Diskussionsanstösse zu amour courtois, Subjektivität in der Dichtung und Strategien des Erzählens, ed. by E. Ruhe and R. Behrens. Munich: Fink 1985
MP	Modern Philology
MS	Mediaeval Studies
NM	Neophilologische Mitteilungen
PL	Migne, Patrologiae cursus completus. Series latina
RF	Romanische Forschungen
RLR	Revue des Langues Romanes
RML	Revue du Moyen Age Latin
RTAM	Revue de Théologie Ancienne et Moderne
SM	Studi Medievali
Studia	Studia Occitanica in Memoriam Paul Remy, 2 vols., ed. by H.E. Keller. Kalamazoo, MI: Western Michigan University Press 1986.
ZFSL	Zeitschrift für französische Sprache und Literatur
ZRP	Zeitschrift für romanische Philologie

PRIMARY SOURCES

Abelard and Heloise. 1974. *Epistolae duorum amantium. Briefe Abaelards und Heloises*, ed. by E. Könsgen. Leiden: Brill

Bibliography

Aimeric de Peguilhan. 1950. *Poems*, ed. by W. Shepard and F. Chambers. Evanston, IL: Northwestern University Press

Alanus de Insulis. 1978. *De planctu Naturae*, ed. by N.M. Häring. In *SM* s. III, 19, 797–880

Alegret. 1907. A. Jeanroy, 'Alegret, jongleurs gascon du XIIe siècle.' In *Annales du Midi* 19, 221–31

Alfanus. 1917. *Premnon Physicon*, ed. by C. Burkhard. Leipzig: Teubner

Alighieri, Dante. 1966. *Il Convivio*, ed. by M. Simonelli. Bologna: Patron

Andreas Capellanus. 1892. *De Amore libri tres*, ed. by E. Trojel. Hauniae: Libreria Gadiana

– 1941. *The Art of Courtly Love*. Intro., trans., and notes by J. Parry. New York: Columbia University Press

– 1947. *Trattato d'amore. Testo latino del sec. XII con due traduzioni toscane inedite del sec. XIV*, ed. by S. Battaglia. Rome: Perrella

– 1974. *Traité de l'amour courtois*. Intro., trans., and notes by C. Buridant. Paris: Klincksieck

– 1980. *De amore* (with a fourteenth-century Toscan translation), ed. by G. Ruffini. Milan: Guanda

– 1982. *On Love*, ed. and trans. by P.G. Walsh. London: Duckworth

[Anonymous] 1891. *Trattato provenzale di penitenza*, ed. by C. De Lollis. In *Studi di Filologia Romanza* 5, 273–340

– 1919. *Las Leys d'Amors*, 4 vols., ed. by J. Anglade. Toulouse: Privat

– 1925. *Jaufre*, ed. by H. Breuer. Göttingen-Halle: Nimeyer

Arnaut Daniel. 1960. *Canzoni*, ed. by G. Toja. Florence: Sansoni

– 1978. *Le canzoni*, 2 vols., ed. by Perugi. Milan-Naples: Ricciardi

– 1981. *The poetry of Arnaut Daniel*, ed. by J.J. Wilhelm. New York: Garland

Arnaut de Maruelh. 1935. *Les Poésies lyriques*, ed. by R.C. Johnston. Paris: Droz

– 1961. *Les Saluts d'amour*, ed. by P. Bec. Toulouse: Privat

– 1969. 'L'ensenhamen di Arnaut de Mareuil,' ed. by M. Eusebi. In *Romania* 90, 14–30

Avicenna. 1966. *Liber Canonis*. Hildezheim: Olms [reprint of the 1507 Venetian edition]

– 1968. *Liber de anima*, ed. by S. van Riet. Louvain: Editions orientalistes

Beatritz de Dia. 1917. 'Les Chansons de la Comtesse Béatrix de Dia,' ed. by Gabrielle Kussler-Ratyé. In *Archivum Romanicum* 1, 161–82

Berenguer de Palol. 1978. *Poesie*, ed. by M. Beretta Spampinato. Modena: STEM Mucchi

Bernart, Marti. 1929. *Les Poésie*, ed. by E. Hoepffner. Paris: Champion (CFMA)

Bernart de Ventadorn. 1966. *Chansons d'amour*, ed. by M. Lazar. Paris: Klincksieck

Bonifacio, Calvo. 1955. *Le rime*, ed. by F. Branciforti. Catania: Università di Catania
Boutière, Jean, Alexander H. Schutz, and I.M. Cluzel, eds. 1964. *Biographies des Troubadours*. Paris: Nizet
Cadenet. 1978. *Les Poésies*, ed. by J. Zemp. Bern–Las Vegas: Peter Lang
Cercamon. 1922. *Les Poésies*, ed. by A. Jeanroy. Paris: Champion (CFMA)
- 1981. *Poesie*, ed. by V. Tortoreto. Modena: STEM Mucchi
- 1983. *The Poetry of Cercamon and Jaufre Rudel*, ed. by G. Wolf and R. Rosenstein. New York: Garland
Cervantes y Saavedra, Miguel de. 1932. *Don Quixote*, English trans. by R. Smith. New York: The Hispanic Society of America
- 1960. *El ingenioso hidalgo Don Quijote de la Mancha*, ed. by J. García Soriano and J. García Morales. Madrid: Aguilar
Cerveri de Girona. 1947. *Obras completas*, ed. by M. de Riquer. Barcelona: Instituto Español de Estudios Mediterráneos
Constantinus Africanus. 1536. *Opera*. Basel: H. Petrum
Dalfin d'Alvernhe. See Perdigon, below.
Daude de Pradas. 1879. *The Romance of Daude de Pradas on the Four Cardinal Virtues*, ed. by A. Stickney. Florence: Würtenberg
- 1933. *Poésies*, ed. by A. Schutz. Toulouse: Privat
Donna H. 1888. *Partimen*, with Rofin, ed. by O. Schultz-Gora
- 1991. Ed. by A. Rieger
Elias de Barjols. 1906. *Le Troubadour Elias de Barjols*, ed. by S. Stroński. Toulouse: Privat
Elias Cairel. 1921. *Der Trobador Elias Cairel*, ed. by H. Jaeschke. Berlin: Ebering
Folquet de Marselha. 1910. *Le troubadour Folquet de Marseille*, ed. by S. Stroński. Cracovie: Académie des Sciences
Fortunatianus Chirius. 1979. *Ars rhetorica*, ed. by L. Calboli Montefusco. Bologna: Patron
Gaucelm Faidit. 1965. *Les poèmes*, ed. by J.D. Mouzat. Paris: Nizet
Gavaudan. 1905. *Poesie*, ed. by S. Guida. Modena: STEM Mucchi
- 1979. *Les poèsies*, ed. by A. Jeanroy. In *Romania* 34, 497–539
Giraut de Bornelh. 1916–19. *Sämtliche Lieder des Trobadors Giraut de Bornelh*, 2 vols., ed. by A. Kolsen. Halle: Niemeyer
- 1989. *The Cansos and Sirventes of the Troubadour Giraut de Borneil*, ed. By Ruth Verity Sharman. Cambridge: Cambridge University Press
Guilhem, Ademar. 1951. *Poésies*, ed. by K. Almqvist. Uppsala: Almqvist and Wiksell
Guilhem de Berguedan. 1971. *Guillem de Berguedá*, 2 vols., ed. by M. de Riquer. Abadía de Poblet: Scriptorium Populeti

Guilhem de Cabestanh. 1924. *Les chansons*, ed. by A. Längfors. Paris: Champion (CFMA)
Guilhem de Montanhagol. 1964. *Les Poésies*, ed. by P.T. Ricketts. Toronto: Pontifical Institute of Medieval Studies
Guilhem de Peitieu. 1973. *Poesie*, ed. by N. Pasero. Modena: STEM Mucchi
Guilhem de Saint-Leider. 1956. *Poésies*, ed. by A. Sakari. Helsinki: Société Néophilologique
Guilhem Magret. 1914. *Der Trobador Guillem Magret*, ed. by Fritz Naudieth. Halle: Niemeyer
Guiraut de Calanso. 1930. 'Die Lieder des provenzalischen Dichters Guiraut von Calanso,' ed. by E. Willy. In *RF* 44, 255–406
– 1930. *Das Sirventes 'Fadet joglar,'* ed. by W. Keller. Erlange: Junge
Guiraut Riquier. 1962. *Las Cansos*, ed. by U. Mölk. Heidelberg: Winter
Hildebertus de Lovardino. *De quattuor virtutibus vitae honestae*. PL 171, 1055–64
Jaufre Rudel. 1924. *Les chansons*, ed. by A. Jeanroy. Paris: Champion (CFMA)
– 1978. *The Songs*, ed. by R. Pickens. Toronto: Pontifical Institute of Medieval Studies
– 1983. *The Poetry of Cercamon and Jaufre Rudel*, ed. by G. Wolf and R. Rosenstein. New York: Garland
– 1985. *Il canzoniere di Jaufre Rudel*, ed. by Giorgio Chiarini. L'Aquila: Japadre
Jausbert de Puycibot. 1924. *Les poésies*, ed. by W.P. Shepard. Paris: Champion (CFMA)
Lanfranc Cigala. 1954. *Il Canzoniere*, ed. by F. Branciforti. Florence: Olschki
Luquet Gatelus. 1957. *[Lucchetto Gattilusio]: Liriche*, ed. by M. Boni. Bologna: Palmaverde
Marcabru. 1909. *Poésies complètes*, ed. by J.M.L. Dejeanne. Toulouse: Privat
– 1957. 'Aujatz de chan, com enans'e meillura,' ed. by A. Roncaglia. In *CN* 17, 20–48
– 1968. 'La tenzone fra Ugo Catola e Marcabruno,' ed. by A. Roncaglia. In *Linguistica e Filologia: Omaggio a Benvenuto Terracini*, 203–54. Milan: Il Saggiatore
Matfre Ermengau. 1862–81. *Le Breviari d'Amor*, 2 vols., ed. by Gabriel Azaïs. Béziers-Paris
Mir Bernart (in a *partimen* with Sifre). 1938. 'Zwei provenzalische "partimen" und zwei "coblas",' ed. by A. Kolsen. In *SM*, n.s. 12, 183–91
Monge de Montaudon. 1885. *Die Dichtungen*, ed. by O. Klein. Marburg: Elwert
– 1975. 'Pois Peire d'Alvernh'a chantat.' See Routledge 1969 and Scarone 1975 under Secondary Sources, below.
N'At de Mons. 1887. *Die Werke*, ed. by W. Bernhardt. Heilbronn: Henninger
Peire Bremon Ricas Novas. 1930. *Les Poésies*, ed. by J. Boutière. Toulouse: Privat

Peire Cardenal. 1957. *Poésies complètes*, ed. by R. Lavaud. Toulouse: Privat
Peire d'Alvernha. 1955. *Liriche*, ed. by A. Del Monte. Turin: Chiantore
Peire Ramon de Tolosa. 1935. *Le poesie*, ed. by A. Cavaliere. Florence: Olschki
Peire Rogier. 1976. *The Poems*, ed. by D. Nicholson. Manchester: Manchester University Press
Peire Vidal. 1960. *Poesie*, 2 vols., ed. by D.S. Avalle. Milan-Naples: Ricciardi
Peirol. 1953. *Peirol Troubadour of Auvergne*, ed. by S.C. Aston. Cambridge: Cambridge University Press
Perdigon. 1926. *Les chansons*, ed. by H.J. Chaytor. Paris: Champion (CFMA)
Pessoa, Fernando. 1983. *Obra poética*, ed. by M. Aliete Galhoz. Rio de Janeiro: Aguilar
Pistoleta. 1914. *Der Trobador Pistoleta*, ed. by E. Niestroy. Halle: Niemeyer
Ponz de Capduoill. 1879. *Leben und Werke*, ed. by M. von Napolski. Halle: Niemeyer
Rabanus Maurus. *Carmina*, in *PL* 113, 1585–1676. ['Carmen ad Eigilum de libro quem scripserat' is on p. 1601.]
Raimbaut d'Aurenga. 1952. *The Life and Works*, ed. by W.T. Pattison. Minneapolis: Minnesota University Press
– 1968. 'Cars douz,' ed. by J.H. Marshall, 'On the Text and Interpretation of a Poem of Raimbaut d'Orange.' In *Medium Aevum* 37, 12–36
Raimbaut de Vaqueiras. 1964. *The Poems*, ed. by J. Linskill. The Hague: Mouton
Raimon Jordan. 1922. *Le Troubadour Raimon Jordan*, ed. by H. Kjellman. Uppsala: Almqvist
Raimon de Miraval. 1971. *Les Poésies*, ed. by L.T. Topsfield. Paris: Nizet
Rambertino de Buvalelli. 1978. *Le poesie*, ed. by E. Melli. Bologna: Patron
Rigaut de Berbezilh. 1960. *Liriche*, ed. by A. Varvaro. Bari: Adriatica
Rofin. See Donna H., above.
Sifre. See Mir Bernart, above.
Sordel. 1954. *Le poesie*, ed. by M. Boni. Bologna: Palmaverde
William of Conches. 1929. *Das Moralium dogma philosophorum*, ed. by J. Holmberg. Uppsala: Almqvist

SECONDARY SOURCES

Agamben, Giorgio. 1977. *Stanze. La parola e il fantasma nella cultura occidentale*. Turin: Einaudi
Akehurst, Frank R.P. 1973. 'Les étapes de l'amour chez Bernard de Ventadour.' *CCM* 16, 133-47
– 1978. 'La folie chez les troubadours.' *Mélanges Charles Camproux*, 19–28. Montpellier: Centre d'Estudis Occitans

Allegretto, Manuela. 1979. *Il luogo dell'amore. Studio su Jaufré Rudel.* Florence: Olschki
Angeli, Giovanna. 1978. *Il mondo rovesciato.* Rome: Bulzoni
Anglade, Joseph. 1929. 'Peire Vidal et le *Liber de nobilitate animi.*' *SM* 2, 445–6
Appel, Carl. 1902. *Provenzalische Chrestomathie,* 2d ed. Leipzig: Reisland
– 1923. 'Zu Marcabru.' *ZRP* 43, 403–69
– 1928. *Raimbaut von Orange.* Berlin: Weidmann
Arnaud, Leonard E. 1942. *French Nonsense Literature in the Middle Ages. The 'Fratras' and Its Later Evolution.* New York: New York University Press
Avalle, D'Arco Silvio. 1977. *Ai luoghi di delizia pieni.* Milan–Naples: Ricciardi
Babcock, Barbara, ed. 1978. *The Reversible World. Forms of Symbolic Inversion Symposium. Toronto 1972.* Ithaca: Cornell University Press 1978
Baeumer, Max L. 1973. *Toposforschung.* Darmstadt: Wissenschaftliche Buchgesellschaft
Battaglia, Salvatore. 1933. 'La poesia di Peire Vidal.' In *Studi Romanzi* 33, 137–64
Bec, Pierre. 1968. 'La douleur et son univers poétique chez Bernard de Ventadour.' *CCM* 11, 549–71
– ed. 1970. *Présence des Troubadours.* Toulouse, *Annales de l'Institute d'études occitanes,* n. 5
– 1971. 'L'antithèse poétique chez Bernard de Ventadour.' *Mélanges Jean Boutière,* 107–37. Liège: Soledi
– 1981. *Burlesque et obscénité chez les troubadours: Pour une approche du contre-texte médiéval.* Paris: Stock
Benton, John F. 1961. 'The Court of Champagne as a Literary Center.' *Speculum* 36, 551–91
– 1968. 'Clio and Venus: An Historical View of Medieval Love.' In Newman, ed., 1968, 19–42
Bezzola, Reto. 1944–63. *Les Origines et la formation de la littérature courtoise en Occident,* 5 vols. Paris: Champion
Boase, Roger. 1977. *The Origin and Meaning of Courtly Love. A Critical Study of European Scholarship.* Manchester: Manchester University Press
Bowden, Betsy. 1979. 'The Art of Courtly Copulation.' *Medievalia et Humanistica* 9, 67–85
Briffault, Robert S. 1945. *Les Troubadours et le sentiment romanesque.* Paris: Les Editions du Chêne
Brinkmann, Hennig. 1925. *Geschichte der lateinischen Liebesdichtung im Mittelalter.* Halle: Niemeyer
– 1926. *Entstehungsgeschichte des Minnesangs.* Halle: Niemeyer
Bruno, Roy, ed. 1977. *L'erotisme au Moyen Age. Etudes présentés au troisième colloque de l'Institut d'études médiévales de l'Université de Montréal.* Montreal: L'Aurore

Bultot, Robert. 1963. *La doctrine du mépris du monde en Occident, de S. Ambrose à Innocent III*, 6 vols. (of which only 4 have appeared). Louvain: Nauwelaerts
Bundy, M.W. 1927. *The Theory of Imagination in Classical and Medieval Thought*. University of Illinois Studies in Language and Literature 12
Burgess, Glyn S. 1970. *Contribution à l'étude du vocabulaire pré-courtois*. Geneva: Droz
Busse, Wilhelm G. 1975. *Courtly Love oder Paramours. Die Liebesauffassungen in der mittelenglischen Literatur vor dem medizinischen und moraltheologischen Hintergrund der Zeit*. Düsseldorf: Stern
Butturff, Douglas R. 1974. 'The Comedy of Coquetry in Andreas' *De Amore*.' *Classical Folia* 28, 181–90
Cahoon, Leslie. 1989. 'The Anxieties of Influence: Ovid's Reception by Early Troubadours.' *Mediaevalia: A Journal of Mediaeval Studies* 13, 119–55
Calin, William. 1980. 'Defense and Illustration of *Fin'Amor*: Some Polemical Comments on the Robertsonian Approach.' In Smith and Snow 1980, 32–48
Camproux, Charles. 1969. 'Les troubadours.' *RLR* 78, 71–97
Canter, H.C. 1930. 'The Figure 'ΑΔΥΝΑΤΟΝ in Greek and Latin Poetry.' *American Journal of Philology* 5, 31–44
Capusso, Maria Grazia. 1987. 'Le tre frecce d'amore nella canzone allegorica di Guiraut de Calanson "Celeis cui am de cor e de saber."' In *Actes du Premier Congrès International de l'Association Internationale d'Études Occitanes*, ed. by Peter T. Ricketts, 157–70. London: Westfield College
Casella, Mario. 1938. 'Poesia e storia. II: Jaufre Rudel.' *Archivio Storico Italiano* 94, 153–99
Chambers, Frank M. 1971. *Proper Names in the Lyrics of the Troubadours*. Chapel Hill: University of North Carolina Press
Chenu, M.D. 1957. *La théologie au douzième siècle*. Paris: Vrin
Cherchi, Paolo. 1971. 'Gli adynata dei trovatori.' *MP* 68: 223–41
– 1972a. '"Mare amoroso" (v.121) e "la flors enversa" di Raimbaut d'Aurenga.' *Romania* 93, 77–84
– 1972b. 'Notula sull'amore lontano di Jaufre Rudel.' *CN* 32, 185–7
– 1979. 'Andreas' *De Amore*: Its Unity and Polemical Origin.' In *Andrea Capellano, i trovatori e altri temi romanzi*, 83–111. Rome: Bulzoni
– 1985. 'New Uses of Andreas' *De Amore*.' *Mittelalterbilder*, 22–30
– 1989. 'Amor cortese.' *Medioevo Romanzo* 14, 161–3
Cherniss, Michael D. 1975. 'The Literary Comedy of Andreas Capellanus.' *MP* 72, 223–37
Chevalier, M., and R. Jammes. 1962. 'Supplément aux coplas de disparates.' *Mélanges M. Bataillon*, 358–93. Bordeaux: Feret
Chiarini, Giorgio. 1985. *Gli artifici del trobar*. Pisa: Cursi

Chydenius, J. 1970. *The Symbolism of Love in Medieval Thought*. Commentationes Humanarum Literarum 44. Helsinki

Ciavolella, Massimo. 1976. *La malattia d'amore dall'antichità al medioevo*. Rome: Bulzoni

Cnyrim, Eugen. 1888. *Sprichwörter, sprichwörtliche Redensarten und Sentenzen bei den provenzalischen Lyrikern*. Marburg: N.G. Elwert

Cocchiara, Giuseppe. 1963. *Il Mondo alla rovescia*. Turin: Boringhieri

Colby, Alice. 1965. *The Portrait in Twelfth-Century French Literature: An Example of the Stylistic Originality of Chrétien de Troyes*. Geneva: Droz

Colie, Rosalie. 1966. *Paradoxia Epidemica*. Princeton, NJ: Princeton University Press

Contini, Gianfranco. 1957. 'Prehistoire de "l'aura" de Pétrarque.' *Actes et mémoires du Ier Congrès International de Langue et Littérature du Midi de la France*, 113–18. Avignon: Palais du Roure

– ed. 1960. *Poeti del Duecento*, 2 vols. Milan-Naples: Ricciardi

Coon, Raymond H. 1928. 'The Reversal of Nature as a Rhetorical Figure.' *Indiana University Studies* 15/80, 1–20

Corti, Maria. 1959. 'Le fonti del Fiore di virtù e la teoria della nobiltà nel Duecento.' *Giornale Storico della Letteratura Italiana* 136, 1–82

Crohns, Hjalmar J. 1905. 'Zur Geschichte der Liebe als Krankheit.' *Archiv für Kulturgeschichte* 3, 66–86

Cropp, Glynnis M. 1975. *Le Vocabulaire courtois des troubadours de l'époque classique*. Geneva: Droz

Curtius, Ernst Robert. 1953 [1948]. *European Literature and the Latin Middle Ages*, trans. by W.R. Trask. Princeton, NJ: Princeton University Press

De Bruyne, Edgar. 1946. *Etudes d'esthétique médiévale*, 3 vols. Bruges: De Tempel

De Cavazzani Sentieri, A. 1919. 'Sulla figura dell'ἀδύνατον.' *Athenaeum* 7, 179–84

Delhaye, Philippe. 1949/1950. 'Une Adaptation du "De officiis" au XIIe siècle: Le "Moralium dogma philosophorum."' *RTAM* 16, 227–58 and 17, 5–28

– 1953. *Gautier de Châtillon est-il l'auteur du 'Moralium dogma philosophorum'? Analecta medievalia namurcensia* 3

– 1958. 'Grammatica et ethica.' *RTAM* 25, 59-100

Del Monte, Alberto. 1953. *Studi sulla poesia ermetica medievale*. Naples: Giannini

Demats, Paule. 1970. 'D'"Amoenitas" à "Déduit": André le Chapelain et Guillaume de Lorris.' *Mélanges Jean Frappier*, 2, 217–33. Geneva: Droz

Dembowski, Peter. 1986. 'Mesura dans la poésie lyrique de l'ancien provençal.' *Studia* 2, 269–80

Demling, Johann. 1898. *De poetarum latinorum ἐκ τοῦ ἀδυνάτου comparationibus*. Würzburg: Programm Neues Gymnasium

Denomy, Alexander J. 1945. '*Fin'Amors*: The Pure Love of the Troubadours, Its Amorality and Possible Source.' *MS* 7, 139–207
- 1946. 'The "De Amore" of Andreas Capellanus and the Condemnation of 1277.' *MS* 8, 107–49
- 1947. *The Heresy of Courtly Love*. New York: D.X. McMullen
- 1949. ' "Jovens": The Notion of Youth among the Troubadours, Its Meaning and Source.' *MS* 14, 1–22
Deroy, Jean P. Th. 1971. 'Mercé ou la quinta linea Veneris.' *Actes du VIIe Congrès International de Langue et Littérature d'Oc et d'Etudes Franco-Provençales*, 309–28. Montpellier: Centre d'Estudis Occitans
Desmond, M.R. 1982. 'Catullus and Bernard de Ventadorn: The Rhetoric of Sincerity.' *NM* 83, 405–13
Di Capua, Francesco. 1959. *Scritti Minori*, 2 vols. Rome: Desclé
Diderot, Denis. 1965. *Oeuvres esthétiques*, ed. by P. Vernier. Paris: Garnier
Diez, Friedrich 1883 [1826]. *Die Poesie der Troubadours*. Leipzig: Barth
Di Girolamo, Costanzo. 1983. 'Trobar clus e trobar leu.' *Medioevo Romanzo* 8, 11–35
Donaldson, Ethelbert Talbot. 1965. 'The Myth of Courtly Love.' *Ventures – Magazine of the Yale Graduate School* 5, 16–23
Dragonetti, Roger. 1959. 'Trois motifs de la lyrique courtoise confrontés avec les "Arts d'aimer."' *Romanica Gandensia* 7, 5–48
- 1960. *La Technique poétique des trouvères dans la chanson courtoise. Contribution à l'étude de la rhétorique médiévale*. Bruges: De Tempel
Dronke, Peter. 1963. Review of Schlösser 1960. *Medium Aevum* 32, 56–60
- 1965–6. *Medieval Latin and the Rise of European Love Lyric*, 2 vols. Oxford: Oxford University Press
Duby, George. 1964. 'Les "jeunes" dans la société aristocratique dans la France du Nord–Ouest au XIIe siècle.' *Annales* 19, 835–46
- 1980. *The Three Orders*, trans. by A. Goldhammer. Chicago: University of Chicago Press. (Pages 338–46 are devoted to Andreas Capellanus.)
Dutoit, Ernest. 1936. *Le Thème de l'adynaton dans la poétique*. Paris: Les Belles Lettres
Ecker, Lawrence. 1934. *Arabischer, provenzalischer und deutscher Minnesang*. Bern-Leipzig: Haupt
Economou, G. 1972. *The Goddess Nature in Medieval Literature*. Cambridge, MA: Harvard University Press
Ehrismann, Gustav. 1919. 'Die Grundlagen der ritterlichen Tugend systems.' *Zeitschrift für deutsches Altertum* 46, 137–216
Eifler, G., ed. 1970. *Ritterliches Tugend System*. Darmstadt: Wissenschaftliche Buchgesellschaft

Erasmus, Desiderius. 1603. *Adagia*. Ursellis: Hackett Winfrid
Errante, Guido. 1948. *Marcabru e le fonti sacre dell'antica lirica romanza*. Florence: Sansoni
Faral, Edmond. 1962 [1924]. *Les Arts poétiques du XIIe et du XIIIe siècles*. Paris: Champion
Favati, Guido. 1945. 'Prodezza e voci affini nei primi secoli della letteratura italiana.' *Annali della Scuola Normale Superiore di Pisa*. s. 2, 14, 45–60
– 1970. 'L'innovazione di Guglielmo IX d'Aquitania e un canto di Marbodo di Rennes.' In Pierre Bec 1970, 65–76. A new version is the first chapter of G. Favati 1975
– 1975. *Inchiesta sul Dolce Stil Nuovo*. Florence: Le Monnier
Fechner, J.U. 1964. 'Zum Gap in der altprovenzalischen Lyrik.' *Germanisch-romanische Monatschrift*, n.s. 16, 15–34
Ferrante, Joan M. 1980a. 'Ab joi mou lo vers e 'l comens.' In *The Interpretation of Medieval Lyric Poetry*, 113–41, ed. by W.T.H. Jackson. New York: Columbia University Press
– 1980b. '"Cortes' Amor" in Medieval Texts.' *Speculum* 55, 686–95
Forster, Leonard W. 1969. *The Icy Fire – Five Studies in European Petrarchism*. Cambridge: Cambridge University Press
Frank, Grace. 1942. 'The Distant Love of Jaufré Rudel.' *Modern Language Notes* 57, 528–34
Frank, István. 1952. *Trouvères et Minnesänger*. Saarbrücken: West-Ost
Frank, K. Donald. 1988. *Naturalism and the Troubadour Ethic*. New York: Peter Lang
Frappier, Jean. 1959. 'Vues sur les conceptions courtoises dans les littératures d'Oc et d'Oïl au XIIe siècle. *CCM* 2, 135–56
– 1963. 'Aspects de l'hermétisme dans la poésie médiévale.' *CCM* 15, 9–24
– 1971. 'Amour courtois.' *Mélanges Jean Boutière*, 33–41. Liège: Soledi
– 1972. 'Sur un procès fait à l'amour courtois.' *Romania* 93, 145–93
– 1976. 'Variations sur le thème du miroir de Bernard de Ventadour à Maurice Scève.' *Histoire, mythes et symboles*, 149–67. Geneva: Droz
Friedman, Lionel J. 1965–6. 'Gradus amoris.' *Romance Philology* 19, 167–77
Fucilla, Joseph G. 1936. 'Petrarchism and the Modern Vogue of the Figure 'ΑΔΥΝΑΤΟΝ.' *ZRP* 56, 671–81
Gaunt, Simon B. 1989. *Troubadour and Irony*. Cambridge: Cambridge University Press
– 1990. 'Marginal Men, Marcabru and Orthodoxy: The Early Troubadour and Adultery.' *Medium Aevum* 59, 55–72
Gauthier, René A. 1951a. *Magnanimité. L'idéal de la grandeur dans la philosophie païenne et dans la théologie chrétienne*. Paris: Vrin

– 1951b. 'Pour l'attribution à Gautier de Châtillon du "Moralium dogma philosophorum."' *RML* 7, 19–64
– 1953. 'Les Deux Recensions du "Moralium dogma philosophorum."' *RML* 9, 171–260
Genette, Gérard. 1966. *Figures*. Paris: Seuil
Georgi, Annette. 1969. *Das lateinesche und deutsche Preisgedicht des Mittelalter in der Nachfolge des genus demonstrativum*. Berlin: Schmidt
Ghil, Eliza M. 1986. 'The Seasonal Topos in the Old Provençal "canzo": A Reassessment.' *Studia* 1, 87–99
Giffen, Lois Anita. 1971. *Theory of Profane Love among the Arabs: The Development of the Genre*. New York: New York University Press
Gillmeister, Heiner. 1972. *Discrecioun – Chaucer und die via regia*. Bonn: Bouvier
Gilson, Etienne. 1947. *La Théorie mystique de Saint Bernard*. Paris: Vrin
Goldin, Frederick. 1967. *The Mirror of Narcissus in the Courtly Love Lyric*. Ithaca, NY: Cornell University Press
Goth, Barbara. 1967. *Untersuchungen zur Gattungsgeschichte der Sottie*. Munich: Fink
Grabmann, Martin. 1932. 'Das Werk "De amore" des Andreas Capellanus und das Verurteilungsdekret des Bischofs Stephan Tempier von Paris vom März 1277.' *Speculum* 7, 75–9
Gregory, Tullio. 1955. *Anima mundi. La filosofia di Guglielmo di Conches e la scuola di Chartres*. Florence: Sansoni
Greimas, Algirdas J. 1970. *Du Sens*. Paris: Seuil
Gruber, Jörn. 1983. *Die Dialektik des Trobar: Untersuchungen zur Struktur and Entwicklung des occitanischen und französischen Minnesangs des 12 Jahrhunderts*. Tübingen: Niemeyer
Guiette, Robert. 1960. 'D'une Poésie formelle en France au moyen âge.' *Romanica Gandensia* 8, 9–32
Hackett, Winfrid M. 1971. 'Le problème de midons.' *Mélanges Jean Boutière*, 1, 285–94. Liège: Soledi
Hauser, Arnold. 1982. *The Sociology of Art*, trans. by K. Northcott. Chicago: University of Chicago Press
Hermanns, Wilhelm. 1913. *Ueber den Begriff der Mässigung in der patristisch–scholastischen Ethik von Clemens v. Alexandrien bis Albertus Magnus*. Aachen
Hissette, Roland. 1977. *Enquête sur les 219 articles condamnés à Paris le 7 Mars 1277*. Louvain: Publications universitaires
– 1983. 'Une "duplex sententia" dans le "De Amore" d'André le Chapelain?' *RTAM* 50, 246–51
Hoepffner, Ernst. 1955. *Les Troubadours dans leur vie et dans leur oeuvres*. Paris: Colin

Holte, R. 1962. *Béatitude et Sagesse. Saint Augustin et le problème de la fin de l'homme dans la philosophie ancienne.* Paris: Etudes augustiniennes

Jaeger, C. Stephen. 1985. *The Origins of Courtliness. Civilizing Trends and the Formation of Courtly Ideals 939–1210.* Philadelphia: University of Pennsylvania Press

Jaeger, Werner. 1945 [1935]. *Paideia: The Ideals of Greek Culture*, 3 vols., trans. by G. Highet. New York: Oxford Univesity Press

Jehn, Peter. 1972. *Toposforschung. Eine Dokumentation.* Frankfurt: Athenaeum

Jensen, Frede. 1983. *Provençal Philology and the Poetry of Guillaume of Poitiers.* Gylling: Odense University Press

Jocelyn, H.D. 'Vergilius Cacozelus (Donatus' Vita Vergilii 44).' *Papers of the Liverpool Latin Seminar* 2, 67–142

Jones, Lowanne E. 1978. 'Guiraut de Calanso's Lyric Allegory of Lady Love.' *Mélanges Charles Camproux*, 105–20. Montpellier: Centre d'Estudis Occitans

Jung, Marc R. 1971. *Études sur les poèmes allégoriques en France au Moyen Age.* Romanica Helvetica n. 82

Kaehne, Michael. 1983. *Studien zur Dichtung Bernarts von Ventadorn*, 2 vols. Munich: W. Fink

Karnein, Alfred. 1985. *De Amore in volksprachlicher Literatur.* Heidelberg: C. Winter–Universitätsverlag

Kasten, Ingrid. 1986. *Frauendienst bei Trobadors und Minnesänger im 12 Jahrhundert.* Heidelberg: C. Winter–Universitätsverlag

Kay, Sarah. 1985. 'La Notion de personnalité chez les troubadours: Encore la question de la sincérité.' *Mittelalterbilder*: 166–82

– 1987. 'Continuation as Criticism: The Case of Jaufre Rudel.' *Medium Aevum* 56, 46–64

– 1991. *Subjectivity in Troubadour Poetry.* Cambridge: Cambridge University Press

Kellermann, Wilhelm. 1968. Über die altfranzösischen Gedicht des uneingeschränkten Unsinns.' *Archiv* 205, 1–22

Kelly, Douglas. 1968. 'Courtly Love in Perspective: The Hierarchy of Love in Andreas Capellanus.' *Traditio* 24, 119–48

Kendrick, Laura. 1988. *The Game of Love: Troubadour Wordplay.* Berkeley: University of California Press

Kertesz, Christopher. 1971. 'The De arte (honeste) amandi and Andreas Capellanus.' *Texas Studies in Literature and Language* 13, 5–16

Klubertanz, G.P. 1952. *The Discursive Power. Sources and Doctrine of the 'vis cogitativa' according to St. Thomas Aquinas.* Saint Louis: Modern Schoolman

Knoespel, Kenneth. 1985. *Narcissus and the Invention of Personal History.* New York/London: Garland

Köhler, Eric. 1952. 'Marcabrus "L'autrier jost'una sebissa"und das Problem der Pastourelle.' *Romanistisches Jahrbuch* 5, 256–68
- 1955–6. 'Bravoure, savoir, richesse et amour dans les jeux-partis des troubadours.' *Estudis Romànics* 5, 95–110
- 1960. 'Zur Diskussion der Adelsfrage bei den Trobadors.' *Festgabeschriften W. Bulst*. Heidelberg: Winter
- 1964a. 'Narcisse et la Fountaine d'Amour et Guillaume de Lorris.' *L'Humanisme médiéval dans les littératures romanes du XIIe siècle*, 147–64. Paris: Klincksieck
- 1964b. 'Observations historiques et sociologiques sur la poésie des troubadours.' *CCM* 7, 27–51
- 1966. 'Sens et fonction du terme "jeunesse" dans la poésie des troubadours.' *Mélanges René Crozet*, 569–83. Poitiers: Société d'études médiévales
- 1970. 'Trobar clus: discussione aperta – Marcabru und die beiden Schulen.' *CN* 30, 300–14

Kohler, Erika. 1935. *Liebeskrieg – Zur Bildersprache der höfischen Dichtung des Mittelalters*. Stuttgart: Kohlhammer

Kolsen, Adolf. 1894. *Guiraut von Bornelh, der Meister der Trobadors*. Berlin: Vogt

Lavis, Georges. 1972. *L'Expression de l'affectivité dans la poésie lyrique française du Moyen Age (XIIe–XIIIe siècles) – Étude sémantique et stylistique du reseau lexical 'joie-dolor.'* Paris: Les Belles Lettres

Lawner, Lynn. 1973. 'Marcabru and the Origins of "Trobar clus."' In *Literature and Western Civilization*, vol. 3, ed. by D. Daiches and A. Thorlby, 485–523. London: Aldus

Lazar, Moshé. 1964. *Amour courtois et 'fin'amours' dans la littérature du XIIe siècle*. Paris: Klincksieck
- 1989. 'Carmina erotica, carmina iocosa: The Body and the Bawdy in Medieval Love Songs.' In *Poetics of Love in the Middle Ages. Texts and Contexts*, ed. by Moshe Lazar and J. Norris Lacy, 249–76. Fairfax, VA: George Mason University Press

Lazzari, Francesco. 1965. *Il 'contemptus mundi' nella scuola di San Vittore*. Naples: Istituto Italiano per gli Studi Storici

Leclercq, Jean. 1963. *La Liturgie et les paradoxes chrétiens*. Paris: Editions du Cerf

Lefèvre, Yves. 1973. 'Jaufré Rudel et son "amour de loin."' *Mélanges Pierre Le Gentil*, 461–77. Paris: SEDES et CDV
- 1987. 'L'Amour c'est le paradis: Commentaire de la chanson IX de Guillaume IX d'Aquitaine.' *Romania* 102, 289–305

Lehman, Paul. 1927. *Pseudo-antike Literatur des Mittelalters*. Leipzig–Berlin: Teubner

Limentani, Alberto. 1977. *L'eccezione narrativa. La Provenza medievale e l'arte del racconto*. Turin: Einaudi

Lottin, O. 1942–60. *Psychologie et morale aux XIIe et XIIIe siècles*, 6 vols. Louvain: Abbaye du Mont César

Lowes, John Livingston. 1913–14. 'The Lovers Maladye of Hereos.' *MP* 11, 491–546

McCash, June Hall Martin. 1979. 'Marie de Champagne and Eleanor of Aquitaine: A Relationship Reexamined.' *Speculum* 54, 698–711

Madec, G. 1974. *Saint Ambroise et la philosophie*. Paris: Etudes augustiniennes

Mancini, Mario. 1984. *La gaia scienza dei trovatori*. Parma: Pratiche

– 1987. 'Tan volh sa senhoria: Sulla metafora feudale dei trovatori.' *Medioevo Romanzo* 12, 211–60

Margoni, Ivos. 1965. *Fin'amors, mezura e cortesia. Saggio sulla lirica provenzale del XII secolo*. Milan-Varese: Istituto Editoriale Cisalpino

Marrou, Henri-Irénée. 1947. 'Au dossier de l'amour courtois.' *RML* 3, 81–9

– 1971. *Les Troubadours*, 2d ed. Paris: Seuil

Meneghetti, Maria Luisa. 1984. *Il pubblico dei trovatori. Ricezione e riuso dei testi lirici cortesi fino al XIV secolo*. Modena: Mucchi

Menocal, Maria Rosa. 1987. *The Arabic Role in Medieval Literary History*. Philadelphia: University of Pennsylvania Press

Milone, Luigi. 1979. 'Retorica del potere e poetica dell'oscuro da Guglielmo IX a Raimbaut d'Aurenga.' *Quaderni del Circolo Filologico-Linguistico Padovano*, 10, 149–77

– 1983a. '"L'amors enversa" di Raimbaut d'Aurenga.' *Museum Patavinum*, 1, 45–66

– 1983b. 'Raimbaut d'Aurenga fra "fin'amor" e "no–poder."' *Romanistische Zeitschrift für Literaturgeschichte*, 7, 1–27

Mölk, Ulrich. 1968. *'Trobar clus, trobar leu.' Studien zur Dichtungstheorie der Trobadors*. Munich: Fink

Monson, Don Alfred. 1981. *Les 'ensenhamens' occitans. Essai de definition et délimitation du genre*. Paris: Klincksieck

– 1984. '"L'amor pur d'André le Chaplain et la poésie des troubadour.' In *Chrétien de Troyes and the Troubadours – Essays in Memory of the Late Leslie Topsfield*, ed. by Peter Noble and Linda M. Paterson, 78–89. Cambridge: St Catherine's College

– 1987. 'Lyrisme et sincérité: Sur une chanson de Bernart de Ventadorn.' *Studia*, 143–59

– 1988. 'Andreas Capellanus and the Problem of Irony.' *Speculum* 63, 539–72

– 1991. 'Bernart de Ventadorn et Tristan.' *Mélanges de langue et littérature occitane en hommage à Pierre Bec*, 385–400. Poitiers: CÉSCM

Monteverdi, Angelo. 1955. 'La "chansoneta nueva" attribuita a Guglielmo d'Aquitania.' *Siculorum Gymnasium* 8, 6–15

Moore, J.D. 1979. 'Courtly Love: A Problem of Terminology.' *Journal of the History of Ideas* 40, 621–32

Moore, Olin H. 1914. 'Jaufré Rudel and the Lady of Dreams.' *PMLA* 29, 517–36

Morani, M. 1981. *La tradizione manoscritta del 'De natura hominis' di Nemesio.* Milan: Vita e Pensiero

Musso, Franco 1971. 'Tono iperbolico e vanterie in Peire Vidal.' *Omaggio a Camillo Guerrieri-Crocetti*, 439–53. Genova: Bozzi

Nardi, Bruno. 1942. *Dante e la cultura medievale.* Bari: Laterza

– 1959. 'L'amore e i medici medievali.' *Studi in onore di Angelo Monteverdi*, 2, 517–42. Modena: Mucchi

Nelli, René. 1963. *L'Erotique des troubadours.* Tolouse: Privat

Nelson, N.E. 1933. 'Cicero's *De officiis* in Christian Thought: 300–1300.' *University of Michigan Publications – Language and Literature* 10, 59–160

Neuman, Eduard. 1951. 'Der Streit um "das ritterliche Tugendsystem."' *Erbe der Vergangenheit. Germanistische Beiträge–Festgabe für Karl Helm zum 80 Geburtstage*, 137–55. Tübingen: Niemeyer

– 1952–3. 'Zum "ritterlichen Tugendsystem."' *Virkendes Wort* 3, 49–61

Newman, F.X., ed. 1968. *The Meaning of Courtly Love – Papers of the First Annual Conference of the Center for Medieval and Early Renaissance Studies*, State University of New York at Binghamton, 17–18 March 1967. Albany: State University of New York Press

Nichols, Stephen G. 1991. 'Voice and Writing in Augustine and in the Troubadour Lyric.' *Vox Intexta. – Orality and Textuality in the Middle Ages*, ed. by A.N. Doane and Carol Braun Pasternack, 137–61. Madison: University of Wisconsin Press

Norberg, Dag. 1958. *Introduction à l'étude de la versification latine médiévale.* Stockholm: Almqvist-Wiksell

Norden, Eduard. 1918. *Die antike Kunstprosa.* Leipzig: Teubner

Olson, Susan. 1976. 'Immutable Love: Two Good Women in Marcabru.' *Neophilologus* 60, 190–91

Paden, William. 1975. 'The Troubadour's Lady: Her Marital Status and Social Rank.' *Studies in Philology* 72, 28–50

– 1986. '"Et ai be faih co·l fols en pon": Bernart de Ventadorn, Jacques de Vitry, and Q. Horatius Flaccus.' *Studia* 1, 181–91

Paepe, Norbert de. 1966. '"Amor" und "verus amor" bei Andreas Capellanus. Versuch einer Lösung des "reprobatio" Problem.' *Mélanges René Crozet*, 2, 921–7. Poitiers: Société d'Etudes médiévales

Palumbo, Pietro. 1969. 'La questione della "reprobatio amoris" nel trattato di Andrea Cappellano.' *Bollettino del Centro di Studi Filologici e Linguistici Siciliani* 7 (*Saggi in memoria di Ettore Li Gotti*) 2, 429–46

Panvini, Bruno. 1949. *Giraldo di Bornelh, trovatore del sec. XII.* Catania: Università di Catania

Paratore, Ettore. 1965. 'Da Plauto al "Mare amoroso."' *Rivista di Cultura Classica e Medievale* 7, 825–60

Paré, G., A. Brunet, and P. Tremblay. 1933. *La Renaissance du XIIe siècle – Les écoles et l'enseignement.* Paris: Vrin

Paris, Gaston. 1883. 'Lancelot du Lac. II. Le conte de la Charrette.' *Romania* 12, 459–533

Paterson, Linda M. 1975. *Troubadours and Eloquence.* Oxford: Clarendon Press

Payen, J.C. 1984. 'Bernart Marti et la légende de Tristan.' In *Chrétien de Troyes and the Troubadours: Essays in Memory of the Late Leslie Topsfield*, ed. by Peter Noble and Linda M. Paterson, 34–43. Cambridge: St Catherine's College

Pfister, Max. 1976. 'La langue de Guilhem IX, comte de Poitiers.' *CCM* 19, 91–113

Picarel, Monique. 1970. 'Le début printanier dans les chansons des troubadours: Marcabru et Bernard de Ventadour.' In Bec, ed., 1970, 169–97

Picone, Michelangelo. 1977. 'Osservazioni sulla poesia di Raimbaut d'Aurenga.' *Vox Romanica* 36, 28–37

– 1977. 'Dante e il mito di Narciso: dal *Roman de la Rose* alla *Commedia*.' *RF* 89, 382–97

– 1979. *'Vita nuova' e tradizione romanza.* Padua: Liviana

Pirot, François. 1967. 'Bibliographie commentée du troubadour Marcabru.' *Le Moyen Age* 73, 87–126

– 1972. *Recherches sur les connaissances littéraires des troubadours occitans et catalans des XIIe et XIIIe siècles: Les Sirventes-ensenhamens de Guiraut de Cabrera, Guiraut de Calanson et Bertrand de Paris.* Barcelona: Real Academia de Buenas Letras

Pirrone, Nicola. 1914. "ΑΔΥΝΑΤΟΝ." *Athenaeum* 2, 38–45

Planche, Alice. 1986. 'Texte à l'endroit, monde à l'envers. Sur une chanson de Raimbaut d'Aurenga: "Ar resplan la flors enversa."' *Studia* 1, 213–26

Pohlenz, Max. 1934. *Antikes Führertum. Ciceros de officiis und das Lebensideal des Panaitios.* Leipzig-Berlin: Teubner

Poirion, Daniel. 1970. 'Narcisse et Pygmalion dan le Roman de la Rose.' *Essays in Honor of L. Solano*, 153–65. Chapel Hill: North Carolina University Press

Pollmann, Leo. 1962. 'Dichtung und Liebe bei Wilhelm von Aquitanien.' *ZRP* 78, 326–57

– 1965. *Trobar clus, Bibelexegese und hispano-arabische Literatur.* Münster: Forschungen zur romanischen Philologie 16. Münster

– 1966. *Die Liebe in der hochmittelalterlichen Literatur Frankreichs. Versuch einer historischen Phänomenologie.* Analecta Romanica 18. Frankfurt: Klostermann

Porter, Lambert C. 1960. *La Fatrasie et le fatras – Essai sur la poésie irrationelle en France au Moyen Age*. Geneva: Droz
Press, Alan R. 1961. 'La Strophe printanière chez les troubadours et chez les poètes latins du Moyen Age.' *Actes et memoires du IIIe Congrès International de Langue et litérature d'Oc* 2, 70–8. Bordeaux: Université de Bordeaux
– 1970a. 'The Adulterous Nature of Fin'amors: A Re-examination of the Theory.' *Forum for Modern Languages Studies* 6, 327–41
– 1970b. 'Amour courtois, amour adultère?' *Actes du VIe Congrès International de Langue et Literature d'Oc*, 435–42. Montpellier: Centre d'Estudis Occitans
Rajna, Pio. 1889. 'Tre studi per la storia del libro di Andrea Cappellano.' *Studi di filologia romanza* 5, 193–265
– 1928. 'Guglielmo, conte di Poitiers, trovatore bifronte.' *Mélanges Alfred Jeanroy*, 349–60. Paris: Droz
Raupach, Manfred and Raupach, Margret. 1979. *Französierte Trobadorlyrik*. Tübingen: Niemeyer
Reiss, Edmond. 1979. '*Fin'Amors*: Its History and Meaning in Medieval Literature.' *Medieval and Renaissance Studies* 8, 74–99
Renier, Rodolfo. 1885. *Il tipo estetico della donna nel Medioevo*. Ancona: Morelli
Renzi, Lorenzo. 1976. 'Lettura contestuale della "flor enversa" di Raimbaut d'Aurenga.' *Poetica e Stile (Quaderni del Circolo Filologico Linguistico Padovano,* n. 8), 25–34. Padua: Liviana
Ricketts, Peter T. 1966. '*Castitatz* chez Guilhem de Montanhagol.' *RLR* 77, 145–50
Riege, Angelica. 1991. *Trobairitz – Der Beitrag der Frau in der altokzitanischen höfischen Lyrik. Edition des Gesamtkorpus*. Tübingen: Niemeyer
Rieger, Dietmar. 1983. 'Kalter Wind und Pferdegewieher. Zwei Sonderfälle des trobadoresken Natureingangs.' *ZFSL* 93, 2–13
Riquer, Martín de. 1975. *Los trobadores*, 3 vols. Barcelona: Planeta
Robertson, D.W., Jr. 1952. 'Amors de terra lonhdana.' *Studies in Philology* 49, 566–82
– 1952–3. 'The Subject of the *De Amore* in Andreas Capellanus.' *MP* 50, 141–61
– 1962. '"Courtly Love" and Andreas Capellanus.' In *A Preface to Chaucer. Studies in Medieval Perpectives*, 291–448. Princeton, NJ: Princeton University Press
– 1968. 'The Concept of Courtly Love as an Impediment to the Understanding of Medieval Texts.' In Newman, ed., 1968, 1–18
Rocher, Daniel. 1964. 'Tradition latine et morale chevaleresque. A propos du "Ritterliches Tugendsystem."' *Etudes Germaniques* 19, 127–41
Rohr, Rupprecht. 1990. 'Liebe als Krankheit bei den Trobadors.' In *Liebe als Krankheit. Kolloquium der Forschungsstelle für europäische Lyrik des Mittelalters,*

ed. by Theo Stemmler, 139–49. Mannheim: Forschungstelle für europäische Lyrik des Mittelalters an der Universität Mannheim

Roncaglia, Aurelio. 1952. 'Can la frej'aura venta.' *CN* 12, 255–64

- 1964. 'Obediens.' *Mélanges Maurice Delbouille*, 2, 597–614. Gembloux: J. Duculot
- 1968. *La generazione trobadorica del 1170*. Rome: De Santis
- 1969. 'Trobar clus: discussione aperta.' *CN* 29, 5–55
- 1975. Review of Zumthor 1974. *CN* 35, 269–72
- 1985. 'Les troubadours et Virgile.' *Lectures Médiévales de Virgile. Actes du Colloque organisé par l'École française de Rome*, 267–83. Rome: Ecole française de Rome

Ross, Werner. 1954. 'Über den sogennanten Natureingang der Trobadors.' *RF* 65, 49–68

Rossi, Luciano. 1987. 'Chrétien de Troyes e i trovatori: Tristan, Linhaura, Carestia.' *Vox Romanica*, 46, 1–47

- 1989. 'Noch einmal: Die Trobadors und Vergil.' *Vox Romanica*, 48, 58–76

Roubaud, Jacques. 1986. *La Fleur inverse*. Paris: Ramsey

Routledge, Michael J. 1969. 'Essai d'établissement du texte du sirventés "Pos Peire d'Alvernhe a chantat."' *RLR* 78, 103–27

Roy, Bruno. 1985. 'André le Chapelain, ou l'obscenité rendue courtoise.' *Mittelalterbilder*, 59–74

Ruiz-Domenec, José Enrique. 1980. *El juego del amor como representación del mundo en Andrés el Capellán*. Barcelona: Universidad Autónoma

Sakari, Aimo. 1949. 'Azalaïs de Porcairagues, le Joglar de Raimbaut d'Orange.' *NM* 50, 23–43; 56–87; 174–98

- 1971. 'A propos d'Azalaïs de Porcairagues.' *Mélanges Jean Boutière*, 517–28. Liège: Soledi

Salverda de Grave, Jean J. 1938. *Observations sur l'art lyrique de Giraut de Borneil*. Amsterdam: Mededellingen der Koninklijke Nederlandsche Akademie van Wetenschappen, Afd. Letterkunde, N.R.1

Sansone, Giuseppe E. ed. 1977. *Testi didattico-cortesi di Provenza*. Bari: Adriatica

- 1980. 'L'allegoria dei tre gradi d'amore in una poesia provenzale inedita.' *Romania* 101, 238–61

Scarone Grassano, N. 1975. 'Per un'edizione critica del sirventese "Pos Peire d'Alvergn'a chantat."' *Studi in ricordo di Guido Favati*, 193–213. Genoa: Tilgher

Scheludko, Dimitri. 1934. 'Ovid und die Trobadors.' *ZRP* 54, 129–74

- 1935–7. 'Zur Geschichte des Natureinganges bei den Trobadors.' *ZFSL* 60, 256–334

- 1937. 'Anlösslich des Liedes von Raimbaut d'Aurenga "Cars douz." (Zur Fragen dem 'trobar clus).' *Archivum Romanicum* 21, 285–97
- 1940. 'Über die Theorien der Liebe bei den Trobadors.' *ZRP* 60, 191–234
Schlösser, Felix. 1960. *Andreas Capellanus. Seine Minnelehre und das christliche Weltbild um 1200*. Bonn: Bouvier
Schnell, Rüdiger. 1982. *Andreas Capellanus. Zur Rezeption des römanischen und kanonischen Rechts in De Amore*. Munich: Fink
- 1985. *Causa amoris. Liebeskonzeption und Liebesdarstellung in der mittelalterlichen Literatur*. Bern-Munich: Francke
- 1989. 'L'amour courtois en tant que discours courtois sur l'amour.' (I) *Romania*, 110, 72–126
Schrötter, Wilibald. 1908. *Ovid und die Troubadours*. Halle: Niemeyer
Schultz-Gora, Oskar. 1888. *Die provenzalischen Dichterinnen – Biographien und Texte*. Altenburg: G. Fock
- 1932. 'Das Adynaton in der altfranzösischen und provenzalischen Dichtung nebst Duzugehörigen.' *Archiv* 161, 196–209
Schutz, Alexander H. 1958. 'Some Provençal Words Indicative of Knowledge.' *Speculum* 33, 508–14
Serper, Arié. 1974. 'Guiraut de Borneil, le "gant" le "trobar clus" et Lignaure.' *RLR* 80, 93–106
- 1986a. 'Amour courtois et amour divin chez Raimbaut d'Orange.' *Studia* 1, 279–89
- 1986b. 'Le vocabulaire de la "connaisance" dans la poésie des troubadours.' *Actes du XVIIe Congrès International de Lingüistique et Philologie Romanes*. Aix-en Provence, 29 August – 3 September, 331–42
Shapiro, Marianne. 1984. '*Entrebescar los motz*: Word Weaving and Divine Rhetoric.' *ZRP*, 100, 355–83
Sharman, Ruth V. 1983. 'Giraut de Borneil: Maestre dels trobadors.' *Medium Aevum* 52, 63–76
Silvestre, Hubert. 1980. 'Du nouveau sur André le Chapelain.' *RML* 36, 99–106
- 1982. 'Du nouveau sur André le Chapelain.' *Bulletin de Théologie ancienne et médiévale* 13, 280–2
Simonelli, Maria. 1966. 'Il tema della nobiltà in Andrea Cappellano e in Dante.' *Dante Studies* 84, 51–64
Singer, Irving. 1973. 'Andreas Capellanus: A Reading of the Tractatus.' *Modern Language Notes* 88, 1288–1315
- 1984. *The Nature of Love*, 2 vols. Chicago: University of Chicago Press
Smith, Nathaniel B., and Joseph T. Snow, eds. 1980. *The Expansion and Transformation of Courtly Literature*. Athens: University of Georgia Press

Spaggiari, Barbara. 1977. 'La poesia religiosa anonima catalana e occitanica.' *Annali della Scuola Normale Superiore di Pisa*, s. III, 7, 177–350
- 1982. 'Cacciare la lepre col bue.' *Annali della Scuola Normale Superiore di Pisa*. s. III, 12, 1333–1403
Spence, Sarah. 1988. *Rhetorics of Reason and Desire: Vergil, Augustine, and the Troubadours*. Ithaca, NY: Cornell University Press
Spies, Alfons. 1931. *Militat omnis amans. Ein Beitrag zur Bildersprache der antiken Erotik*. Tübingen: Laupp
Spitzer, Leo. 1944. *L'Amour lointain de Jaufré Rudel et le sens de la poésie des troubadours*. Chapel Hill: North Carolina University Press
Sutherland, Dorothy R. 1961. 'The Love Meditation in Courtly Literature (A Study of the Terminology and Its Development in Old Provençal and Old French).' In *Studies in Medieval French Presented to Alfred Ewert*, 165–93. Oxford: Clarendon Press
- 1961. 'L'élément théâtral dans la "canso" chez les troubadours de l'époque classique.' *Actes et Mémoires du IIIe Congrès International de Langue et Littérature d'Oc*, 2, 95–101. Bordeaux: Université de Bordeaux
Taiana, Franz. 1977. *Amor purus und die Minne*. Freiburg: Universitätsverlag
Tavera, Antoine. 1986. 'Farai chansoneta nueva.' *Studia* 1, 301–12
Taylor, Robert A. 1977. *La littérature Occitane du Moyen Age. Bibliographie sélective et critique*. Toronto: University of Toronto Press
Thamin, Raymond. 1895. *Saint Ambroise et la morale chrétienne au IVe siècle. Etude comparée des traités 'des devoires' de Cicéron et de Saint Ambroise*. Paris: Masson
Thiolier-Méjean, Suzanne. 1978. *Les poésies satiriques et morales des troubadours du XIIe siècle à la fin du XIIIe siècle*. Paris: Nizet
Thomas, Antoine. 1929. 'Le *Liber de nobilitate animi* et les troubadours.' *SM* 2, 163–72
Toja, Gianluigi. 1959. 'Postilla arnaldiana. La fame del "nebot Sain Guillem."' *CN* 19, 239–50
Topsfield, Leslie T. 1956. 'Raimon de Miraval and the Art of Courtly Love.' *Modern Language Review* 51, 33–41
- 1975. *Troubadours and Love*. Cambridge: Cambridge University Press
- 1979. '*Malvestatz* versus *Proeza* and *Leautatz* in Troubadour Poetry and the Lancelot of Chrétien de Troyes.' *L'Esprit Créateur* 19, 37–53
Tortoreto, Valeria. 1976. 'Cercamon maestro di Marcabru?' *CN* 36, 61–93
Utley, Francis Lee. 1972. 'Must We Abandon the Concept of Courtly Love?' *Medievalia et Humanistica* 3, 299–324
Vallone, Aldo. 1950. *La cortesia dai Provenzali a Dante*. Palermo: Palumbo

Van Vleck, Amelia E. 1991. *Memory and Re-Creation in Troubadour Lyric.* Berkeley: University of California Press

Vecchi, Giuseppe. 1958. *Poesia latina medievale.* Parma: Guanda

Vinay, Gustavo. 1951. 'Il *De Amore* di Andrea Cappellano nel quadro della letteratura amorosa e della rinascita del secolo XII.' *SM* n.s. 71, 203–76

Viscardi, Antonio. 1970 [1948]. 'La poesia trobadorica e l'Italia.' In *Ricerche e interpretazioni mediolatine e romanze,* 345–81. Milan: Cisalpina

– 1970 [1969]. 'Il *De Amore* di Andrea Cappellano e l'amore cortese.' *Ricerche e interpretazioni mediolatine e romanze,* 783–97. Milano: Cisalpina

Vuijlsteke, Marc. 1981. 'La langue poétique de Raimbaut d'Orange: tradition et création.' In *Court and Poet: Selected Proceedings of the Third Congress of the International Courtly Literature Society,* ed. by G.S. Burgess, A.D. Deyermond, W.H. Jackson, A.D. Mills, and P.T. Ricketts, 329–38. Liverpool: Cairns

– 1991. 'Eléments de definition d'un mode de l'enoncé poétique: Raimbaut d'Orange et le trobar clus.' In *Mélanges de langue et literature occitane en hommage à Pierre Bec,* 587–98. Poitiers: CÉSCM

Wack, Mary Frances. 1990. *Lovesickness in the Middle Ages. The 'Viaticum' and Its Commentaries.* Philadelphia: University of Pennsylvania Press

Warning, Rainer. 1979. 'Lyrisches Ich und Öffentlichkeit bei den Trobadors.' In *Deutsche Literature im Mittelalter: Kontakte und Perspektiven – Hugo Kuhn zum Gedenken,* ed. C. Cormeau, 120–59. Stuttgart: Metzler

Wechssler, Eduard. 1909. *Das Kulturproblem des Minnesangs. I: Minnesang und Christentum.* Halle: Niemeyer

Weinrich, Harold. 1971. *Tempus. Besprochene und erzählte Welt,* 2d ed. Stuttgart: Kohlhammer

Wetherbee, Winthrop. 1971. *Platonism and Poetry in the Twelfth-Century.* Princeton, NJ: Princeton University Press

Wettstein, Jacques. 1945. *Mezura. L'Idéal des troubadours, son essence et ses aspect.* Zürich: Leemann

Whorf, Benjamin L. 1956. *Language, Thought and Reality. Selected Writings.* Ed. and with an intro. by John B. Carroll. Cambridge, MA: Technology Press of MIT

Wind, Bartina Harmina. 1964. Review of F. Schlösser 1960. *CCM* 7, 346–50

Wolfson, H.A. 1935. 'The Internal Senses in Latin, Arabic and Hebrew Philosophical Texts.' *Harvard Theological Review* 28, 69–133

Zonta, Giuseppe. 1908. 'Rileggendo Andrea Cappellano.' *SM* 3, 49–68

Zorzi, Diego. 1955. 'L'*amor de lonh* di Jaufre Rudel.' *Aevum* 29, 124–44

Zuddy, Zara P. 1965. 'The Definition of Sleep in Andreas Capellanus.' *Medium Aevum* 34, 129–30

Zumthor, Paul. 1963. *Langue et techniques poétiques à l'époque romane (XIe–XIIIe siècles)*. Paris: Klincksieck
- 1972. *Essai de poétique médiévale*. Paris: Seuil
- 1974. 'Des paragrammes chez les troubadours?' *Romanic Review* 65, 1–12
- 1975. *Langue, texte, énigme*. Paris: Seuil

Index of Names

Abelard, 6, 45, 78
Abraham, 120
Adam, 34, 139
Aeneas, 85
Agamben, Giorgio, 138
Agamemnon, 149
Aimeric de Peguilhan, 19, 115, 135
Akehurst, Frank R.P., 135, 147
Alanus de Insulis, 84–5, 136
Albertanus of Brescia, 133
Aldobrandino da Siena, 30
Alegret, 22, 86
Alfanus of Salerno, 67, 148
Alfonso, King of Aragon, 8, 13, 26
Allegretto, Manuela, 146
Ambrose, Saint, 44, 143
Andreas Capellanus, ix–x, xiv, 10–14, 16–17, 20–1, 25–34, 37–41, 54, 57–9, 66–70, 85, 124, 127, 131–42, 148–9
Angeli, Giovanna, 151, 160
Anglade, Joseph, 139, 159
Apollo, 147
Appel, Carl, 98, 137, 153–5
Arachne, 118, 163
Aristotle, 30
Arnaud, Leonard E., 160

Arnaut Daniel, 16, 27, 81, 83, 90, 98 106–16, 121–2, 151, 156, 160–1, 164
Arnaut de Maruelh, 8, 16, 23, 25–6, 36, 56, 59, 141, 162
Arnaut Guillem de Marsan, 49
Arthur, 104–5, 117, 120, 160
Atalanta, 109, 121
Aude, 120
Augustine, Saint, 44, 60, 143, 146, 149, 154
Avalle, D'Arco Silvio, 54, 60, 105, 118–19, 135, 146, 154, 160, 163
Avicenna, 28, 68
Aya, 120
Azalais de Porcairagues, 14, 17, 157

Babcock, Barbara, 151
Baeumer, Max L., 151
Barthes, Roland, 148
Battaglia, Salvatore, 136, 142, 160
Baudri de Bourgueil, 6
Beatritz, Comtessa de Dia, 17, 18, 23
Bec, Pierre, 56, 130, 147
Benton, John F., 129, 132
Berenguer de Palol, 58, 155, 162
Beretta Spampinato, Margherita, 58, 155, 162

Index of Names

Bernard, Saint, 136
Bernart de Ventadorn, 10, 14, 27, 55, 60, 78, 100, 106, 117, 118–20, 122–3, 134, 141, 154, 157, 163
Bernart Marti, 154
Bernhardt, Wilhelm, 49, 145
Beroe, 146
Bertolme Zorzi, 81
Bertran D'Alamon, 79
Bertrand de Born, 137
Bezzola, Reto, 131, 150
Blanchefleur, 119
Boase, Roger, 129
Boer, Cornelis de, 147
Boethius (Boeci), 21, 137
Boni, Marco, 58, 118
Bonifacio Calvo, 65
Boutière, Jean, 157, 161
Bowden, Betsy, 139
Breuer, Hermann, 146
Briffault, Robert S., 40, 143
Brinkmann, Hennig, 130
Brizard, 149
Brunet, Adrien, 144
Bruno, Roy, 130
Bultot, Robert, 152
Bundy, M.W., 148
Burgess, Glyn S., 137
Burgundius of Pisa, 148
Buridant, Claude, 137
Burkhard, C., 148
Busse, Wilhelm G., 138
Butturff, Douglas R., 139

Cadenet, 8, 162
Cahoon, Leslie, 163
Calboli Montefusco, Lucia, 152
Calin, William, 130
Camproux, Charles, 130
Canter, H.C., 151
Caplan, Harry, 156

Capusso, Maria Grazia, 136
Casella, Mario, 40, 143
Castiglione, Baldesar, 50
Cato, 103–4
Catullus, 84
Cercamon, 18, 22, 86, 101, 153
Cerveri de Girona, 65
Chambers, Frank M., 19, 115, 135, 164
Charybdis, 84–5
Chaytor, Henry J., 139
Chenu, M.-D., 150
Cherchi, Paolo, 130, 137–8, 146, 151, 157
Cherniss, Michael D., 139
Chevalier, Maxime, 160
Chiarini, Giorgio, 146
Chrétien de Troyes, 133
Christ, Jesus, 9
Chydenius, J., 132
Ciavolella, Massimo, 138
Cicero, 43–5, 47–8, 84, 132, 143, 146
Claudian, 84
Cluzel, Irénée M., 157, 161
Cnyrim, Eugen, 162–3
Cocchiara, Giuseppe, 151
Colby, Alice, 146
Colie, Rosalie, 151
Constantinus Africanus, 28
Contini, Gianfranco, 146, 149
Coon, Raymond H., 151
Corti, Maria, 139
Crohns, Hjalmar J., 138
Cropp, Glynnis M., 131, 135–6, 153
Curtius, Ernst Robert, 46, 83, 111, 137, 144, 151, 161

Dalfin d'Alvernhe, 26, 139
Dante Alighieri, 41, 42, 45, 72, 88, 102, 106, 128, 132, 137, 143, 160–3

Index of Names 189

Daude de Pradas, 48, 116, 135, 143, 145, 162
De Bruyne, Edgar, 144
De Cavazzani Sentieri, Aida, 151
De Lollis, Cesare, 137
Dejeanne, Jean M.L., 13, 22, 27, 85–8, 145, 153
Del Monte, Alberto, 22, 89, 90, 154, 161, 163
Delhaye, Philippe, 48, 143
Demats, Paule, 139
Dembowski, Peter, 145
Demling, Johann, 151
Denomy, Alexander J., 134, 138, 142
Deroy, Jean P. Th., 135
Desmond, Marilynn R., 149
Di Capua, Francesco, 50, 145
Di Girolamo, Costanzo, 163
Diderot, Denis, 70, 149
Diez, Friedrich, 52, 81, 146
Don Quixote, 79
Donaldson, Ethelbert Talbot, 129
Donna H., 20
Dragonetti, Roger, 134, 151
Dronke, Peter, 5, 130, 132
Druart La Vache, 21
Duby, George, 138–9
Dulcinea, 79, 150
Dutoit, Ernest, 151

Ebles de Ventadorn, 86
Ecker, Lawrence, 146
Economou, George, 150
Ehrismann, Gustav, 45, 144
Eifler, Gunter, 144
Eleanor of Aquitaine, 133
Elias Cairel, 114, 121
Elias de Barjols, 120
Elias d'Ussel, 19
En Barral, 104

Erasmus, Desiderius, 84, 152, 156, 161
Errante, Guido, 153
Eugenius Vulgarius, 156
Eusebi, Mario, 23, 137

Faral, Edmond, 146, 159
Fauriel, Claude, 130
Favati, Guido, 132, 137
Fechner, Jorg-Ulrich, 158
Ferrante, Joan M., 129–30
Flore, 119
Folquet de Marselha, 8, 14, 22, 52, 72, 76–7, 116–17, 154, 160
Forster, Leonard W., 157
Fortunatianus Chirius, 83, 152
Frank, Grace, xii, 129
Frank, István, 160
Frank, K. Donald, 150
Frappier, Jean, 129–30, 148, 163
Frederick the Great, 44
Fucilla, Joseph G., 151
Fulgentius, 154

García Morales, Justo, 150
García Soriano, Justo, 150
Garin Lo Brun, 47, 126
Gaucelm Faidit, 18, 19, 55–6, 117
Gaunt, Simon B., 147, 153–5
Gauthier, René A., 143–4
Gavaudan, 120–1, 155
Genette, Gérard, 151
Geoffrey of Brittany, 160
Georgi, Annette, 146
Ghil, Eliza M., 156
Giacomo da Lentini, 69, 149
Giffen, Lois Anita, 132
Gillmeister, Heiner, 145
Gilson, Etienne, 136
Giraut de Bornelh, 8, 10, 22, 26, 92, 102–4, 117, 135, 155, 158

Goldin, Frederick, 148
Goth, Barbara, 160
Grabmann, Martin, 142
Gregory, Tullio, 150
Greimas, Algirdas J., 64, 147
Gruber, Jörn, 151, 156
Guida, Saverio, 154
Guiette, Robert, 151
Guilhem Ademar, 135
Guilhem de Berguedan, 115, 162
Guilhem de Cabestanh, 15, 78, 137
Guilhem de Montanhagol, 16, 50, 117, 134–5
Guilhem de Saint-Leider, 14, 135
Guilhem Magret, 114
Guilhem IX de Peitieu, Duke of Aquitaine, 7, 8, 10, 13, 22, 78, 86, 90, 130–2, 138–9, 150
Guillaume, 161
Guillem, Sain, 109, 121
Guiraut de Calanso, 136
Guiraut Riquier, 62, 64, 81

Hackett, Winfrid M., 131
Hadoard, 44
Häring, Nicholas M., 152
Hartmann von Aue, 46
Hauser, Arnold, 149
Hector, 119
Hecuba, 150
Helen, 164
Helm, Rudolf, 154
Heloïse, 78
Hermanns, Wilhelm, 145
Hero, 119
Hildebert de Lavardin, 6, 46, 143–4, 154
Hissette, Roland, 142
Hoepffner, Ernst, 154, 161
Holmberg, John, 143–4

Holte, Ragnar, 143
Homer, 83
Horace, 82, 161
Hugh of Orléans, 6

Irigaray, Luce, 148
Isaiah, 155
Isolde, 119

Jaeger, C. Stephen, 144
Jaeger, Werner, 146
Jaeschke, Hilde, 114, 162
Jammes, Robert, 160
Jaufre Rudel, xi, xii, 59, 60, 86, 90, 116, 138, 146
Jausbert de Puycibot, 118, 137
Jean de Meung, 41
Jeanroy, Alfred, 18, 59, 116, 135, 138, 153
Jehn, Peter, 151
Jensen, Frede, 130
Joannicius, 29, 138
Jocelyn, H.D., 152
Jocglar, 100
Johnston, Ronald C., 8, 16, 26, 36, 59, 141, 162
Juvenal, 83

Kaehne, Michael, 150
Karnein, Alfred, 133, 137–8, 143
Kasten, Ingrid, 129, 132
Kay, Sarah, 149, 151, 156
Kellermann, Wilhelm, 160
Kelly, Douglas, 142
Kendrick, Laura, 129
Kertesz, Christopher, 139
Kjellman, H., 119, 139
Klein, Otto, 23, 161
Klubertanz, G.P., 148
Knoespel, Kenneth, 148

Köhler, Eric, 131-2, 137-8, 148, 154, 163
Kohler, Erika, 163
Kolsen, Adolf, 8, 14, 22, 102–3, 117, 135, 159
Könsgen, Edwald, 158
Kussler-Ratyé, Gabrielle, 18, 23

Lacan, Jacques, 148
Landouzy, Louis, 138
Landric, 119
Lanfranc Cigala, 120
Långfors, Arthur, 15, 137
Lavis, Georges, 147
Lawner, Lynn, 153
Lazar, Moshé, 14, 27, 40, 55, 60, 101, 117, 119–20, 122–3, 130, 134, 141, 143, 154, 157
Lazzari, Francesco, 152
Le Kain, 149
Leander, 119
Leclercq, Jean, 152
Lefèvre, Yves, 129, 132
Lehman, Paul, 147
Limentani, Alberto, 61, 147
Linhaure, 102
Lottin, Odon, 144
Lowes, John Livingston, 138
Lucchetto Gattilusio, 118, 163
Lucretius, 160

McCash, June Hall Martin, 134
Macrobius, 45, 47
Madec, Goulvan, 143
Mancini, Mario, 131, 148
Marbod, 6, 160
Marcabru, 10, 21, 22, 26, 27, 49, 53, 62, 85–8, 90, 120–1, 145, 152–5, 158, 163
Marcoat, 86
Margoni, Ivos, 145

Maria de Vertfuoil, 157
Marie de France, 133
Marrou, Henri-Irénée, 130
Martin of Bracara, 44, 46
Matfre Ermengau, 124–7, 148
Matthew, 155
Matthew of Vendôme, 6, 137, 146
Meleagre, 109, 121
Melicertes, 85
Meneghetti, Maria Luisa, 151, 156
Menocal, Maria Rosa, 132
Milone, Luigi, 155
Minerva, 118
Mir Bernart, 135
Mölk, Ulrich, 130, 156, 163
Monclin, 110, 121
Monge de Montaudon, 22–3, 111, 160
Monson, Don Alfred, 133, 136, 140, 145, 149, 163
Monteverdi, Angelo, 130
Moore, John D., 129
Moore, Olin H., 147
Morani, Moreno, 148
Mostacci, Jacopo, 149
Mouzat, Jean D., 18, 55, 117
Musso, Franco, 160

Narcissus, 67, 120, 123
Nardi, Bruno, 137–8, 149
N'At de Mons, 49, 50
Naudieth, Fritz, 115
Nelli, René, 17, 20, 86, 135, 153
Nelson, Norman E., 143
Nemesius of Emesa, 67, 148
Nero, 85
Nestor, 85
Neuman, Eduard, 144
Newman, F.X., 129
Nichols, Stephen G., 147
Norberg, Dag, 157

Index of Names

Norden, Eduard, 152
Odierna, 110, 121
Olson, Susan, 154
Ovid, 29, 36, 131, 134, 146–7, 161–3

Paden, William, 131, 146, 156
Paepe, Norbert de, 139
Pallas, 163
Palumbo, Pietro, 142
Panvini, Bruno, 158
Paratore, Ettore, 154
Paré, Gérard, 144
Paris, Gaston, 4, 130
Paris, 85, 164
Parry, John J., 133–4
Pasero, Nicolò, 7, 8, 21, 57, 130–2, 138–9
Paterson, Linda M., 150, 155, 161, 163
Pattison, Walter T., 7, 15, 18, 91–4, 100, 114, 138, 155, 160, 164
Paul, Saint, 140
Payen, Jean C., 163
Peire Bremon Ricas Novas, 120
Peire Cardenal, 53, 163
Peire d'Alvernha, 22, 88–90, 120–2, 130, 155
Peire Ramon de Tolosa, 120
Peire Vidal, 54, 60, 104–6, 117–19, 146, 154, 160, 163
Peirol, 18
Penelope, 84
Pépin, Roger, 138
Perdigon, 26, 139
Perugi, Maurizio, 16, 27, 107, 109–13, 161, 164
Pessoa, Fernando, 70, 127
Petrarch, Francis, 95, 160
Petrocchi, Giorgio, 160
Pfister, Max, 130
Picarel, Monique, 156

Pickens, Rupert T., 146
Picone, Michelangelo, 148, 155, 161
Pierre de Blois, 6
Pirot, François, 133, 136, 153
Pirrone, Nicola, 151
Pistoleta, 120
Planche, Alice, 158
Plautus, 83–4, 93
Pliny, 160
Plutarch, 161
Poestat, 135
Pohlenz, Max, 143
Poirion, Daniel, 148
Pollmann, Leo, 132, 163
Ponz de Capduoill, 163
Porter, Lambert C., 160
Press, Alan R., 146, 156
Priam, 150
Propertius, 146
Pujol, 135
Pyramus, 119, 122, 147

Quintilian, 84, 99, 128, 154

Rabanus Maurus, 122
Rachel, 119–20
Raimbaut d'Aurenga, 7, 10, 15, 17, 18, 81, 90–5, 97–104, 106, 114, 118, 121, 135, 138, 155–8, 160, 164
Raimbaut de Vaqueiras, 135
Raimon de Miraval, 115, 135
Raimon Jordan, 119, 139
Rajna, Pio, 133, 153
Rambertino de Buvalelli, 120
Raphael, Saint, 119–20
Raupach, Manfred, 134
Raupach, Margret, 134
Reiss, Edmond, 130
Renier, Rodolfo, 146
Renzi, Lorenzo, 158

Ricketts, Peter T., 16, 51, 117, 134
Riege, Angelica, 135
Rieger, Dietmar, 156
Rigaut de Berbezilh, 22
Rilke, Rainer Maria, xiii, 60, 162
Riquer, Martín de, 8, 63, 130, 135, 153, 159, 160, 162
Robertson, Durant W., Jr, 129, 138, 139
Rocher, Daniel, 144
Rofin, 20
Rohr, Rupprecht, 148
Roland, 120
Roncaglia, Aurelio, 5, 131, 137, 146, 152–3, 156, 163
Roques, Mario, 147
Roscius, 150
Rosenstein, Roy, 146, 153
Ross, Werner, 156
Rossi, Luciano, 133–4, 137, 163
Roubaud, Jacques, 158
Routledge, Michael J., 161
Roy, Bruno, 140
Ruffini, Graziano, 136
Ruiz-Domenec, José Enrique, 139

Sakari, Aimo, 14, 134–5, 157
Salverda de Grave, Jean J., 158
Sansone, Giuseppe E., 136, 145
Scarone Grassano, Nives, 161
Scheludko, Dimitri, 98, 131, 134, 156
Schlösser, Felix, 133–4, 141
Schnell, Rüdiger, 130, 133, 137, 139, 141
Schrötter, Wilibald, 163
Schultz-Gora, Oskar, 135, 152
Schutz, Alexander H., 116, 145, 157, 161–2
Scylla, 85
Seneca, 45, 137, 160

Serlo of Winton, 6
Serper, Arié, 145, 155, 158
Shapiro, Marianne, 158
Sharman, Ruth Verity, 159
Shepard, William, 19, 115, 118, 135, 137
Sifre, 135
Silvestre, Hubert, 139, 142
Simonelli, Maria, 139
Singer, Irving, 141
Sismondi, Jean-Charles-Léonard Simonde de, 130
Smith, R., 150
Sordel, 26, 49, 57
Spaggiari, Barbara, 157, 161
Spence, Sarah, 149
Spies, Alfons, 163
Spitzer, Leo, xii, xiii, 129
Stendhal, xii, 61
Stickney, Austin, 48, 143
Stimming, Albert, 137
Strecker, Karl, 153
Stroński, Stanisław, 8, 15, 22, 73, 116, 145, 154
Sutherland, Dorothy R., 146, 160

Taiana, Franz, 141
Tavera, Antoine, 130
Taylor, Robert A., 153, 161
Tempier, Stephan, 142
Terence, 84
Thamin, Raymond, 143
Thiolier-Méjean, Suzanne, 146, 163
Thisbe, 119, 147
Thomas, Antoine, 139
Thomas Aquinas, 134
Toja, Gianluigi, 161
Topsfield, Leslie T., 115, 134–7, 153–5, 161
Tortoreto, Valeria, 154, 158

Tremblay, Pierre, 144
Tristan, 119, 122, 133, 164
Trojel, E., 134
Tydeus, 85

Utley, Francis Lee, 129

Valéry, Paul, 150
Vallone, Aldo, 143
Van Vleck, Amelia E., 164
Varchi, Benedetto, 130
Varvaro, Alberto, 22
Vecchi, Giuseppe, 158
Venantius Fortunatus, 6
Vernière, Paul, 149
Vinay, Gustavo, 132, 139
Virgil, 137, 163
Viscardi, Antonio, 134, 138
Vivien, 161
Vuijlsteke, Marc, 155

Wack, Mary Frances, 138
Walfrid Strabo, 84, 120
Walsh, P.G., 134

Walter (Gualterus), 32, 34
Walter of Châtillon, 143, 152
Warning, Rainer, 146
Wechssler, Eduard, 5, 40, 143
Weinrich, Harold, 64, 147
Wetherbee, Winthrop, 150
Wettstein, Jacques, 137, 145
Whorf, Benjamin L., 144
Wilhelm, James J., 161
William, Saint, 161
William of Conches, 44–9, 53–4, 87, 138, 143
Wind, Bartina Harmina, 133
Wolf, George, 146, 153
Wolfram von Eschenbach, 46
Wolfson, Harry A., 148

Zemp, Josef, 8, 162
Zeno, 42–3
Zonta, Giuseppe, 134
Zorzi, Diego, 129
Zuddy, Zara P., 138
Zumthor, Paul, xi, xii, 129–30, 133, 150–1, 156, 160

252
60.00